Theory of Knowledge
The 1913 Manuscript

Theory of Knowledge
The 1913 Manuscript

BERTRAND RUSSELL

Edited by
Elizabeth Ramsden Eames
in collaboration with
Kenneth Blackwell

London and New York

First published in 1984 by George Allen & Unwin

Paperback edition first published in 1992
by Routledge
11 New Fetter Lane, London EC4P 4EE

Simultaneously published in the USA and Canada
by Routledge
a division of Routledge, Chapman and Hall, Inc.
29 West 35th Street, New York, NY 10001

Funds to edit this volume were provided by the National Endowment for the Humanities, the Social Sciences and Humanities Council of Canada and McMaster University.

Printed in Great Britain by
T.J. Press (Padstow) Ltd, Padstow, Cornwall

British Library Cataloguing in Publication Data

Russell, Bertrand
Theory of knowledge: the 1913 manuscript
I. Title   II. Eames, Elizabeth Ramsden
III. Blackwell, Kenneth
121

Library of Congress Cataloging in Publication Data

Russell, Bertrand, 1872–1970.
Theory of knowledge.
Bibliography: p.
includes index.
1. Knowledge, theory of.   I. Eames, Elizabeth Ramsden.
II. Blackwell, Kenneth.   III. Title.
B1649.R91   192 (121) 84–2983

ISBN 0–415–08298–6

Contents

THEORY OF KNOWLEDGE

PART I. ON THE NATURE OF ACQUAINTANCE

PART II. ATOMIC PROPOSITIONAL THOUGHT

Introduction

I. BACKGROUND

IN HIS AUTOBIOGRAPHY Bertrand Russell gives a vivid description of his life and work for the first ten years of the century: the long struggles with the writing of *Principia Mathematica* which occupied him to the exclusion of almost every other intellectual project during those years; the day by day frustration of facing a blank page when he was unable to resolve the contradictions in logic that he had himself found; the intensity of the effort of thought involved in this activity; and the personal unhappiness which made the work harder to bear.[1] All of this makes it easy for us to share Russell's experience and understand the direction of his thought. But for the second decade of the century the account in the *Autobiography* is much less satisfactory. Partially this is because there are a number of divergent themes: the continued sharing of his work and friendship with the co-author of *Principia Mathematica*, A. N. Whitehead, and the end of this close collaboration; the return to Cambridge, and the friendship and philosophical interactions with Ludwig Wittgenstein; the love affair with Lady Ottoline Morrell with its rapture and pain, and later affairs with others; the war and the exhausting and ultimately futile opposition to it. All these different stories, and the striking omission of any but a superficial discussion of his own intellectual development during those years, have made it difficult to obtain a clear view of how changes occurred in his thought between 1910 and 1920. The most common view of Russell's philosophy during this period sees it as the rapid sequence from the outright epistemological and Platonic realism of *The Problems of Philosophy* of 1912, through the phenomenalist constructionism of *Our Knowledge of the External World* of 1914, to the logical atomism of "The Philosophy of Logical Atomism" of 1918.[2] In this view the influence of Wittgenstein, which

---

1 Russell *1967*, 144–200.

2 Russell commentary has come in several phases: in the first phase, his contemporaries seemed bemused by the changes of his philosophy and established the reputation of fickleness which has clung to his work. An example of this is C. D. Broad's remark that Russell develops a new philosophy every few years (in "Critical and Speculative Philosophy", *1924*, 79). More recent commentary has focused on two aspects of Russell's

Russell referred to as coming in "two waves",[3] was evident in the last of the three phases mentioned, and a fairly sharp dichotomy was supposed to exist between each of the phases of the decade. It is strange that Russell, who seldom retreated from recounting his own failures or faults, should have not reported the fact that he had written a large part of a major work on theory of knowledge which had been intended as his first important philosophical work after *Principia Mathematica* and which he was forced to abandon under circumstances which constituted an "event of first-rate importance in my life", as he reported later to Ottoline Morrell.[4] In fact the existence of the partial book manuscript was not known until Bertrand Russell's papers were catalogued in 1967, prior to their sale, and, at that time, Russell did not respond to inquiries about it.[5] It is tempting to speculate on the reasons for this silence on Russell's part, but, in any case, we can see that the changes in Russell's thought between 1910 and 1920 may be illuminated in an important way by the book.

Since the Bertrand Russell Archives have been acquired by McMaster University in Hamilton, Ontario, Canada, the incomplete manuscript has been available for study, and several commentators have noted it, and have sought to interpret its incompleteness and its position in Russell's life and thought.[6] Editorial investigation has virtually established that the missing first 142 pages of the manuscript were published in a series of six articles in *The Monist* of 1914 and 1915, that Russell stopped writing at page 350 (the

---

work, his logical work, especially theory of types and theory of descriptions, for which the *locus classicus* is *Principia Mathematica* (1910–13), and his epistemology in which the main interest has been in work done by Russell either prior to 1918, his theory of acquaintance, or his logical atomism which is linked with Wittgenstein's work and dated by "The Philosophy of Logical Atomism". An example of the interest in acquaintance is the work of Chisholm, "On the Nature of Acquaintance: A Discussion of Russell's Theory of Knowledge", in Nakhnikian *1974*. An example of the interest in logical atomism as formulated in the period immediately after World War I is Urmson, *Philosophical Analysis* (1956). Some critics who have progressed to an interest in the later work of Russell still make the assumption that there is a sharp break between it and the "phenomenalism" of the work prior to *The Analysis of Matter* (1927). See Maxwell, "The Later Bertrand Russell: Philosophical Revolutionary", in Nakhnikian *1974*. See Eames, *Bertrand Russell's Theory of Knowledge* (1969), for a discussion of the critical views of Russell's philosophy.

3 Russell, *My Philosophical Development* (*1959*, 112).

4 Russell to Ottoline Morrell, #1,123, [4 Mar. 1916]. (As in the case of all of Russell's letters to Morrell cited here, the original is in the Humanities Research Center, University of Texas at Austin, and a microfilm copy is in the Bertrand Russell Archives, McMaster University [hereafter abbreviated "RA"]. In citing the dates of these letters, "pmk." means "postmarked".) This letter is extracted and printed in Russell's *Autobiography* (*1968*, 57), in the appendix to Chapter 1 of Volume 2.

5 Blackwell and Eames, "Russell's Unpublished Book on Theory of Knowledge" (*1975*, 4).

6 See Clark, *The Life of Bertrand Russell* (*1975*, 204–6). Also there are short discussions in: McGuinness, "Bertrand Russell and Ludwig Wittgenstein's 'Notes on Logic'" (1972); Blackwell, "Wittgenstein's Impact on Russell's Theory of Belief" (1974); McGuinness,

last page of the manuscript) and did not resume writing, and that Wittgenstein's criticisms of one or more major theses of the book could not be answered by Russell and led him to give up his work on it. These are the results of our study of the book and of the historical documents which are available concerning it. Now that the entire text in published form is available for study, it is possible to see its full significance in the development of Russell's thought. This significance can be evaluated only in the light of the historical context in which the work was planned, undertaken, and, finally, left unfinished. Our study also reveals the probable revision by which, apparently, the present fourth chapter was added to the first draft of the manuscript. It is the object of this Introduction to make that historical context as clear as possible, given the availability of the records of the events of the period.

The period under consideration is that between the time that Russell finished his share of the work on *Principia Mathematica*, in 1910, and the time that he completed work on the sixth *Monist* article, in February of 1915. The sources for our knowledge of this period are several: Russell's own retrospective account of the period, which we know suffers from serious omissions;[7] the other writings by Russell of this period, published and unpublished; Russell's correspondence with Ottoline Morrell, which began in late March of 1911 when they became lovers and continued almost daily during the period in question; his correspondence with others with whom he discussed his work: his student Ludwig Wittgenstein,[8] his philosophically interested acquaintance Oliver Strachey,[9] his friend and the European editor of the *Monist* P. E. B. Jourdain,[10] his niece and philosophic

"The *Grundgedanke* of the *Tractatus*" (1974); Eames, "Philip E. B. Jourdain and the Open Court Papers" (1975); Pears, "Russell's Theories of Memory" and "Wittgenstein's Treatment of Solipsism in the *Tractatus*" in his *Questions in the Philosophy of Mind* (1975), "The Relation between Wittgenstein's Picture Theory of Propositions and Russell's Theories of Judgment" (1977), and "Wittgenstein's Picture Theory and Russell's *Theory of Knowledge*" (1979); Sommerville, "Types, Categories and Significance" (1979); Perkins, "Russell's Unpublished Book on Theory of Knowledge" (1979); Eames, "Response to Mr. Perkins" (1979); Griffin, "Russell on the Nature of Logic" (1980); Sommerville, "Wittgenstein to Russell (July, 1913): 'I Am Very Sorry to Hear ... My Objection Paralyses You'" (1980); Blackwell, "The Early Wittgenstein and the Middle Russell", in Block *1981*; Lackey, "Russell's 1913 Map of the Mind" (1981); Pears, "The Function of Acquaintance in Russell's Philosophy" (1981), and "The Logical Independence of Elementary Propositions", in Block *1981*; Griffin, "Russell's Multiple-Relation Theory of Judgment" (1982).

7 This period is discussed by Russell in the second volume of the *Autobiography* (1968) and in his *1959*, 102–9, 112. Russell's faulty memory of this period is discussed in Blackwell, "Our Knowledge of *Our Knowledge*" (1973).

8 Wittgenstein *1974*.

9 Correspondence between Russell and Oliver Strachey, RA.

10 Correspondence between Russell and Philip Jourdain, RA; also letters of Philip Jourdain to Paul Carus and to Open Court, Open Court papers, Special Collections, Morris Library,

protégée Karin Costelloe (later Stephen),[11] and the chairman of the Philosophy Department at Harvard and leading neo-realist R. B. Perry;[12] correspondence relating to the publication of three of the *Monist* articles in the 1956 collection, *Logic and Knowledge*, with the editor, Robert Charles Marsh,[13] and the publisher of the volume, George Allen & Unwin;[14] the papers of the Open Court Publishing Company,[15] the publishers of the *Monist* and *Our Knowledge of the External World*; and the notebooks and papers from Russell's seminar on theory of knowledge given at Harvard in 1914 and kept by students in that seminar, Victor Lenzen and T. S. Eliot.[16]

We find in Russell's work and correspondence of the period immediately following *Principia Mathematica* a kind of vacillation concerning work in what he called "technical philosophy". What he meant by "technical philosophy" was, first of all, the kind of mathematical logic done in that book, and second, the application of the techniques developed there to problems in philosophy, in science, and in common sense. A description of what the programme for such a philosophy should be and what truths it could be expected to yield can be found in two lectures which Russell gave in Paris in March of 1911. In the first lecture he sets forth the position of "analytic realism" and introduces the term "logical atomism".[17] He describes his position as a commitment to realism in theory of knowledge and with respect to universals, and to the use of logical techniques in the analysis of complexes into the simples which are their constituents—the logical atoms which are the result of the analysis. Sense-data and a priori knowledge of universals and logical truths are the basic ingredients of knowledge on this view. In this lecture he recommends a method of piecemeal, precise analysis of limited topics as appropriate to the philosophy he calls "analytic realism", or "logical atomism". In the second lecture, "The Philosophical Importance of Mathematical Logic", he claims for that discipline success in the analysis of infinity and continuity, and asserts that it will provide the

---

Southern Illinois University at Carbondale.

11 Letters of Karin Costelloe to Russell, RA.

12 Russell's letters to R. B. Perry, Harvard University Archives, with photocopies in RA; Perry's letters to Russell are in RA with some carbons at Harvard.

13 Letters of Robert Charles Marsh to Russell, and photocopies of letters of Russell to R. C. Marsh in RA, with the originals in the Houghton Library, Harvard University.

14 Correspondence between George Allen & Unwin and Russell in RA.

15 Open Court papers, Special Collections, Morris Library, Southern Illinois University at Carbondale.

16 Victor Lenzen's notebook is in RA. His "A Theory of Judgment", Thesis, Phil. 9c, 16 May 1914, is in the Bancroft Library, University of California, Berkeley (photocopy in RA). T. S. Eliot's notes on the seminar on theory of knowledge, and two papers on theory of objects which appear to be drafts of papers for the seminar, are in the T. S. Eliot papers in the Houghton Library of Harvard University.

17 Russell, "Le Réalisme analytique" (1911).

most formal, contentless, abstract, and hence the most fundamental truths on which philosophy can build a sound theory of space, time, and matter.[18]

In spite of this commitment to technical philosophy, Russell expressed in letters to Ottoline Morrell a revulsion toward this kind of philosophy.[19] He remarked in later autobiographical writing that this attitude followed the long years of concentrated logical work on "the big book", *Principia Mathematica*.[20] But he also told Ottoline Morrell that he had not forsaken technical philosophy and had begun rereading philosophers of the past as a preparation for his next major work, which he was not yet ready to begin writing.[21] In fact, he may have been influenced by a desire to work at the kind of philosophy which was of interest to Ottoline Morrell, who was a woman of sophisticated artistic, intellectual, and political interests, but uneducated in symbolic logic and mathematics. Russell attributed to her a broadening of his tastes, interests, and sympathies,[22] and he longed to share his intellectual life with her; at their lovers' meetings they read Plato and Spinoza, and from their discussions a book emerged which they referred to as "Prisons", dealing with the ability of philosophy to free the mind and spirit from the trammels of the here and now. This book, the text of which is lost, reached the stage of typescript, and part of it was published in modified form by Russell as a journal article.[23] The borderline between philosophy on the one hand, and religion and normative ethics on the other, occupied part of Russell's interest, and can be seen in the final chapter of *The Problems of Philosophy*.

At the same time that Russell was most influenced by Ottoline Morrell, he met, in October of 1911, a young Austrian engineering student who had come to Cambridge to study mathematical logic with him.[24] This was Ludwig Wittgenstein, who became an important part of Russell's life and thought over two decades. Devoted as a student, brilliant as a neophyte logician, vulnerable to anguishing depressions and sensitivities, alive with aesthetic and philosophical insights, he provided the delights, fascinations, and alarms associated with erratic genius. After two terms at Cambridge, Wittgenstein became a close personal friend whom Russell loved "as a son", and a valued philosophical colleague whom Russell dreamed of as his successor.[25] Wittgenstein's influence on Russell was at least as portentous

---

18 Russell, "L'Importance philosophique de la logistique" (1911). A translation of this article by P. E. B. Jourdain, "The Philosophical Importance of Mathematical Logic", appeared in the *Monist* (1913).

19 Russell to Morrell, #286, 11 Dec. 1913.

20 Russell *1959*, 102; *1967*, 153 (the latter passage was composed in 1931).

21 Russell to Morrell, #220, 15 Oct. 1911.

22 Russell *1967*, 205.

23 Russell to Morrell, #336, pmk. 9 Feb. 1912. Russell, "The Essence of Religion" (1912).

24 Russell to Morrell, #225, 18 Oct. 1911.

25 For Wittgenstein as a "son", Russell to Morrell, #548, [21 Aug. 1912]; for Wittgenstein as

and enduring as that of Ottoline Morrell, although the two pulled him in opposite directions. We will have occasion to say more of Wittgenstein's influence on Russell's book, but, at the moment, we can see his influence in Russell's reports to Ottoline Morrell of Wittgenstein's criticisms of his views on religion, ethics, and the value of philosophy. According to Russell Wittgenstein held ethics and religion to be irrelevant to philosophy, and too personal for discussion. If one is interested in philosophy, he said, one will pursue it, and that is the end of the matter.[26] The "shilling shocker", *The Problems of Philosophy*, was "hated" by Wittgenstein, and, although Russell seemed amused by the younger man's "tyranny", he confessed that it had made him much more sceptical.[27] Russell also told Ottoline Morrell of his "delightful lazy feeling" in relinquishing logical problems which he himself was too old to solve to the fresh insights and vigour of Wittgenstein.[28] On the other hand, during the same period that Russell was expressing these lotus-eating sentiments to Ottoline Morrell, he was fully engaged in teaching his course "Principles of Mathematics" at Cambridge, going through the "big book" with Wittgenstein, presiding with gusto over philosophical discussions with colleagues and students, and writing page after page of articles and drafts of articles on a range of technical topics.[29]

The main technical topics of the period between 1910 and 1913 to which Russell addressed himself were those connected with his attempt to analyze the data of sensation in such a way that they could provide a basis for the "construction" of space, time, matter, and cause. To this project belonged his recurrent work on matter, an exemplification of the analysis of a scientific concept. During the winter and spring of 1912 Russell wrote a good deal on such topics, and this work bore fruit in his 1914 publications. In his published work we find traditional philosophical topics under discussion but with the employment of concepts developed in mathematical logic. The Aristotelian Society address of March 1911 on "Knowledge by Acquaintance and Knowledge by Description" takes the technical work done in "On Denoting" in 1905, and incorporated into *Principia*, and develops its epistemological implications. The Aristotelian address of October 1911, on universals and particulars, is devoted to a traditional philosophical topic but the argument rests on relational logic. In addition Russell's reviews and responses to critics involved the use of the tools of technical philosophy. If these tools were occasionally set aside, they were not abandoned and could be expected to emerge in Russell's next major work.

Russell seemed to stand, and many commentators today still see him as

---

his successor, Russell to Morrell, #422, pmk. 23 April 1912.

26 Russell to Morrell, #388, pmk. 17 Mar. 1912.

27 Russell to Morrell, #459, pmk. 21 May 1912.

28 Russell to Morrell, #564, pmk. 4 Sept. 1912.

29 These projects are referred to in the letters to Morrell of this period, and are present in

standing, with a foot in two worlds, the old and the new.[30] The old world of philosophy sought insight, synthesis, an overarching human meaning which carried ethical enlightenment; the new world of scientific philosophy eschewed the comprehensive, the theologically orthodox, the schema intended to shore up ethical insights, and sought instead the scientific model of the piecemeal, the modest, the precise, with the method of logical analysis as the scientific method of philosophy. This contrast was made by Russell in "Mysticism and Logic" and in *Our Knowledge of the External World* of 1914 where, although he expressed respect for the intuitive and holistic, he committed himself to the new method of philosophizing. But in doing so he did not leave the older philosophical questions behind, or find them totally meaningless or irrelevant; they were still important and philosophy must answer them or show them to be unanswerable.

From the conflicting tendencies in Russell's thought at this time emerged a concept of what needed to be done in philosophy. In speaking of his long-run hopes for philosophy, Russell wrote to Ottoline Morrell of his collaboration with Whitehead, saying that Whitehead was working on the technical end (the projected fourth volume of *Principia* for which Whitehead was to have primary responsibility, applying logical techniques to the definition of points in space and moments in time, and to the geometry of physics), and that he would work at the same problems from the psychological end, and that they hoped to meet in the middle.[31] In fact, Russell was working from both ends and attempting a synthesis on his own. His attempts at analyzing sense-data, his work on the analysis of matter, his discussions with Whitehead on spatial and temporal series were on the technical end, while his work on theory of knowledge, of which *The Problems of Philosophy* was a first sketch, approached the same problems from the less technical end. In asking himself what projects remained in philosophy worth working at, Russell had two answers: the prescribing of a new technical way of doing philosophy, and the pursuit of the question: What can be known?[32] The two projects turned out to be intimately connected, for the exploration of what can be known involves technical considerations of propositional formulation and analysis of relational complexes using symbolic logic, while the construction of concepts of space, time, and matter employs technical means but presupposes assumptions about what it is possible to know and how. What emerged as Russell's next major work, then, was one on theory of knowledge; it asked the old philosophical question of what can be known; it took account of the answers

---

manuscript drafts in RA.

30 In Ayer *et al.*, *The Revolution in Philosophy* (*1956*, 46ff.). This point is also familiar from the commentary of Warnock in *English Philosophy Since 1900* (*1958*, 31).

31 Russell to Morrell, #667, 28 Dec. 1912.

32 *Ibid.*; see also #220, 15 Oct. 1911.

provided by philosophers from Plato to Meinong, but it formulated an answer in terms of a technical analysis of experience and a technical formulation of what knowledge can be derived from experience and from the a priori. Theory of knowledge thus provided a ground for technical work, and a bridge to allow the analysis of sense-data and the analysis of scientific concepts to meet. It was this project which became Russell's next major book, on a scale comparable in importance and extent to *Principia*; this is the text with which we are presently concerned, *Theory of Knowledge*. No title-page is extant for the book; however, Russell referred to what he was doing by this title in his letters, it was the title of the seminar at Harvard, and it appears on numerous outlines. In one passage he surrounded the phrase with quotation marks in speaking of the progress of the book. Accordingly, the editors have adopted "*Theory of Knowledge*" as its title.[33]

The immediate occasion of the writing of the book was Russell's invitation to Harvard University to teach logic and theory of knowledge during the spring term of 1914, and to deliver the Lowell Lectures. The invitation was extended more than a year in advance, and early in 1912 Russell was explaining to Ottoline Morrell that, although he had been unwilling to accept an invitation to be a permanent member of the Harvard Department of Philosophy, he felt he ought not to neglect the opportunity of the Lowell Lectureship. He later described his mission as that of converting the American realists to a proper appreciation and mastery of the new logical techniques by which alone their right-minded but inept attempts to answer epistemological problems could be made effective.[34]

II. CREATION AND CRITICISM

Early in the spring of 1913, then, Russell's various plans for future work crystallized around theory of knowledge. The whole project would include an analytic section in which all the components of knowledge would be separated out and formulated, and a constructive section in which on this basis points in space, moments of time, and units of matter would be logically constructed.[35] In the 1890s Russell, walking in the snow of the Tiergarten, when he was under the influence of neo-Hegelianism, had dreamed of writing a series of books of increasing concreteness from mathematics to biology, and a series of books of increasing abstractness from social philosophy on, ending in a grand synthesis.[36] As he said, something of this dream survived, and can be seen in the form of the scheme

---

33 See below, 155: 12–13; see also Appendix A.3.
34 Russell to Morrell, #1032, 26 May 1914.
35 Russell to Morrell, #768, pmk. 8 May 1913; #782, pmk. 21 May 1913.
36 Russell, "My Mental Development" (*1944*, 11).

for the epistemological synthesis of 1913.[37] Thus, he planned to begin work
on a book on theory of knowledge which would prepare him for the seminar
he was to teach at Harvard and mark the start of the next major project of his
career. His other projects included the Lowell Lectures, which Russell
referred to as his "popular lectures" and which, at that time, he conceived as
devoted to "the place of good and evil in the universe", the other side of the
technical-nontechnical dualism. (The topic suggested by Russell was rejected by the Lowell committee because the subjects of religion and ethics
were excluded under the terms of the will which endowed the lectureship.[38]) This dualism, however, the full scale of the new work would
help to overcome as it bound together the groundwork of theory of knowledge with the techniques of logical construction. The other project was to
prepare a course and even a textbook in advanced logic (see Appendix A.2),
in which the ideas of *Principia* would be presented along with whatever new
ideas could be gleaned to add to it. But "theory of knowledge", as he
referred to his new major work, had priority both in time and in importance.

The scope of the book on theory of knowledge can be seen in the
description Russell gave of it to Ottoline Morrell on 8 May 1913, the day
after he began to write.

> There will be an introductory chapter, which I shall probably leave
> to the last—the first substantial chapter, which I have nearly
> finished, is called "Preliminary description of Experience". Then I
> shall set to work to refute James's theory that there is no such thing
> as consciousness, then the idealist theory that there is nothing else.
> Then I shall classify cognitive relations to objects—sense, imagina-
> tion, memory. Then I shall come on to belief, error, etc.; then to
> inference; then finally to "construction of the physical world"—
> time, space, cause, matter. If I go on on the scale on which I have
> begun, it will be quite a big book—500 pages of print I should
> think.[39]

Two weeks later he wrote that the book was to have three parts: acquaintance, judgment, and inference, and that it would amount to 500 *manuscript*
pages. This discrepancy is accounted for by Russell's having two different
ideas: one was for one large book which would have both an analytic and a
constructive section, and this idea involved the larger estimate of pages; the

---

37 Russell to Morrell, #768, pmk. 8 May 1913.
38 Letter from A. Lawrence Lowell to Russell, 6 June 1913, RA, copy in Harvard University
    Archives. Russell's comments on receiving Lowell's letter are in #835, Sun. mg. [15?] June
    1913].
39 Russell to Morrell, #768, pmk. 8 May 1913. For his first report on his writing, see #770,
    Wed. night [7 May 1913].

other idea was to write two books, the first analytic, the second constructive. The tripartite division belonged to both schemes. The dual scheme is evident when, in June, Russell wrote that he had finished the first two parts, acquaintance and judgment, and was going to try to finish inference before Ottoline returned, leaving the constructive book until after she would be back. He also revealed his hesitation in a letter in which he remarked that it might be one or two books.[40] As a matter of fact, Russell wrote only the first two parts of the analytic section of the project, and did not write either the third part on inference, "Molecular Propositional Thought", or the constructive section.

The full view of what Russell had proposed as the scope of the work, whether it ended as one or two books, is important because it enables us to understand the fragment which we have in the surviving manuscript. This fragment consists of leaves numbered 143 to 350 inclusive, and comprises Chapters VII, VIII, and IX of Part I (on acquaintance) and Chapters I through VII of Part II (on judgment). (See Appendix C for a complete list of the manuscript chapters, with folio numbers.) The understanding of Russell's intention is important, then, in that it provides the framework within which we can reconstruct the portion of the book which he completed, that is, the text here presented.

Russell began writing 7 May, 1913, the day after Ottoline had left for Lausanne where she was to take treatment from a fashionable doctor, R. Vittoz. Russell planned to write ten pages a day and have at least one important section of his work (the analytic section) completed before she returned in late June, or before he left to join her there for a holiday.[41] His daily letters (as summarized in the Chronology) show us the progress of his work and the topics discussed in it: On 9 May he was working on James and Mach and keeping up his ten pages a day; by the 11th he had written fifty-five pages, finished the refutation of James, and gone on to his own view of consciousness; on 13 May he was puzzling over "the present time"—he worked until midnight and finished eighty pages, and spent the next morning thinking of sensation and imagination. As of 15 May he was "12 pages up on my average", i.e. to page 102, since he had been writing for nine days. By 16 May he had finished 110 pages and found that the treatment of sensation and imagination helped with the analysis of dreams; a day later he was working on the analysis of our knowledge of time, and had finished it by 19 May. The 20th was a day off. On 21 May he reported that he had finished the segment which dealt with acquaintance with particulars

40 Russell to Morrell, #792, [4 June 1913]. For the division of the work into three parts, see #782, pmk. 21 May 1913; for its length, see #784, pmk. 23 May 1913.
41 Russell to Morrell, #764, pmk. 4 May 1913; #798, pmk. 5 June 1913.

and had started on acquaintance with universals.[42] Thus he had completed one-sixth of the outlined analytic section of the work. From here on the reports to Ottoline Morrell can be compared with the chapters of the manuscript. Thus we may conclude that the portion already written, by 19 May, corresponds to the missing 142 leaves of the manuscript, and to the articles which have been identified as the missing six chapters.

On 22 May Russell reported that he had passed page 160; by the next day's letter we know that he had completed Chapter VII. On 23 May he finished Chapter VIII and was anticipating the chapter on logical form. The end of Chapter VIII had brought him to page 180. With the completion of the chapter on logical form, he said, a third of the analytic section of the work would be done. In fact, he completed Part I the same day, writing twenty pages in all, i.e. to page 190.[43]

Russell next started on the second part of the section, that on judgment, and wrote on 24 May that he had a new way of dividing the subject. On 25 May he was working on what is meant by understanding a sentence, and by 30 May he had reached page 273, the end of the treatment of belief, disbelief, and doubt (Chapter IV of Part II). On 1 June he reached page 300 and finished a treatment of truth which he thought superior to his former discussion of that topic.[44] Russell's earlier euphoria, his delight in what he was doing, and his feeling that all that slowed him down was the physical obstacle of getting the words on paper were ebbing. By 5 June he had told Ottoline Morrell that his "work fit" was coming to an end but that he would be able to finish the analytic section before he stopped; he had "all but finished 'self-evidence'", that is, Part II, Chapter VI, which ends on page 323. On 7 June, he reported that the day before he had reached page 350, and hoped to finish the third part on inference before she came home, but apparently he wrote no more since page 350 is the last extant manuscript page. On 8 June he thought he would not try to complete the analytic section—the next part was to be on inference and it required a lot of thought. Two things were depressing Russell: Wittgenstein's criticisms, which he said he had recovered from "only superficially"; and Ottoline's withdrawal of her invitation for him to join her in Lausanne. "I will take a holiday till you come home", wrote Russell.[45] With 350 pages written in thirty-one days, one could say that he had earned a holiday.

---

42 Russell to Morrell, #769, pmk. 9 May 1913; #772, pmk. 11 May 1913; #774, pmk. 13 May 1913; #775, [14 May 1913]; #777, pmk. 16 May 1913; #781, pmk. 20 May 1913; #782, pmk. 21 May 1913.

43 Russell to Morrell, #783, pmk. 22 May 1913; #784, pmk. 23 May 1913.

44 Russell to Morrell, #785, 24 May 1913; #786, pmk. 25 May 1913; #789, pmk. 30 May 1913; #791, pmk. 31 May 1913.

45 Russell to Morrell, #798, pmk. 5 June 1913; #799, pmk. 7 June 1913; #801, pmk. 9 June 1913.

This account records only the order and the dates involved in Russell's progress on the manuscript; we will return to discuss the intervention of Wittgenstein, which is also described in the letters to Ottoline Morrell. But, obviously, the description given in the letters confirms what is suggested by the review of topics at the end of the first part of the manuscript (see below, 99–101): that the missing six chapters are indeed the *Monist* articles. That identification also suggests why the chapters are missing: probably this portion of the manuscript was taken out to be typed, and, since it would then exist in printed form, not retained. If further evidence is necessary, there are many forward references in the *Monist* articles which lead us to expect a treatment of later topics in theory of knowledge.[46] These never appeared in the *Monist*, but some of them are treated in later chapters of the manuscript, while others belong to the part and section of the work which were projected but never written. There is also a slip where a reference to another "chapter" survived the revision of the text to replace "chapter" by "article".[47] What other revisions there may have been between the manuscript as Russell wrote it in May of 1913, and the articles as they were published between January of 1914 and April of 1915, is the topic of a later discussion (see sec. IV).

When the manuscript was found, the only clue suggesting the connection of the book with Wittgenstein was the letter to Ottoline Morrell of 1916 to be published in Russell's *Autobiography*, in which Russell referred to the time when she was seeing Vittoz in Switzerland, "and I wrote a lot of stuff about Theory of Knowledge which Wittgenstein criticized with the greatest severity". Russell went on to say that this criticism was "an event of first-rate importance in my life, and affected everything I have done since. I saw he was right, and I saw that I could not hope ever again to do fundamental work in philosophy. My impulse was shattered, like a wave dashed to pieces against a breakwater."[48] In the perspective of three years, and taking into account that Russell had gone on to do important work (at least *Our Knowledge of the External World* could be so considered), we may be tempted to understand this as an overstatement. The context of the passage is a letter in which Russell in effect was explaining why he was no longer close to Ottoline—trouble with his work and her withdrawal and failure to understand his suffering caused him to feel less intensely for her.

Turning again to Russell's letters of 1913 to Ottoline Morrell, we can trace in the contemporary account how and when Wittgenstein launched his attack, and how Russell responded to it. The exact points on which the criticism bore were not explained in detail to her, and are a matter of

---

46 E.g., *Monist*, 24 (Oct. 1914): 589; see below, 49: 26–7 and 38–40, and also the list of Editorial Emendations.

47 *Monist*, 25 (April 1915): 215; see below, 66: 15.

48 Russell *1968*, 57 (for a full citation, see n. 4). See also #1,467, 27 July 1917.

interpretation. The first reference to Wittgenstein's responses comes in a letter of 14 May 1913, in which Russell described how his protégé was "shocked to hear I am writing on theory of knowledge—he thinks it will be like the shilling book, which he hates."[49] The tone suggests that Russell was able to bear up very well under his friend's hatred of *The Problems of Philosophy* and was in no way deterred from pursuing theory of knowledge. On 20 May, when Russell was about to begin the segment on acquaintance with universals, he reported that Wittgenstein had come with a "refutation of the theory of judgment which I used to hold."[50] This seems not to have been received seriously either, since the tense Russell used suggests that he no longer held this theory, and hence that the criticisms were not germane to the present work. Russell also saw Wittgenstein on the 23rd, at the beginning of the composition of the chapter on logical form. But a few days later Russell showed Wittgenstein a "crucial part of what I have been writing", and Russell reported that Wittgenstein had said that it was "all wrong, not realizing the difficulties—that he had tried my view and knew it wouldn't work."[51] Since Russell had been working for just two days on the second part, that dealing with judgment, it seems likely that this was what Wittgenstein criticized. Russell was disturbed by the criticism, felt he could not understand it, and believed that Wittgenstein had not understood the problem. In any case, Russell pushed ahead with his writing. On 31 May he wrote that he could "circumvent Wittgenstein's problems" if he couldn't solve them, and that he had recovered from the criticisms.[52]

In mid-June Russell's view was darker. In a letter arranging a luncheon with his mother and Russell for June 18, Wittgenstein wrote:

> I can now express my objection to your theory of judgment exactly: I believe it is obvious that, from the prop[osition] "A judges that (say) a is in the Rel[ation] R to b", if correctly analysed, the prop[osition] "aRb . **v** . ~ aRb" must follow directly *without the use of any other premiss.* This condition is not fulfilled by your theory.[53]

There may have been discussion of Russell's problems that day, for the day following the luncheon Russell wrote to Ottoline that "yesterday" he had felt "ready for suicide", and confessed: "All that has gone wrong with me lately comes from Wittgenstein's attack on my work—I have only just realized this. It was very difficult to be honest about it, as it makes a large

49 Russell to Morrell, #775, [14 May 1913].
50 Russell to Morrell, #782, pmk. 21 May 1913.
51 Russell to Morrell, #787, pmk. 28 May 1913. This letter, written on the 27th, records Wittgenstein's visit on the 26th.
52 Russell to Morrell, #791, pmk. 31 May 1913.
53 Wittgenstein *1974*, R.12, [June 1913].

part of the book I meant to write impossible for years to come probably." It was, he said, the first time that he had ever failed in honesty over his work.[54] No further details were given of the points on which Wittgenstein's criticisms made his work impossible, and Russell still spoke as if he were laying aside his book only for a holiday. But it is difficult to avoid the conclusion that Wittgenstein's criticisms were seen as affecting such a vital part of Russell's whole epistemology that there seemed no way of either avoiding or solving the problems. Later that summer, Russell wrote to Wittgenstein about these problems. Wittgenstein responded that he was sorry his criticisms had "paralyzed" Russell but that he thought Russell needed "a correct theory of propositions".[55] We do not know how much of the book was shown to Wittgenstein; it is possible that the whole work was discussed between them. The confrontation was the more painful as it was accompanied by personal conflict; Russell talked of "bad times" with Wittgenstein, and, in an interesting and extended comparison, told Ottoline that he knew how he depressed and irritated her by seeing how Wittgenstein depressed and irritated him.[56] At any rate, Russell's work on the book ceased, and the rest of his summer was unhappy with personal and work worries.

III. HARVARD AND PUBLICATION IN "THE MONIST"

After he stopped writing the book, Russell turned briefly to sketching out ideas for the Lowell Lectures. On 20 June 1913, Oliver Strachey acknowledged receiving Russell's manuscript, which may have been the chapters on relations, as this had been a topic discussed between them. In fact, he discussed with Strachey the use of the term "relating relation", which Russell employed in the book to distinguish the relating relation binding the terms of a complex from a relation which does not bind the terms of a complex. In the context of belief the relation between the subject and the complex of what is believed is the relating relation of believing, while the relating relation internal to the complex believed is the relation between the terms of the complex believed.[57] On 26 June Russell wrote to R. B. Perry asking the permission of the Harvard Department to publish criticisms of James and the neo-realists in the *Monist* in order that his students could read them prior to the seminar. Perry's favourable reply is dated 7 July.[58] These

---

54 Russell to Morrell, #811, pmk. 20 June 1913.
55 Wittgenstein *1974*, R.13, 22 July 1913.
56 Russell to Morrell, #798, pmk. 5 June 1913.
57 See 80–4 and 114–15 below. Besides the topic of relating relations, Strachey discusses the distinction between "proposition" and "complex" (made on 111 below) and that between permutative and non-permutative beliefs (Chapter V of Part II).
58 Russell to Perry, 26 June 1913, Harvard University Archives; Perry to Russell, 7 July 1913, RA.

criticisms are to be found mainly in the second of the first three *Monist* articles: I—"Preliminary Description of Experience", II—"Neutral Monism", and III—"Analysis of Experience". They were published under the common heading "On the Nature of Acquaintance" in January, April and July of 1914.

Shortly after Ottoline came home, late in June, Russell left for a walking holiday in Cornwall with Whitehead's two sons. When he returned he told her that he had sent off a new syllabus of the Lowell Lectures but would not work on them until September.[59] Again he went on holiday to Italy for a second walking tour, this time with C. P. Sanger, and returned toward the end of August. He began the drafting of the lectures and finished the first draft on 25 September;[60] these lectures became *Our Knowledge of the External World*. Wittgenstein visited him briefly late in August and was said to have "done extraordinarily good work".[61] By 1 October, Russell was planning to begin work on logic and his lectures on theory of knowledge for Harvard.

Early in October Wittgenstein came with a great number of new ideas, prior to going to Norway to live in solitude until he should have perfected them. Russell realized the importance and originality of the ideas but could persuade Wittgenstein neither to stay in Cambridge nor to write them out. Finally Wittgenstein agreed to talk in the presence of a shorthand stenographer, and Russell was thus able to obtain a record of the new thoughts on logic. These notes were the basis of the "Notes on Logic", which Russell took to the United States to use in his logic course. The process of extracting some statement of these ideas from Wittgenstein was not an easy one, and, as Russell wrote to Lucy Donnelly, it took up all his time and thought for a week.[62] Wittgenstein departed on 14 October, leaving Russell exhausted, relieved, and anxious for his friend's mental stability.

Soon after, Whitehead came, and they shared Wittgenstein's new ideas, the work Whitehead had been doing in geometry, and the work Russell had been doing on the construction of scientific concepts as part of the preparation for the Lowell Lectures. A new spirit of hope and accomplishment seems to have appeared, and as Russell continued his revision of the Lowell Lectures he expressed confidence and pleasure in what he was doing.

On 24 October Russell wrote to Ottoline Morrell that he was preparing a talk on "time" to be given to the Moral Sciences Club[63] and had gone over

59 Russell to Morrell, #831, [19 July 1913].
60 Russell to Morrell, #876, pmk. 25 Sept. 1913.
61 Russell to Morrell, #856, [c. 29 Aug. 1913]. See also, in Wittgenstein *1974*, R.15, [Summer 1913], Wittgenstein's account of his work, a criticism of *Principia*'s axiom of reducibility.
62 Russell to Lucy Martin Donnelly, 19 Oct. 1913, RA. For Wittgenstein's "Notes on Logic", see his *1979*, and McGuinness *1972*.
63 The minutes of the Cambridge University Moral Sciences Club record that Russell read a paper on "The Perception of Time" on 24 October 1913 and provide a summary of the

"the stuff on theory of knowledge that I wrote last spring". He found that
the early portion was as good as he had thought, but that "it goes to
pieces" where Wittgenstein said it did. Russell remarked that he had not
thought that Wittgenstein would have been able to get out as much work as
in fact he had, and now this work had put a "completely new face upon
whole vast regions".[64] In the meantime, Russell was finishing the lectures
and sending them to be typed. In early November he turned to the work of
the Cambridge term, and to correcting the typescripts of the lectures. He
also wrote to Perry and sent a syllabus for each of his courses. It is
interesting that in the accompanying letter he said that "In my lectures, B
will be shorter than it should be, because I can't arrive at satisfactory views
on the subjects concerned; on the other hand, I shall have a lot to say about
physics and sense-data and realism."[65] As the enclosed syllabus is missing,
one cannot be sure of what the letter B designates. We note that in one
outline of the work, which appears from its rearrangement to have been
tentative, and hence, earlier than the manuscript, "B" refers to the second
part of the analytic section of the work, that is, the part on judgment, or
belief. (See Appendix A.3.) It is likely that, since there were three parts, "B"
would refer to the same part in any outline that Russell would have sent.
This suggestion is supported by the fact that the same material receives the
lightest treatment in the Victor Lenzen notes of the seminar on theory of
knowledge discussed below.

On 18 November Jourdain, who was instrumental in placing Russell's
work in the *Monist*, wrote to ask for the return of two "parts" of "On the
Nature of Acquaintance" when he had finished correcting them.[66] These
could have been the first and second segments of the three-article series, as
we know the journal often had a short interval between the receipt of an
article and the printing of it. Or the two segments could have been the
second and third articles, to appear in the April and July issues. (Russell had
told Perry on 9 November that the *Monist* had delayed publication.) But we
know (see below) that the Chicago office of Open Court may not have had
the third segment on hand even in late May. Of course, Jourdain could have

---

paper: "... Mr. Russell then read a paper entitled 'The Perception of Time'. The subject
was treated psychologically, the essayist's aim being to determine the fundamental experiences upon which our notions of time are based. To do this a series of propositions was laid
down, embodying the most important points which must go to form the finished theory of
time. Great emphasis was laid upon the distinction between present, past and future which
constitute mental time, and succession and co-existence which constitute physical time: the
former are relations between subject and object, the latter relations between object and
object, or rather between the constituted elements of one complex object ..." (Cambridge
University Library).
64 Russell to Morrell, #900, [24 Oct. 1913].
65 Russell to Perry, 9 Nov. 1913, Harvard University Archives.
66 Jourdain to Russell, 18 Nov. 1913, RA.

kept typescripts of the articles in his possession, sending them only when they were required (although the end of May seems late for the July issue). It is possible that the November reference is to proofs rather than typescripts; Jourdain's letter expresses concern about getting proofs of her article to Karin Costelloe in time for her to return them for the January issue. But as Russell reported reading proofs of the second article in February of 1914, this seems unlikely. It is probable that the reference is to correcting typescripts of the first two of the articles, a stage which Russell did not happen to mention to Ottoline Morrell when he prepared the revisions.[67]

After a Christmas holiday in Rome, Russell returned to Trinity and a period of intensive work. He listed among his activities: preparation of theory of knowledge lectures for Harvard, work on important philosophical discoveries which went into both the Lowell Lectures and "The Relation of Sense-Data to Physics", and a lecture on evolution. All of this was five days' work, with the aid of Jourdain's shorthand secretary.[68] Soon afterwards he wrote the essay "Mysticism and Logic", and a preface to the translation of Poincaré's *Science and Method*.

From January to early March Russell was lecturing at Cambridge University; actually he was giving the Lowell Lectures there,[69] and correcting and revising them as he did so. The lectures went to the publisher (Open Court) at the end of January, and Russell then turned to reworking Wittgenstein's notes on logic, in preparation for his course on logic at Harvard. On February 26 he corrected proofs for the second *Monist* article (the one on "Neutral Monism") and left for the United States on 7 March.

Of the work that he did for the Harvard seminar on theory of knowledge, all that has survived is the description of the course which was entered in the Harvard *Official Register*, which was submitted before the book was written, and the notes that were taken by Lenzen and Eliot.[70] Because of the brevity of the Eliot notes only Lenzen's notes will be analyzed in detail. Like

---

67 At any rate, it is certain that by this time there were to be three articles, for on 18 February 1914 Jourdain wrote to C. K. Ogden, editor of *The Cambridge Magazine*, that one reason that "*The Monist* this year will, I hope, be really good" is "Russell's three articles" (letter in Ogden papers, McMaster).

68 Russell to Morrell, #960, 8 Jan. 1914.

69 Florence, "Cambridge 1909–1919 and Its Aftermath" (*1977*, 26); Wood, *Bertrand Russell: The Passionate Sceptic* (*1957*, 93).

70 Notebook of Victor Lenzen from Russell's seminar at Harvard, Spring term, 1914, RA. For the course descriptions, see Appendices A.1 and A.2. T. S. Eliot was a student in Russell's class in logic and in his seminar on theory of knowledge. The notes from these classes are among the Eliot manuscripts in the collection of the Houghton Library of Harvard University. The theory of knowledge notes are extremely brief, consisting of seven manuscript pages of a notebook, and dating from 17 March to 28 April 1914. The last page of notes is torn and there are no notes from 28 April to 23 May. What notes there are are very brief equivalents to Lenzen's much fuller notes. There are also two rough draft typescripts

most lecture notes, Lenzen's have gaps and incomplete sentences, and we have no way of knowing if he attended every session, or recorded each session equally carefully. The notes are handwritten in a notebook which is sewn together; so there is little chance that pages have escaped. Also there is a continuity in the notes; the earlier ones have decipherable dates on them, beginning with 17, 19 and 21 March. The 149 pages of notes on Russell's lectures are, however, full enough to be compared with the six *Monist* articles and the rest of the manuscript of the book. Russell began with an introductory lecture which seems designed for the specific seminar and which corresponds very little with any portion of the book, except that there is a discussion of the relation of theory of knowledge to logic and to psychology which also occurs in the fourth article. The second and succeeding lectures follow in a general way the order of topics and the argument of the *Monist* articles. The preliminary description of experience and the analysis of neutral monism are close to the articles, and readings are assigned from the books from which Russell quotes in the articles. There is a particularly close similarity between the conclusion of the third article and a detailed discussion in the seminar of the problems of "contents" and of Alexius Meinong's view. The notes are also especially close to the text of the fourth article where the numbering of points, the examples used, and the wording are strikingly similar. The discussion of premisses, for instance, is almost word for word the same. The discussion of sensation and imagination is considerably shorter in the seminar notes than in the article, but the points made and the summary of the kinds of acquaintance with particulars are the same in substance. The notes headed "Experience of Time" are again in very close correspondence with the *Monist* article of the same title. The difference is that in the notes there is a further development of the technical definition of moments in time, similar to that given in *Our Knowledge of the External World* (*1914*, 116–22). Since we know from the correspondence with Ottoline Morrell that the article on time was revised after the seminar, we can assume that Russell decided not to include this technical detail in the *Monist* article.

When Russell turned to the discussion of acquaintance with universals, the part of the seminar which would correspond to the seventh, eighth, and ninth chapters of Part I of the book, the correspondence between the book and the lecture notes is less close. Russell headed the seminar discussion "Acquaintance with Universals" and said that he subsumed traditional universals and predicates under relations. But the treatment of relations is

---

of what appear to be papers written for the theory of knowledge seminar; both deal with theory of objects and make references to Meinong, to Russell, and to an idealist position. See also Lenzen, "Bertrand Russell at Harvard, 1914" (1971), and Costello, "Logic in 1914 and Now" (1957).

much slighter than in the book. In particular, it does not include the discussion of the troublesome problem of the "sense" of the relation, nor the solution that Russell offered in the manuscript by postulating acquaint-ance with the form of the complex, in addition to acquaintance with the terms and the relation itself. Instead, in the seminar notes there is a discussion of the direct perception of a fact; this is distinguished from the proposition referring to a fact, which involves the possibility of error. When one is acquainted with or perceives a fact, one may not be aware of its components but only have a direct perception that it is the way it is. The "fact" here replaces the "complex" of the manuscript discussion, and there seems to be perception on one end of the relation of acquaintance and the fact on the other. There is no treatment in the lecture notes of the other topics of Chapter IX, "Logical Data", and no reference to the most general of the forms of logic which are known directly and a priori.

The lecture notes contain only a brief treatment of belief, or judgment, and of propositions. There is a distinction made between atomic and molecular propositions, and a reference to the multiple relation theory of judgment. The treatment of the other topics of the second part of the book is cursory, and no developed theory of truth is given. Instead there is an abrupt break and Russell begins a new topic headed "Epistemology of Physics". This is essentially the material he was dealing with in the Lowell Lectures and in "The Relation of Sense-Data to Physics", but which he treated more technically here. This topic covers the last sixty-one pages of the Lenzen notebook, except for the notes on his reading assignments at the very end.

It should be mentioned that judgment was the topic of the paper which Lenzen presented as a requirement of the seminar, and that a copy of the paper with detailed commentary by Russell has been preserved in the Bancroft Library. The notes show Russell still maintaining a "realist" multiple relation theory of judgment, at least in so far as this is the standpoint from which he criticizes Lenzen's paper. It might be mentioned also that Russell held Lenzen in high regard as a student and as a person, referring to him kindly in his letters to Ottoline Morrell, and later accepting him as a private student in England during the war.

After the term was finished at Harvard Russell made some visits and delivered some lectures in various cities and universities before returning home in June. In late May, when he visited Chicago, he was to lunch with Paul Carus, the head of the Open Court Publishing Company.[71] A few days later, on 29 May, Dr. Carus' secretary, Lydia Robinson, wrote to Miss Cook, the head of his Chicago office, and informed her that Russell's three articles "On the Nature of Acquaintance" would be published by them as a

71 Paul Carus to Miss Cook, 21 May 1914, Open Court papers.

book. She asked Miss Cook: "Counting the July installment as about the same length as the others, what price would you put on this?" This is interesting for several reasons: this and other inter-office correspondence[72] in the Open Court papers is the only indication we have at this time of a plan for the publication of these articles as a book; this information might explain why the first three articles had a common title as well as individual titles while the second three had only individual titles, although we know from other evidence that they all belonged to the part of the book devoted, in nine chapters, to "On the Nature of Acquaintance"; it reveals that the publisher's office did not have in hand the third article, which was due to be published in July; and it raises the question of whether in preparing the chapters for publication Russell revised them so that the first three would constitute a self-contained unit. But whether the third chapter was already at the printer's, or whether Russell had it in his possession, or whether it had been left in England for Jourdain to send on, we do not know. Nor do we know if the plan for issuing the first three articles as a monograph came early, and influenced the revising, or developed over lunch while Russell and Carus talked shop. We do not know why, in the end, they were not so issued. If it seems unusual for a book to be so brief, it should be mentioned that it was not uncommon for Carus to publish series of articles from the journal as short monographs. Russell's criticism of Henri Bergson had elicited a great deal of response, and Carus entertained the idea of publishing it, along with some answers to it, as a small book. This too did not come to fruition.

After Russell returned to England there is little mention of his philosophical work or of the articles and the book in his correspondence. He became increasingly preoccupied with the threat of war, and then with its actuality. First he corrected the proofs of *Our Knowledge of the External World*. He referred in a letter to Ottoline Morrell of 16 July 1914 to working on the topic of sensation and imagination; this may have been for the article of that title (Chapter v of Part I) which appeared in the *Monist* of January 1915.[73] In February of 1915 he reported to her that he was revising an article on "Time" for the *Monist*—published as "On the Experience of Time" in April 1915 (Chapter VI of Part I).[74]

In the inter-office correspondence of Open Court during 1914–16 most of the attention given to Russell concerned the publication of the first and

72 Miss Lydia Robinson to Miss Cook, 29 May 1914, Open Court papers.
73 Russell to Morrell, #1,053, pmk. 16 July 1914.
74 Russell to Morrell, #1,216, 2 Feb. 1915. The only other known reference by Russell to the time article (or, indeed, to any of the six *Monist* articles) comes in his review in 1919 of Dewey's *Essays in Experimental Logic*. Russell complains that Dewey fails to take account of the analysis of time-order suggested in *Our Knowledge of the External World*, Chap. IV, and in his *Monist* article (Russell *1919b*, 23).

second editions of *Our Knowledge of the External World* and of *Justice in War-Time*. A few references to "On the Nature of Acquaintance" occur. In August of 1914 Dr. Carus was asked by his secretary what Jourdain had said about the relation of "this last short essay of Russell's" to "On the Nature of Acquaintance".[75] A customer inquired as to the availability of this book, and in August of 1915 there was a discussion of whether the book should be withdrawn from the list as they did not have it.[76] In October of 1915 inquiries were to be made of Jourdain concerning the status of the book.[77] In February of 1916 a customer was to be told that Open Court was still planning to publish it when the author had made "some additions".[78] After that no reference to the book occurs in the extant correspondence, and apparently the project was dropped. We do not know whether Russell was too preoccupied with the war, or whether he did not know how to revise it satisfactorily, or whether he, Jourdain, or Carus lost interest in its publication.

IV. THE QUESTION OF REVISIONS

Now that the narrative of the writing of *Theory of Knowledge*, the publishing of the articles, the seminar on theory of knowledge, and the projected publication of a book composed of the first three articles is complete, we have an overview of the project and its place in Russell's life and thought. It seems certain that the book as it was originally conceived was to have had two main sections, analytic and constructive, and that the first of these was to have had three parts, devoted to acquaintance, belief, and inference. Of the first of these three parts, two main segments were to consist of acquaintance with particulars and acquaintance with universals. Of the segment concerning acquaintance with particulars, six chapters (or the equivalent of

75 L. G. R. [Lydia G. Robinson] to Dr. Carus, 10 Aug. 1914. It seems likely that the "last short essay" refers to "Definitions and Methodological Principles in Theory of Knowledge", published in the *Monist* in October of 1914.

76 Miss Cook to Percy Morley of Open Court, 7 Aug. and 11 Aug. 1915. The list concerned first appeared in the publisher's supplement to the July 1914 *Monist*. Under Russell's name (p. 8) there are two entries—*Our Knowledge of the External World* and *On the Nature of Acquaintance*. The latter, no. 501, was priced at $1.25.

77 The La Salle office of Open Court wrote to Miss Cook, 6 Oct. 1915, and asked that inquiries be made of Jourdain concerning two projected books: Mach's *Theory of Heat* and Russell's *On the Nature of Acquaintance*. The letters from Jourdain to Open Court of this period make frequent mention of the Mach book but not of the Russell book; all extant letters seem to discuss only *Our Knowledge of the External World* (1914) or *Justice in War-Time* (1916), or the articles which became *Principles of Social Reconstruction* (1916). No answer to the Chicago office query has been found, and neither title was published.

78 Paul Carus to Miss Cook, 9 Feb. 1916. This letter affirmed his intention to publish *On the Nature of Acquaintance* as a book.

six chapters) appeared as articles in the *Monist*, but are missing from the manuscript. The remaining portion of the part on acquaintance (Chapters VII–IX) is extant in the manuscript, as is the entire second part of the analytic section, that on belief or judgment (Chapters I–VII of Part II). Thus there are ten chapters present in the manuscript.

The second, or constructive, section, which was to have dealt with the use of logical techniques in the construction of space, time, cause, and matter, was not written as the second half of the original book, nor as a second book, but is represented in the constructive work done in the Lowell Lectures. Thus, in preparing the lectures Russell borrowed from what would have been the entire concluding section of his major project, and provided an example of what such constructive philosophy would be, as is indicated in the full title *Our Knowledge of the External World as a Field for Scientific Method in Philosophy*. "The Relation of Sense-Data to Physics" (see below, this section) and the section of the theory of knowledge seminar headed "Epistemology of Physics" belong to the same category. It seems, then, that the re-evaluation which Wittgenstein's criticisms and new work in logic forced on Russell left the theory of belief irretrievably undermined and added further difficulties to those already besetting the problem of the definition of a proposition. He still found the work on acquaintance with particulars viable, and he still believed in the method of construction, but the link between them, the theory of belief and the treatment of inference, was damaged beyond repair. A gaping hole had appeared in Russell's theory of knowledge.

Although the information presented thus far has shown that the missing six chapters are the *Monist* articles of 1914 and 1915, and thus that the entire text of *Theory of Knowledge* presented here can be accepted as an integrated piece of work, a question may still be raised about the extent of revision that the original chapters may have undergone prior to their publication in the *Monist*. If that revision could be inferred to be extensive, then it might be asked if the reconstructed text is a coherent piece of work. Since we have not found the manuscript of the first six chapters, no definitive answer can be given to this challenge, but several kinds of indirect evidence can be adduced as to the extent and nature of possible revisions.

One line of evidence depends on our knowledge of the intervals between the writing, revising, and publishing of each of the six chapters. We know that all, or most, of them were written in May of 1913, and we know the date of the publication of each; we also have a few clues to the period in which work was done on some of the articles. The first article, which was published in January of 1914, was almost certainly revised sometime in late October or early November; we know that it was revised, at least minimally, by the replacement of references to "chapters" with references to "articles". We know, too, that Russell was fully engaged in other activities from the end of the first week in June until Wittgenstein left for Norway in mid-October. It seems that there would not have been enough time to thoroughly rework the material.

The second article was published in April of 1914, and Russell read proofs in late February. He may also have worked on it at the same time that he revised the first article, and these may be the two parts of "On the Nature of Acquaintance" which Jourdain had asked to be returned on 18 November 1913.

The third article was published in July, and we saw that the *Monist* may not have had a text of it by late May. But we find no references to Russell working on it, or reading proof for it. Russell referred in this article (at 43: 35 below) to the publication of "The Relation of Sense-Data to Physics" in *Scientia* in July of 1914. This article was read as a paper during his visit to America—Russell referred to it in his letter to Ottoline Morrell as the one he had written "the day at Leysin", that is, when he visited her there at the beginning of January 1914. The third article could have been revised while he was in the United States, or left with Jourdain before he came to the United States. July publication would have been impossible if he had left the revision and typing until after his return in late June.

There are no references of any kind to revising or reading proof for the fourth article, which appeared in the October *Monist*; the closeness of the Lenzen notes to the text might suggest that Russell had that text in front of him when he lectured. The reference in the article (at 46n. below) to work done by Wittgenstein means that it is unlikely that the passage was written prior to October of 1913. The work referred to in the footnote is the problem of finding the appropriate logical form to fit the fact of judgment. In any case it seems likely that there were no substantive revisions after the lectures were given.

The fifth article, on "Sensation and Imagination", was apparently referred to as a topic on which Russell was working on 16 July 1914; he said he was doing a "great deal of work".[79] This suggests that he was doing some extending and, perhaps, revising; there was plenty of time, since it did not appear until January of 1915. In article form it is longer than the Lenzen notes for the lectures would suggest.

In a letter to Ottoline Morrell on 2 February 1915, Russell reported revising the article "On the Experience of Time" for the *Monist*, and it was published in April. The time would not exclude extensive revision, but we saw that this article was closely akin to the Lenzen notes—except that the notes include a longer and more technical development. This might suggest that it was in the deletion of this long discussion that the chapter was

---

79 Russell to Morrell, #1,053, pmk. 16 July 1914. This work included going through the proofs of Keynes' *Treatise on Probability* and discussing it with Broad and Keynes.

changed. Of course, the Lenzen notes may record a longer treatment appropriate for the seminar because of its later discussion of what Russell usually called the "constructive" part of theory of knowledge.

There may be some significance in the fact that all of the footnotes in the six articles are numbered except for one in the third article, which is marked with an asterisk. This note refers to an emended formula in the text.[80] To avoid the necessity of renumbering the footnotes, the preferred formula might have been put in and marked by an asterisk for a minimal disturbance of the text in proof. Since the improved formula found in the footnote occurs in the running text of the corresponding passage of the Lenzen notes, it suggests that Russell had submitted the typescript of the third article before giving the material as a lecture, and hence before the May meeting with Carus.

A feature of the surviving manuscript which raises speculation about possible revision is the renumbering of the manuscript chapters of the first part of the work. What we have as Chapter VII, "On the Acquaintance Involved in Our Knowledge of Relations", originally was numbered "VI" and has had added to it an extra "I". Chapter VIII has similarly been converted from "VII"; and Chapter IX was so numbered after the original "VIII" was crossed out. Does this indicate that a chapter was added to the original sequence of chapters in a revision prior to the presentation of the articles for publication? If so, then the first 142 pages might originally have comprised five chapters, and the later numbers may have been altered to match the new numbering. On the other hand, Russell may simply have made a mistake in the original numbering of these chapters.

Another approach to estimating the probability of extensive revision between the manuscript and the articles is to compare the estimated length of the chapters as they formed part of the missing 142 pages of manuscript, and the actual length of the articles. This is difficult to do with precision because of Russell's habit of varying the length of the manuscript page, depending on when he came to the end of a paragraph (see sec. II of "Textual Principles and Methods"). A preliminary estimate of the number of words found by counting the average number of words on about thirty pages of manuscript, and the average number of words on about ten *Monist* pages, leads us to expect that there were about 5,000 more words in the articles than in the missing manuscript. However, a more careful calculation of the average number of characters per word, and the average number of characters on a page, narrows the margin to just 1,200 more words in the articles, not a large discrepancy in the light of the limitations of the estimate.

The comparison of the gross length of the first 142 pages of manuscript and the first six articles suggests a more refined comparison. By using the

---

80 *Monist*, 24 (July 1914): 444. See below, 38.

passages in letters to Ottoline Morrell where Russell reported what topic and what page he had reached, we are able to chart those areas where the closest correlation of word-count occurs, and those where the greatest discrepancy appears. If we compare the length of the manuscript, as described in the letters, with the length of the same topic's treatment in the articles, we find the following. On 11 May Russell told her that he had reached page 55, had finished the refutation of neutral monism, and was going on to his own view; by character-count method this would be 231 words a page, multiplied by 55, for a total of 12,705 words. This is nearly equivalent to the total at the end of the second article, 12,864 words. Next, Russell said by 13 May he had reached page 80 and had finished the discussion of "the present time". That discussion takes place just past the middle of Chapter III (38 below), and he carried on working that day. The next morning he was thinking of sensation and imagination. Thus he would now have reached the end of Chapter III, which would yield 18,480 words. The first three articles, which bring the discussion up to the same point, total 18,623 words. On 16 May, Russell had reached 110 pages, and had finished sensation and imagination; thus we project that he had written 25,410 words. By the end of the fifth article of the *Monist*, which is devoted to sensation and imagination, there are 27,198 printed words. There is thus a discrepancy of over 1,600 words by which the *Monist* material seems to be longer than the manuscript treatment of the topics of Chapters IV and V. Finally, on 19 May, Russell had reached 142 pages, and the end of Chapter VI or 32,802 words; the end of the *Monist* articles marks the accumulation of 33,997 words; here there is a discrepancy of 1,200 words.

Perhaps the additional 1,200 words can be located more accurately. We noted that in his letters Russell went directly from "the present time" to "sensation and imagination", but the first topic occurs considerably before the end of the third article, the second throughout the fifth article. The topic of the fourth article was not mentioned at all by Russell in his chapter by chapter report in the letters. Let us suppose, then, that the fourth article was added in its entirety when the work was revised for the publication of the articles. But, in that case, as the fourth article is 3,453 words long (the equivalent of fifteen manuscript pages), the total length of the six articles would be more than 2,200 words greater than that of the six *Monist* articles. Yet the total discrepancy is only 1,200 words by which the *Monist* articles are longer than the 142 holograph pages. We must assume either that some addition and rearrangement took place, or that, if the fourth article was a sheer addition, some deletions in the manuscript occurred when the articles were prepared for publication.

Are there any other discrepancies between the description given to Ottoline Morrell of what Russell was writing and what, in fact, is discussed in the articles? There is no mention of the discussion of "contents" and no reference to Meinong in Russell's account of the third chapter—but perhaps he reported only what he expected his correspondent to understand. It is possible that he simply omitted to mention some topics of his manuscript, such as "contents" and "definitions and methodological principles". But, from the standpoint of the topics discussed, the discussion in the fourth chapter is oddly placed in the series if one thinks of the articles as comprising a book. Logically one might expect definitions, the discussion of the relation of psychology, logic, and theory of knowledge, and the statement of method in an introductory chapter. In fact, Russell told Ottoline Morrell there would be such a chapter but that he would write it later. Could this material have been added later in order to supply what was missing from the manuscript but after the first chapter was already in print (or in the press)? The later addition of the fourth chapter is also suggested by Jourdain's letter to Ogden (see xxxi, note 67) and by the inquiry to Carus (xxxv, note 75).

In addition to the question of discrepancy, there is the question of what Russell informed Ottoline Morrell he would do if he changed the manuscript. There were three significant alterations that his letters mentioned he intended to make: add an introductory chapter, put in more controversy and discussion of the positions of other philosophers, and weaken the conclusions.[81] Do the articles seem to incorporate revisions of any of these kinds? One possible revision, perhaps, is the acknowledgement to Wittgenstein already mentioned, and the treatment of Meinong is a second possibility. The text refers to many philosophers, but it is not, as it stands, heavily laden with references; hence it is unlikely that this kind of revision was carried out. Some weakening of conclusions can be seen in some of the authorial alterations in the holograph; these alterations seem to have occurred during the writing of the work. Perhaps the insertion of Chapter IV, that is, of what normally would have been an introductory chapter, is the most likely change for Russell to have made in revision. If we turn to the outline of the book (see Appendix C) which shows a detailed plan for the third part of the analytic section—that is, the part labeled "Molecular Propositional Thought" but referred to in the letters as the third part on inference—we find that a considerable number of the chapter headings refer to premisses of theory of knowledge, epistemological and logical premisses, and the inference involved in them. And, as we have seen, the fourth article also deals with the topic of logical and epistemological premisses. It is thus possible that some of this chapter, in a rewriting, could have borrowed ideas originally intended for the third part of the analytic section and not touched by the criticism of the second part. At any rate, it seems that the fourth article, with its discussion of the relation of epistemology to psychology and logic, its definition of terms to be used, its many forward references, its

81 Russell to Morrell, #768, pmk. 8 May 1913; #785, 24 May 1913.

discussion of premisses, and its acknowledgement of the unpublished work of Wittgenstein, is a plausible candidate for the location of changes undertaken during revision for publication.

It should be noted that in the fourth article Russell both acknowledged in a footnote Wittgenstein's contribution in recognizing that "a fact of a different logical form" is involved in judgment, and referred forward, in the phrase "as soon as we reach the theory of judgment" (46: 17–18), to later portions of the book. This suggests that Russell had not abandoned the hope of salvaging the book, even when he seemed to be admitting Wittgenstein's criticism. The passage to which the footnote is appended is ambiguous. The recognition of a difference of form between subject–predicate and relational facts, and propositional facts involving judgment, could be read as that between acquaintance as a two-term relation and judgment as involving two levels of relations and the possibility of error. But this distinction was part of the basic structure of the epistemological argument and could scarcely be attributed to Wittgenstein since it appears in the earliest outlines and sketches of the proposed book. On the other hand, if the reference is to Wittgenstein's criticism of his treatment of judgment, a criticism which the letters to Ottoline Morrell and to Wittgenstein lead us to believe caused Russell to abandon his work "as impossible for years to come probably", why would Russell be making a forward reference to the theory of judgment when it was still vulnerable to that criticism? In some passages Russell makes a distinction between logical and epistemological problems and puts aside the logical problems as not presently relevant to the argument, but in the passage in question he specifically concludes that no complete separation can be made between epistemology and logic. One other explanation might be that Russell was referring forward to other portions of theory of knowledge as a field of inquiry rather than to his own book. But Russell may have hoped for a solution to the problem, and this hope would explain the inclusion of both the acknowledgement to Wittgenstein and the references to unwritten parts of the book, the saving of the manuscript, and the renumbering of the chapters.

In our review of the Lenzen notes we noted three places where there seemed an especially close resemblance between the articles and the notes. Since these notes were taken between March and May of 1914, it is likely that Russell would have followed the text more closely if the writing in question had been material he was currently revising. If this was the case, the discussion of Meinong and of "contents" at the end of the third article, the fourth article, and the discussion of time from the sixth article, would be candidates for possible and contemporary revision. All of the material mentioned could have been revised at that time, in terms of publication schedules.

A further question can be asked concerning possible revisions: Are there places in the manuscript of Chapter VII of Part I through the seven chapters of Part II where there are signs of conflict of meaning, of inconsistency of sense, or of the author signalling a change of opinion? Since the book circles back to discuss some topics from different perspectives, it ought to be possible to note such changes. Inevitably there will be slight differences of wording as one topic is discussed in different contexts, for example, as time is discussed in relation to acquaintance, and, later, in the context of belief. In our view a careful study of the entire body of the work does not reveal any substantial revision in thought, or any inconsistency between what is said in the first six chapters and what is said elsewhere in the text, or between earlier and later chapters of the manuscript, with the important exception of the acknowledgement of the problems pointed out by Wittgenstein.

Our conclusion is that there is no evidence of other changes of philosophical position between the writing of the book and the preparation of the articles for publication. We can, however, construct several explanations of the evidence of some reworking of the text. A plausible but not provable hypothesis is that when Russell came to prepare the first three of his manuscript chapters for publication he revised them sufficiently to make a self-contained unit. This would not necessarily mean that he added or subtracted any material, although he may have balanced an insertion with a deletion; the closeness of the estimated word-count precludes any major change in length. Perhaps he took out some of the definitions of terms from the original third chapter, since they would obviously have referred forward to their use in an extended analysis; and perhaps he replaced this section with a discussion of "contents". This material, if it was deleted, would have been put into a separate article, the fourth.

Whether Russell made such changes or not, it seems likely that he decided to put into a new fourth article material which would have gone into the introduction, or into the third part of the analytic section of the book. These sections would have included a discussion of the relation of epistemology to logic and psychology and a discussion of the status of premisses in theory of knowledge, and would have been the appropriate place to acknowledge Wittgenstein's contribution to logical theory and his discovery of an unsolved problem. It may also be the case that some of the definitions of terms came from an originally quite long chapter on sensation and imagination, which, when the fourth article was added, became "v" (although it followed immediately after the third in the account in the letters). This is suggested by the larger word-count discrepancy at the end of the chapter on sensation and imagination than at other points, including that at the end of Chapter VI. It seems that to account for the word-count parallels it must be assumed that the fourth article contains material not in the first 142 pages of manuscript, and probably some reworked material that originally had another location in the proposed book. This hypothesis would also account for the renumbering of the present Chapters VII, VIII and IX, although one wonders why the chapters would be renumbered if they were not to be published. They were not thrown out, however, and perhaps Russell thought he might find some way of salvaging the material. Further archival research may uncover new clues to the revision of the manuscript of *Theory of Knowledge*; meanwhile, it seems that the book is marked by a high degree of unity and continuity, and affords an overview of the work Russell did during those years, and of the direction of his development.

V. CONCLUSION

How did Russell go on with philosophy with this large breach in his theory of knowledge? The answer is, with great difficulty. He seems to have forced himself to leap over the gap, and to do the constructive work without the epistemological foundation he had hoped to give it. His correspondence with Whitehead shows that his undertaking to make construction the topic of the Lowell Lectures was an act of desperation.[82] At the same time he made an effort to understand and incorporate into his own work on logic the new ideas that Wittgenstein had shared with him. The continuance of the war prevented any further sharing of ideas, and while Wittgenstein, in the Austrian army, was carrying his notebooks with him and revising and rewriting what was to become, by 1919, the *Logisch-Philosophische Abhandlung*, Russell, in England, was engaged in efforts to end the war and to protect internees and conscientious objectors.[83] He had no teaching except occasional private students, as Trinity College declined to renew the lectureship of such a traitorous philosopher.[84] He did little writing of philosophy until late in 1917, when he came to believe that further opposition to the war was futile.[85] It was at this time that he again planned to write a book in nontechnical terms giving a presentation of the new work in logic. He also gave a series of lectures on philosophy under the sponsorship of H. Wildon Carr and other friends between 22 January and 12 March 1918.[86] They were published in the *Monist* in 1918 and 1919, and no authorized republication of them occurred until 1956. Yet, it is these lectures on "The Philosophy of Logical Atomism" which are taken as initiating a new and

---

82 Russell *1968*, 57, 78. See also Russell to Morrell, #813, pmk. 21 June 1913; #816, 27 June 1913; #825, [9 July 1913].

83 For Russell's activities, see his *1968*. For Wittgenstein's activities, see von Wright's historical introduction to Wittgenstein's *Prototractatus* (1971).

84 Russell *1968*, 68ff.

85 *Ibid.*, 33, 81.

86 Thompson, "Some Letters of Bertrand Russell to Herbert Wildon Carr" (*1975*, 13). "The Philosophy of Logical Atomism" (1918–19): eight lectures given at Dr. Williams' Library, Gordon Square, London, and reprinted in *Logic and Knowledge* (1956).

radically different philosophy from any that Russell had espoused before. As we have seen, the term and method recommended were enunciated in 1911, and all the major themes were addressed in *Theory of Knowledge* in 1913. Even the new way of speaking of the fact and the proposition appeared in the Lenzen notes of 1914. The lectures are of interest in giving a fuller treatment in published form of Russell's attempt to naturalize some of the ideas of Wittgenstein and to avoid some of the targets of his criticism. It is noteworthy, however, that some form of the multiple relation theory of belief is defended in spite of the earlier criticisms.

Both Wittgenstein and Russell appear to have finished important work in prison in 1918–19: Wittgenstein at Monte Cassino as a prisoner of war was seeking to send his now completed book to Russell; Russell in prison for anti-war activities was completing work on *Introduction to Mathematical Philosophy*.[87] This work, in introducing nonmathematicians to mathematical logic, acknowledges the work of Wittgenstein, and ends by discussing, but not accepting, what Russell understood to be the meaning of Wittgenstein's statement that logic and mathematics consist of tautologies.[88] In an article written early the next year, "On Propositions: What They Are and How They Mean", Russell offers an amalgam of logical analysis and psychological explanation of the nature and epistemological status of propositions; neither is identical with the realist view of his earlier work.[89] In 1921 *The Analysis of Mind* brought into systematic relation the behaviourism which Russell had been studying and sought to use in conjunction with neutral monism, and the earlier method of logical constructions in order to develop a systematic view of mind, belief, emotion and knowledge.[90] It might be said that J. B. Watson's behaviourism, James' neutral monism, and Wittgenstein's logic were all involved in Russell's post-war efforts to patch the hole that had first appeared when Wittgenstein in late May of 1913 launched the devastating criticism of *Theory of Knowledge*.

As far as the influence of Wittgenstein is concerned, it was only at the end of 1919, when Russell had the opportunity to read his book and to talk with him about it,[91] that he was able to assess the extent to which his own views could be made compatible with Wittgenstein's. By that time neither philosopher held the views with which he had confronted the other in May and June of 1913. The Introduction which Russell wrote for the *Tractatus*

87 Russell *1968*, 34.
88 Russell, *Introduction to Mathematical Philosophy* (*1919*, 203–5).
89 Russell, "On Propositions: What They Are and How They Mean" (1919). Reprinted in his *1956*.
90 Russell, *The Analysis of Mind* (1921).
91 Russell *1968*, 99–100. Russell to Morrell, #1,542, 20 Dec. 1919.

Logico-Philosophicus,[92] as the *Logisch-Philosophische Abhandlung* came to be called, and the revision of *Principia Mathematica* for the edition of 1925–27,[93] represent the high-water mark of Wittgenstein's influence on Russell—an influence which, by then, was far from the actual position that Wittgenstein held.

The text that follows gives us a picture of a mind at work; since no final revision was made and the book was left incomplete, it is possible to see the unsolved problems left without disguise or evasion. The discussion of the nature of the proposition, which in a number of chapters is introduced and postponed, reveals a problem left unsolved. The theory of relations, with all the detailed analysis of the concepts of relation, terms, form, the distinction of two levels of relation, the logical classification of homogeneous and heterogeneous, and of permutative and non-permutative complexes, is unique to this work, and, apparently, not successful in dealing with the problem, since Russell did not return to the scheme. The theory of judgment, renamed belief, that attempts to avoid the errors of psychologism (or monistic absolutism) and of the reification of nonexistent complexes is vividly presented, and the reasons for the persistence of this view and of its difficulties are clearly evident. If one puts together the theses of *Theory of Knowledge* and the 1913 "Notes on Logic" of Wittgenstein, in the historical context which has been explored, a fresh understanding of the interactions of the two philosophers emerges.

Perhaps most important of all, *Theory of Knowledge* illuminates for us the continuity of development, the changes and the reasons for the changes, which heretofore seemed mysteriously to appear between 1910 and 1919. The contrast between realist epistemology and "phenomenalist" constructionism can be seen as two phases in the development of a hoped-for philosophical synthesis. The "new" ideas of logical atomism can be seen as the development of a long history from 1911 on. The progressive erosion of the Platonic realism of universals, and of the claims that logical truths are known a priori and that they provide the fundamental truths of philosophy, can all be clearly traced.

Elizabeth Ramsden Eames.

---

92 Wittgenstein, *Tractatus Logico-Philosophicus* (1922, 7–23 [Russell's introduction]).
93 Whitehead and Russell, *Principia Mathematica*, 2nd ed. (1925–27).

Acknowledgements

THE EDITORS OF this volume wish to acknowledge the generous assistance of their respective institutions, Southern Illinois University at Carbondale and McMaster University. Grants from the former institution and a grant from the National Endowment for the Humanities (U.S.A.) supported the first phase of the work, while a Major Editorial Grant from the Social Sciences and Humanities Research Council of Canada supported the completion of the work as part of the Bertrand Russell Editorial Project at the latter institution. The responsibility for the content of this volume is solely the editors'.

The work could not have been carried out without the support of President Warren E. Brandt of Southern Illinois University at Carbondale; Vice-Presidents Frank C. Horton and John C. Guyon and their staffs; Deans Ralph McCoy and Kenneth Peterson of Morris Library; Dean Lon R. Shelby of the College of Liberal Arts; and the Executive Officers of the Department of Philosophy, David S. Clarke, Jr., and George McClure.

McMaster University provided substantial financial and technological resources both before and after the award of the Major Editorial Grant. In particular, gratitude is extended to the following University administrators: the late William Ready, University Librarian 1966–79, who brought the Russell papers to McMaster; Alwyn Berland, former Dean of Humanities and now Chairman of the Project's Board of Management and the Bertrand Russell Archives Academic Advisory Board; and Assistant Vice-President Alan C. Frosst, the Project's advisor on budgetary matters. Other administrators have been helpful: former President A. N. Bourns, President Alvin A. Lee, Vice-President Leslie J. King, Associate Vice-President J. P. Evans, former Acting Dean S. M. Najm, former Associate Dean Chauncey Wood, Dean D. P. Gagan and Associate Dean William J. Slater.

This volume could not have been undertaken without the permission and cooperation of the Bertrand Russell Estate. The late Countess Russell graciously assisted in searching for needed references in the library at Plas Penrhyn, Penrhyndeudraeth, Wales, and in encouraging our efforts to bring this work to publication.

The resources of the following research institutions were employed and are gratefully acknowledged: the Humanities Research Center of the University of Texas at Austin (Lady Ottoline Morrell papers), the Bancroft

Library of the University of California, Berkeley (Victor Lenzen papers), the Houghton Library (T. S. Eliot and R. C. Marsh papers) and the University Archives (R. B. Perry papers) of Harvard University, the British Library, the Special Collections of Morris Library, Southern Illinois University at Carbondale (Open Court papers), Cambridge University Library (Minutes of the Moral Sciences Club), and, of course, the Bertrand Russell Archives in the Division of Archives and Research Collections in the Mills Memorial Library, McMaster University (where the C. K. Ogden papers are housed as well).

For research assistance at Southern Illinois University at Carbondale, Morris Library, special thanks are due to Kenneth Duckett, David Koch and Katharine Lockwood, the Director and staff of the Special Collections, and to Alan M. Cohn and Kathleen Eads of the Humanities Library. The advice on editing the text given by Jo Ann Boydston, Director of the Center for Dewey Studies, and by Donald Cook, University of Indiana, Bloomington, both of the Center for Scholarly Editions, was valuable. The Center for Scholarly Editions granted its award of Approved Text to the first phase of the work.

Among those who read and commented on some or all aspects of the volume at various stages were Lewis E. Hahn, Jo Ann Boydston, Patricia Baysinger, Nicholas Griffin, Brian McGuinness, Richard A. Rempel, John G. Slater and Katharine Tait. Jack Pitt helped with the Minutes of the Cambridge University Moral Sciences Club. Hans Rudnick of the Department of English of Southern Illinois University utilized his linguistic and philosophical skills to check Russell's translations of passages from Meinong.

At McMaster University the Russell Editorial Project has had the cooperation of the entire library staff—in particular, that of the University Librarian, Graham R. Hill, and the staffs of Archives and Research Collections, Interlibrary Loan, Reference and Serials. The Assistant Russell Archivist, Carl Spadoni, and the Archival Assistant in the Russell Archives, Cheryl Walker, were always helpful. Gerald Field in Mathematical Sciences drew the diagrams in the text and Appendices. Audio-Visual Services supplied the plates.

At Southern Illinois University at Carbondale, Clarice Keegan, Beverly Browning and Janet Trapp Slagter assisted in the collations and the bibliographical and proofreading tasks. At McMaster University, John King assisted in the annotations and textual notes, commented on the Introduction and the "Textual Principles", and proofread the volume. Bernd P. Frohmann, the Project's Bibliographical Assistant, researched the Bibliographical Index and drafted the General Index. Sheila Turcon drafted the Chronology and assisted in the General Index. A doctoral student in philosophy, Michael O'Connor, researched many of the annotations. Undergraduate assistants were Jill LeBlanc and James O'Meara.

Diane M. Kerss, Production Manager of the Project, has had a long involvement with *Theory of Knowledge*. As the sole photocompositor in the early years of the Russell Editorial Project, she keyboarded the whole text. Since then she has supervised the production of camera-ready copy. She was assisted by Joy Drew, Jacqueline S. Hassan and Nancy Scott (who did the paste-up). At Carbondale, Cathy Hamer prepared the typescript of the editorial matter.

Our work was facilitated by McMaster's Printing Services, managed by Don Henwood, with the aid of Sue Fletcher in the phototypesetting department.

Finally, we wish to thank the Humanities Research Center, the University of Texas at Austin, for permission to quote from its letters from Bertrand Russell to Lady Ottoline Morrell, and the Cambridge University Moral Sciences Club for permission to quote from its Minutes. Eugene Freeman, editor of *The Monist*, encouraged the reprint of the first six chapters of *Theory of Knowledge* from that journal.

Chronology:
Russell's Life and Writings, 1910–18

Theory of Knowledge was written in May and June 1913. Although this chronology is devoted chiefly to the events of those months, relevant events from the years before and afterwards are included to provide context.

	Life	Writings
Dec. 1910		*Principia Mathematica*, Vol. 1, published.
6 Mar. 1911		"Knowledge by Acquaintance and Knowledge by Description" read to Aristotelian Society.
Mar. 1911	Beginning of love affair with Lady Ottoline Morrell.	Delivers lectures in Paris on "Le Réalisme analytique", "L'Importance philosophique de la logistique" and "Sur les Axiomes de l'infini et du transfini".
17 May 1911	Invited by Perry to lecture at Harvard.	
15 Oct. 1911		Rereading major philosophers to prepare for new work.
18 Oct. 1911	Meets Wittgenstein.	
30 Oct. 1911		"On the Relations of Universals and Particulars" read to Aristotelian Society.
Jan. 1912		*The Problems of Philosophy* published.
8 Feb. 1912	Santayana renews Perry's invitation to lecture at Harvard.	
17 May 1912		"On Matter" read at Cardiff.
July 1912		"The Philosophy of Bergson" published in *Monist*.
Oct. 1912		"What Is Logic?" attempted and "The Essence of Religion" published in *Hibbert Journal*.

16 Nov. 1912	Agrees to three-month visit to U.S.A. in 1914 to lecture at Harvard.	
30 Dec. 1912– c.14 Jan. 1913	At the Beetle and Wedge, Moulsford.	Works on matter.
14 Jan.– 8 Mar. 1913	Lent term at Cambridge.	
4 Mar. 1913		Sends Perry descriptions of Harvard courses (Appendix A.1).
17 Apr. 1913		Writes sketch of *Theory of Knowledge*.
18 Apr. 1913	Easter term begins.	
6 May 1913	Ottoline leaves for six weeks in Lausanne.	
7 May 1913		Begins Chap. I of analytic section of *Theory of Knowledge*, intending to average 10 pp. daily.
9 May 1913		Writes on James and Mach.
11 May 1913		Finishes refutation of James; begins own view of consciousness. 55 pp. of MS. completed.
13 May 1913		Writes on "the present time"; 80 pp. completed.
14 May 1913	Wittgenstein is "shocked" to hear of *Theory of Knowledge*.	Thinking of sensation and imagination.
15 May 1913		12 pp. up on his average, i.e. to p. 102.
16 May 1913		110 pp. completed; finds his treatment of sensation and imagination aids analysis of dreams.
17 May 1913		Begins analysis of time.
19 May 1913		Finishes analysis of time (p. 142) and segment on acquaintance with particulars.
20 May 1913	Wittgenstein refutes a theory of judgment Russell used to hold.	
21 May 1913		Begins acquaintance with universals. From this point MS. is extant.
22 May 1913		More than 160 pp. completed, finishing Chap. VII.

23 May 1913	Sees Wittgenstein between chapters.	Works on Chaps. VIII and IX, finishing at p. 190 (end of Pt. I).
24 May 1913		Begins new part, on judgment; thinks of new way of dividing the subject.
25 May 1913		Works on what is meant by understanding a sentence.
26 May 1913	Wittgenstein delivers more criticisms.	
30 May 1913		Reaches p. 273, end of treatment of belief, disbelief and doubt (Chap. IV, Pt. II).
1 June 1913		Finishes treatment of truth, reaching p. 300.
5 June 1913		All but finished Chap. VI of Pt. II, i.e. to p. 323.
6 June 1913	Topic for Lowell Lectures found unsatisfactory by President Lowell of Harvard.	Reaches p. 350.
7 June 1913		Hopes to finish 3rd part, on inference, before Ottoline's return.
8 June 1913		Decides not to do part on inference now.
13 June 1913	Easter term ends.	
18 June 1913	Lunches with Wittgenstein and his mother. Ottoline returns.	
19 June 1913	Tells Ottoline that Wittgenstein's criticisms make *Theory of Knowledge* impossible.	
26 June 1913		Writes to Perry asking permission to publish criticisms of James.
July 1913	Vacations in Cornwall.	
19 July 1913		Submits new syllabus for Lowell Lectures.
22 July 1913	Wittgenstein writes that he is sorry his criticisms have paralyzed Russell.	
Aug. 1913	Vacations on Continent.	

25 Sept. 1913		Finishes 1st draft of Lowell Lectures.
early Oct. 1913	Wittgenstein visits Russell and dictates "Notes on Logic".	
10 Oct. 1913	Michaelmas term begins.	
24 Oct. 1913		Reads "The Perception of Time" to Cambridge Moral Sciences Club.
9 Nov. 1913		Sends Perry syllabus (now lost) of "Theory of Knowledge" lecture course.
8 Dec. 1913	Michaelmas term ends.	
Jan. 1914		"Preliminary Description of Experience" published in *Monist*.
*c.*1 Jan. 1914	Returns from vacation in Italy to period of intense work.	Begins "The Relation of Sense-Data to Physics" and other papers.
16 Jan. 1914	Lent term begins.	
22 Jan.–5 Mar. 1914		Weekly delivery of *Our Knowledge of the External World* (Lowell) lectures at Trinity College.
7–13 Mar. 1914	Travelling to U.S.A.	
14 Mar.–26 May 1914	At Harvard.	Lectures on logic and theory of knowledge.
16 Mar. 1914		Begins bi-weekly delivery of Lowell Lectures in Boston.
Apr. 1914		"Neutral Monism" published in *Monist.*
18–25 Apr. 1914	Lecture tour of eastern American colleges.	
26 May–6 June 1914	Lecture tour (Chicago, Madison, Ann Arbor).	
late May 1914		Open Court decides to publish "On the Nature of Acquaintance" as a book.
31 May 1914	In Chicago; beginning of affair with Helen Dudley.	
June 1914	Returns to England.	
July 1914		"Analysis of Experience" published in *Monist*. "The Relation of Sense-Data to Physics" and "Mysticism and Logic" published in *Scientia* and *Hibbert Journal*, respectively.

16 July 1914		Works on "Sensation and Imagination".
Aug. 1914	First World War begins; takes decision to oppose War.	*Our Knowledge of the External World* published.
Oct. 1914		"Definitions and Methodological Principles in Theory of Knowledge" published in *Monist*.
Jan. 1915		"Sensation and Imagination" published in *Monist*.
2 Feb. 1915		Revises article on time for *Monist*.
Apr. 1915		"On the Experience of Time" published in *Monist*.
4 Mar. 1916	Recalls Wittgenstein's criticism as an event of first-rate importance in his life.	
22 Jan.–12 Mar. 1918		Delivers lecture series on "The Philosophy of Logical Atomism" in London (published in *Monist*).

Theory of Knowledge

by

Bertrand Russell

Part I
On the Nature of Acquaintance

Chapter I
Preliminary Description of Experience

THE PURPOSE OF what follows is to advocate a certain analysis of the simplest and most pervading aspect of experience, namely what I call "acquaintance". It will be maintained that acquaintance is a dual relation between a subject and an object which need not have any community of nature. The subject is "mental", the object is not known to be mental except in introspection. The object may be in the present, in the past, or not in time at all; it may be a sensible particular, or a universal, or an abstract logical fact. All cognitive relations—attention, sensation, memory, imagi- 10 nation, believing, disbelieving, etc.—presuppose acquaintance.

This theory has to be defended against three rival theories: (1) the theory of Mach and James, according to which there is no distinctive relation such as "acquaintance", involved in all mental facts, but merely a different grouping of the same objects as those dealt with by non-psychological sciences; (2) the theory that the immediate object is mental, as well as the subject; (3) the theory that between subject and object there is a third entity, the "content", which is mental, and is that thought or state of mind by means of which the subject apprehends the object. The first of these rivals is the most interesting and the most formidable, and can only be met by a full 20 and detailed discussion, which will occupy a second chapter. The other theories, along with my own, will be considered in a third chapter, while the first chapter will consist of an introductory survey of data.

The word "experience", like most of the words expressing fundamental ideas in philosophy, has been imported into the technical vocabulary from the language of daily life, and it retains some of the grime of its outdoor existence in spite of some scrubbing and brushing by impatient philosophers. Originally, the "philosophy of experience" was opposed to the a priori philosophy, and "experience" was confined to what we learn through the senses. Gradually, however, its scope widened until it included every- 30 thing of which we are in any way conscious, and became the watchword of an emaciated idealism imported from Germany. The word had, on the one hand, the reassuring associations of the "appeal to experience", which seemed to preclude the wilder vagaries of transcendental metaphysicians; while on the other hand it held, as it were in solution, the doctrine that nothing can happen except as the "experience" of some mind. Thus by the use of this one word the idealists cunningly forced upon their antagonists the odium of the a priori and the apparent necessity of maintaining the bare dogma of an unknowable reality, which must, it was thought, be either wholly arbitrary or not really unknowable.

In the revolt against idealism, the ambiguities of the word "experience" have been perceived, with the result that realists have more and more avoided the word. It is to be feared, however, that if the word is avoided the confusions of thought with which it has been associated may persist. It seems better to persevere in the attempt to analyze and clarify the somewhat
10 vague and muddy ideas commonly called up by the word "experience", since it is not improbable that in this process we may come upon something of fundamental importance to the theory of knowledge.

A certain difficulty as regards the use of words is unavoidable here, as in all philosophical inquiries. The meanings of common words are vague, fluctuating and ambiguous, like the shadow thrown by a flickering street-lamp on a windy night; yet in the nucleus of this uncertain patch of meaning, we may find some precise concept for which philosophy requires a name. If we choose a new technical term, the connection with ordinary thought is obscured and the clarifying of ordinary thought is retarded; but if
20 we use the common word with a new precise significance, we may seem to run counter to usage, and we may confuse the reader's thoughts by irrelevant associations. It is impossible to lay down a rule for the avoidance of these opposite dangers; sometimes it will be well to introduce a new technical term, sometimes it will be better to polish the common word until it becomes suitable for technical purposes. In the case of "experience", the latter course seems preferable, since the actual process of polishing the word is instructive, and the confusions of thought which it covers cannot well be otherwise dispelled.

In seeking the central idea embodied in the word "experience", we shall
30 at the same time be performing the analysis required for a definition of "mind" and "mental". Common sense divides human beings into souls and bodies, and Cartesian philosophy generalized this division by classifying everything that exists as either mind or matter. This division is so familiar, and of such respectable antiquity, that it has become part of our habits, and seems scarcely to embody a theory. Mind is what we know from within—thoughts and feelings and volitions—while matter is what is in space outside our minds. Nevertheless, almost all the great philosophers since Leibniz have challenged the dualism of mind and matter. Most of them, regarding mind as something immediately given, have assimilated to it what appeared
40 to be "matter", and have thus achieved the monism of the idealist. We may define an idealist as a man who believes that whatever exists may be called "mental", in the sense of having a certain character, known to us by introspection as belonging to our own minds. In recent times, however, this

theory has been criticized from various points of view. On the one hand, men who admitted that we know by introspection things having the character we call "mental" have urged that we also know other things not having this character. On the other hand, William James and the American realists have urged that there is no specific character of "mental" things, but that the things which are called mental are identical with the things which are called physical, the difference being merely one of context and arrangement.

We have thus three opinions to consider. There are first those who deny that there is a character called "mental" which is revealed in introspection. These men may be called "neutral monists", because, while rejecting the division of the world into mind and matter, they do not say "all reality is mind", nor yet "all reality is matter". Next, there are "idealistic monists", who admit a character called "mental", and hold that everything has this character. Next, there are "dualists", who hold that there is such a character, but that there are things which do not possess it. In order to decide among these views, it is necessary to decide whether anything is meant by the word "mental"; and this inquiry brings us back to the meaning of "experience".

When we consider the world without the knowledge and the ignorance that are taught by philosophy, we seem to see that it contains a number of things and persons, and that some of the things are "experienced" by some of the persons. A man may experience different things at different times, and different men may experience different things at the same time. Some things, such as the inside of the earth or the other side of the moon, are never experienced by anybody, but are nevertheless believed to exist. The things which a man is said to experience are the things that are given in sensation, his own thoughts and feelings (at any rate so far as he is aware of them), and perhaps (though on this point common sense might hesitate) the facts which he comes to know by thinking. At any given moment, there are certain things of which a man is "aware", certain things which are "before his mind". Now although it is very difficult to define "awareness", it is not at all difficult to say that I am aware of such and such things. If I am asked, I can reply that I am aware of this, and that, and the other, and so on through a heterogeneous collection of objects. If I describe these objects, I may of course describe them wrongly; hence I cannot with certainty communicate to another what are the things of which I am aware. But if I speak to myself, and denote them by what may be called "proper names", rather than by descriptive words, I cannot be in error. So long as the names which I use really are names at the moment, i.e. are naming things to me, so long the things must be objects of which I am aware, since otherwise the words would be meaningless sounds, not names of things. There is thus at any given moment a certain assemblage of objects to which I could, if I chose, give proper names; these are the objects of my "awareness", the objects "before my mind", or the objects that are within my present "experience".

There is a certain unity, important to realize but hard to analyze, in "my present experience". If we assumed that "I" am the same at one time and at another, we might suppose that "my present experience" might be defined as all the experience which "I" have "now". But in fact we shall find that "I" and "now", in the order of knowledge, must be defined in terms of "my present experience", rather than vice versa. Moreover, we cannot define "my present experience" as "all experience contemporaneous with *this*"
10 (where *this* is some actual part of what I now experience), since that would ignore the possibility of experience other than mine. Nor can we define it as "all experience which I experience as contemporaneous with *this*", since that would exclude all that part of my experiencing of which I do not become introspectively conscious. We shall have to say, I think, that "being experienced together" is a relation between experienced things, which can itself be experienced, for example when we become aware of two things which we are seeing together, or of a thing seen and a thing heard simultaneously. Having come to know in this way what is meant by "being experienced together", we can define "my present contents of experience" as "everything experi-
20 enced together with *this*", where *this* is any experienced thing selected by attention. We shall return to this topic on several subsequent occasions.

I do not propose as yet to attempt a logical analysis of "experience". For the present, I wish to consider its extent, its boundaries, its prolongation in time, and the reasons for regarding it as not all-embracing. These topics may be dealt with by discussing successively the following questions: (1) Are faint and peripheral sensations included in "experience"? (2) Are all or any of our present true beliefs included in present "experience"? (3) Do we now "experience" past things which we remember? (4) How do we come to know that the group of things now experienced is not all-embracing? (5)
30 Why do we regard our present and past experiences as all parts of *one* experience, namely the experience which we call "ours"? (6) What leads us to believe that "our" total experience is not all-embracing? Many of these questions will have to be discussed again more fully at a later stage; for the present, we are not discussing them on their own account, but in order to become familiar with the notion of experience.

(1). Are faint and peripheral sensations included in "experience"? This question may be asked, not only with regard to sensations, but also with regard to faint wishes, dim thoughts, and whatever else is not in the focus of attention; but for illustrative purposes, the case of sensation, which is the
40 simplest, may suffice. For the sake of definiteness, let us consider the field of vision. Normally, if we are attending to anything seen, it is to what is in the centre of the field that we attend, but we can, by an effort of will, attend to what is in the margin. It is obvious that, when we do so, what we attend to is

indubitably experienced. Thus the question we have to consider is whether *attention* constitutes experience, or whether things not attended to are also experienced. It seems we must admit things to which we do not attend, for attention is a selection among objects that are "before the mind", and therefore presupposes a larger field, constituted in some less exclusive manner, out of which attention chooses what it wants. In cases, however, where, in spite of the physical conditions which might be expected to produce a sensation, no sensation appears to exist, as for example when we fail to hear a faint sound which we should hear if our attention were called to it, it would seem that there is no corresponding "experience"; in such cases, in spite of the physical existence of the sound-stimulus, there seems to be sometimes no answering "mental" existent.

(2). Our mental life is largely composed of beliefs, and of what we are pleased to call "knowledge" of "facts". When I speak of a "fact", I mean the kind of thing that is expressed by the phrase "that so-and-so is the case". A "fact" in this sense is something different from an existing sensible thing; it is the kind of object towards which we have a *belief*, expressed in a proposition. The question I am asking now is not whether believing is experienced, for that I take to be obvious; the question is, whether the facts towards which beliefs are directed are ever experienced. It is obvious at once that most of the facts which we consider to be within our knowledge are not experienced. We do not experience that the earth goes round the sun, or that London has six million inhabitants, or that Napoleon was defeated at Waterloo. I think, however, that some facts are experienced, namely those which we see for ourselves, without relying either upon our own reasoning from previous facts, or upon the testimony of others. These "primitive" facts, which are known to us by an immediate insight as luminous and indubitable as that of sense, must, if I am not mistaken, be included in the original matter of experience. Their importance in the theory of knowledge is very great, and we shall have occasion to consider them very fully in the sequel.

(3). Do we now experience past things which we remember? We cannot of course discuss this question adequately without a consideration of the psychology of memory. But in a brief preliminary way, something may be said to indicate an affirmative conclusion. In the first place, we must not confound true memory with present images of past things. I may call up now before my mind an image of a man I saw yesterday; the image is not in the past, and I certainly experience it now, but the image itself is not memory. The remembering refers to something known to be in the past, to what I saw yesterday, not to the image which I call up now. But even when the present image has been set aside as irrelevant, there still remains a distinction between what may be called "intellectual" memory and what may be called "sensational" memory. When I merely know "that I saw

Jones yesterday", this is intellectual memory; my knowledge is of one of those "primitive facts" which we considered in the preceding paragraph. But in the immediate memory of something which has just happened, the thing itself seems to remain in experience, in spite of the fact that it is known to be no longer present. How long this sort of memory may last, I do not profess to know; but it may certainly last long enough to make us conscious of a lapse of time since the thing remembered was present. Thus it would seem that in two different ways past things may form parts of present experience.

10   The conclusion that past things are experienced in memory may be reinforced by considering the difference between past and future. Through scientific prediction, we may come to know, with greater or less probability, many things about the future, but all these things are *inferred*: not one of them is known immediately. We do not even know immediately what we mean by the word "future": the future is essentially that period of time when the present will be past. "Present" and "past" are given in experience, and "future" is defined in terms of them. The difference between past and future, from the standpoint of theory of knowledge, consists just in the fact that the past is in part experienced now, while the future still lies wholly
20 outside experience.

(4). How do we come to know that the group of things now experienced is not all-embracing? This question arises naturally out of what has just been said concerning the future; for our belief that there will be a future is just one of those that take us beyond present experience. It is not, however, one of the most indubitable; we have no very good reason to feel sure that there will be a future, whereas some of the ways in which reality must transcend present experience seem as certain as any knowledge.

This question is one of great importance, since it introduces us to the whole problem of how knowledge can transcend personal experience. For
30 the present, however, we are not concerned with the *whole* of our individual experience, but only with the experience of a given moment. At first sight, it might seem as though the experience of each moment must be a prison for the knowledge of that moment, and as though its boundaries must be the boundaries of our present world. Every word that we now understand must have a meaning which falls within our present experience; we can never point to an object and say: "*This* lies outside my present experience." We cannot know any particular thing unless it is part of present experience; hence it might be inferred that we cannot know that there are particular things which lie outside present experience. To suppose that we can know
40 this, it might be said, is to suppose that we can know what we do not know. On this ground, we may be urged to a modest agnosticism with regard to everything that lies outside our momentary consciousness. Such a view, it is true, is not usually advocated in this extreme form; but the principles of

solipsism and of the older empirical philosophy would seem, if rigorously applied, to reduce the knowledge of each moment within the narrow area of that moment's experience.

To this theory there are two complementary replies. The one is empirical, and consists in pointing out that in fact we do know more than the theory supposes; the other is logical, and consists in pointing out a fallacy in the inference which the theory draws from the data. Let us begin with the empirical refutation.

One of the obvious empirical refutations is derived from the knowledge that we have forgotten something. When, for example, we try to recall a person's name, we may be perfectly certain that the name came into our experience in the past, but for all our efforts it will not come into our present experience. Then again, in more abstract regions we know that there are facts which are not within our present experience; we may remember that there are 144 entries in the multiplication-table, without remembering them all individually; and we may know that there are an infinite number of facts in arithmetic, of which only a finite number are now present to our minds. In both the above cases, we have certainty, but in the one case the thing forgotten did once form part of our experience, while in the other, the fact not experienced is an abstract mathematical fact, not a particular thing existing in time. If we are willing to admit any of the beliefs of daily life, such as that there will be a future, we of course have a great extension of what exists without being experienced. We know by memory that hitherto we have constantly become aware, in sensation, of new particulars not experienced before, and that therefore throughout the past our experience has not been all-embracing. If, then, the present moment is not the last moment in the life of the universe, we must suppose that the future will contain things which we do not now experience. It is no answer to say that, since these things are future, they do not yet form part of the universe; they must, at all times, be included in any complete inventory of the universe, which must enumerate what is to come just as much as what is and what has been. For the above reasons, then, it is certain that the world contains some things not in my experience, and highly probable that it contains a vast number of such things.

It remains to show the logical possibility of the knowledge that there are things which we are not now experiencing. This depends upon the fact that we may know propositions of the form: "There are things having such-and-such a property", even when we do not know of any instance of such things. In the abstract mathematical world, it is very easy to find examples. For instance, we know that there is no greatest prime number. But of all the prime numbers that we shall have ever thought of, there certainly is a greatest. Hence there are prime numbers greater than any that we shall have ever thought of. But in more concrete realms, the same is true: it is perfectly possible to know that there are things which I have known, but have now forgotten, although it is obviously impossible to give an instance of such things. To recur to our former example, I may perfectly remember that yesterday I knew the name of the lady I was introduced to, although today the name is lost to me. That I was told her name, is a fact which I know, and which implies that I knew a particular thing which I no longer know; I know that there was such a particular thing, but I do not know what particular thing it was. To pursue this topic farther would require an account of "knowledge by description", which belongs to a later stage. For the present, I am content to have pointed out that we know that there are things outside present experience and that such knowledge raises no logical difficulty.

(5). Why do we regard our present and past experiences as all parts of one experience, namely the experience which we call "ours"? This question must be considered before we can advance to the further question, whether we can know that there are things which transcend the whole of "our" experience. But at our present stage we can only give it a brief preliminary consideration, such as will enable us to speak of one person's total experience with some realization of what we mean and of what are the difficulties involved.

It is obvious that *memory* is what makes us call past experiences "ours". I do not mean that only those experiences that we now remember are considered as ours, but that memory always makes the links in the chain connecting our present with our past. It is not, however, memory *per se* that does this: it is memory of a certain sort. If we merely remember some external object, the experiencing is in the present, and there is not yet any reason to assume the past experience. It would be logically possible to remember an object which we had never experienced; indeed, it is by no means certain that this does not sometimes occur. We may hear a striking clock, for instance, and become aware that it has already struck several times before we noticed it. Perhaps, in this case, we have really experienced the earlier strokes as they occurred, but we cannot remember to have done so. Thus the case serves to illustrate an important difference, namely the difference between remembering an outside event and remembering our experiencing of the event. Normally, when we remember an event, we also remember our experiencing of it, but the two are different memories, as is shown by the case of the striking clock. The memory which prolongs our personality backwards in time is the memory of our experiencing, not merely of the things which we experienced. When we can remember experiencing something, we include the remembered experiencing with our present experiencing as part of one person's experience. Thus we are led to include also whatever experience we remembered at that earlier period, and so back, hypothetically, to earliest infancy. In the same hypothetical manner, we stretch our personality forward in time to all experiences which will remember our present experiences directly or indirectly.[1] By this extension of the present experience into a series of experiences linked by memory, we include within our own total experience all those particulars, spoken of under our last heading, which are known to have existed, though they do not form part of present experience; and in case time should continue beyond the present moment, we include also those future experiences which will be related to our present as our present is related to our past.

(6). What leads us to believe that "our" total experience is not all-embracing? This is the question of solipsism: What reason have we for believing that anything exists or has existed or will exist except what forms part of our total experience in the sense explained in the preceding paragraph?

The logical argument by which we showed that it is *possible* to know of the existence of things that are outside *present* experience applies, without change, to the existence of things that lie outside our *total* experience. Thus the only question we have to consider is whether, as a matter of empirical fact, we know anything which proves the existence of such things. In abstract logical and mathematical regions, it is easy, by means of the very examples which we used before, to *prove* that there are facts which do not form part of our total experience. It seems certain that we shall not think of more than a finite number of arithmetical facts in the course of our lives, and we know that the total number of arithmetical facts is infinite. If this example be thought inconclusive, on the ground that perhaps we survive death and become more interested in arithmetic hereafter, the following example will be found more stubborn. The number of functions of a real variable is infinitely greater than the number of moments of time. Therefore even if we spent all eternity thinking of a new function every instant, or of any finite or small infinite number of new functions every instant, there would still be an infinite number of functions which we should not have thought of, and therefore an infinite number of facts about them which would never enter our experience. It is therefore certain that there are mathematical facts which do not enter into our total experience.

With regard to existing particulars, no such cogent argument, so far as I know, can be produced. We naturally suppose that other people's bodies are inhabited by minds more or less like ours, which experience pleasures and pains, desires and aversions, of which we have no direct awareness. But although we naturally suppose this, and although no reason can be alleged for believing that our supposition is mistaken, yet it would seem also that there is no *conclusive* reason for believing it not mistaken. Exactly the same

---

1 In the language of the logic of relations, if M is the relation "remembering", N the sum of M and its converse, and x is any moment of experience, the total experience to which x belongs is all moments of experience which have to x the relation N_*. Cf. *Principia Mathematica*, *90.

degree of doubt attaches to the inside of the earth, the other side of the moon, and the innumerable physical facts which we habitually assume without the warrant of direct experience. If there is good reason to believe in any of these things, it must be derived from induction and causality by a complicated process which we are not at present in a position to consider. For the present, let us assume as a working hypothesis the existence of other people and of unperceived physical things. From time to time we shall reconsider this hypothesis, and at the end we shall be in a position to sum up the evidence as to its truth. For the present, we must be content with the conclusions: (a) that there is no logical reason against it, (b) that in the logical world there certainly are facts which we do not experience, (c) that the common-sense assumption that there are particulars which we do not experience has been found thoroughly successful as a working hypothesis, and that there is no argument of any sort or kind against it.

The conclusion to which we have been led by the above discussion is that some of the things in the world, but not all, are collected together at any given moment of my conscious life into a group which may be called "my present experience"; that this group embraces things existing now, things that existed in the past, and abstract facts; also that in my experiencing of a thing, something more than the mere thing is involved, and may be experienced in memory; that thus a total group of my experiences throughout time may be defined by means of memory, but that this group, like the momentary group, certainly does not contain all abstract facts, and appears not to contain all existent particulars, and in especial does not contain the experiencing which we believe to be associated with other people's bodies.

We have now to consider what is the analysis of "experiencing", i.e. what is the bond which combines certain objects into the group forming a momentary experience. And here we must first consider the theory which we have called "neutral monism", due to William James; for the questions raised by this theory are so fundamental that until they are answered, in one way or in another, no further progress can be made.

Chapter II
Neutral Monism

"NEUTRAL MONISM"—AS opposed to idealistic monism and materialistic monism—is the theory that the things commonly regarded as mental and the things commonly regarded as physical do not differ in respect of any intrinsic property possessed by the one set and not by the other, but differ only in respect of arrangement and context. The theory may be illustrated by comparison with a postal directory, in which the same names come twice over, once in alphabetical and once in geographical order; we may compare the alphabetical order to the mental, and the geographical order to the physical. The affinities of a given thing are quite different in the two orders, and its causes and effects obey different laws. Two objects may be connected in the mental world by the association of ideas, and in the physical world by the law of gravitation. The whole context of an object is so different in the mental order from what it is in the physical order that the object itself is thought to be duplicated, and in the mental order it is called an "idea", namely the idea of the same object in the physical order. But this duplication is a mistake: "ideas" of chairs and tables are identical with chairs and tables, but are considered in their mental context, not in the context of physics.

Just as every man in the directory has two kinds of neighbours, namely alphabetical neighbours and geographical neighbours, so every object will lie at the intersection of two causal series with different laws, namely the mental series and the physical series. "Thoughts" are not different in substance from "things"; the stream of my thoughts is a stream of things, namely of the things which I should commonly be said to be thinking *of*; what leads to its being called a stream of *thoughts* is merely that the laws of succession are different from the physical laws. In my mind, Caesar may call up Charlemagne, whereas in the physical world the two were widely sundered. The whole duality of mind and matter, according to this theory, is a mistake; there is only one kind of *stuff* out of which the world is made, and this stuff is called mental in one arrangement, physical in the other.[1]

---

1 For statements of this theory, see William James, *Essays in Radical Empiricism* (Longmans, 1912), especially the first of these essays, "Does 'Consciousness' Exist?" See also Mach, *Analysis of the Sensations* (Chicago, 1897) (the original was published in 1886). Mach's theory seems to be substantially the same as James's; but so far as I know James does not

A few quotations may serve to make the position clearer.
Mach says (*op. cit.*, pp. 14–15):

> That traditional gulf between physical and psychological re-
> search, accordingly, exists only for the habitual stereotyped method
> of observation. A color is a physical object so long as we consider its
> dependence upon its luminous source, upon other colors, upon heat,
> upon space, and so forth. Regarding, however, its dependence upon
> the retina ..., it becomes a psychological object, a sensation. Not the
> subject, but the direction of our investigation, is different in the two
> domains.
>
> The primary fact is not the *I*, the ego, but the elements (sensa-
> tions). The elements *constitute* the *I*. *I* have the sensation green,
> signifies that the element green occurs in a given complex of other
> elements (sensations, memories). When *I* cease to have the sensation
> green, when *I* die, then the elements no longer occur in their
> ordinary, familiar way of association. That is all. Only an ideal
> mental-economical unity, not a real unity, has ceased to exist.
>
> If a knowledge of the connection of the elements does not suffice
> us, and we ask, *Who* possesses this connection of sensations, *Who*
> experiences the sensations, then we have succumbed to the habit of
> subsuming every element (every sensation) under some unanalyzed
> complex. (Pp. 19–20)
>
> Bodies do not produce sensations, but complexes of sensations
> (complexes of elements) make up bodies. If to the physicist bodies
> appear the real abiding existences, while sensations are regarded
> merely as their evanescent transitory show, the physicist forgets, in
> the assumption of such a view, that all bodies are but thought-
> symbols for complexes of sensations (complexes of elements). (P.
> 22)
>
> For us, therefore, the world does not consist of mysterious en-
> tities, which by their interaction with another equally mysterious
> entity, the ego, produce sensations which alone are accessible. For
> us, colors, sounds, spaces, times, ... are the ultimate elements,
> whose given connection it is our business to investigate. (P. 23)

---

refer to him on this subject, so that he must have reached his conclusions independently of
Mach. The same theory is advocated in Perry's *Present Philosophical Tendencies* and in *The
New Realism* (1912).

Mach arrived at his opinions through physics. James, whose opinions are essentially the same, arrived at them through psychology. In his *Psychology* they are not yet to be found, though there is a certain approach to them. The various articles containing the opinions which concern us at present are collected in the posthumous book called *Essays in Radical Empiricism*. The following quotations will, I hope, serve to make it clear what these opinions are.

"'Consciousness'", says James,

is the name of a nonentity, and has no right to a place among first principles. Those who still cling to it are clinging to a mere echo, the faint rumor left behind by the disappearing "soul" upon the air of philosophy. For twenty years past[2] I have mistrusted "consciousness" as an entity; for seven or eight years past I have suggested its nonexistence to my students, and tried to give them its pragmatic equivalent in realities of experience. It seems to me that the hour is ripe for it to be openly and universally discarded.

To deny plumply that "consciousness" exists seems so absurd on the face of it—for undeniably "thoughts" do exist—that I fear some readers will follow me no farther. Let me then immediately explain that I mean only to deny that the word stands for an entity, but to insist most emphatically that it does stand for a function. There is, I mean, no aboriginal stuff or quality of being, contrasted with that of which material objects are made, out of which our thoughts of them are made; but there is a function of experience which thoughts perform, and for the performance of which this quality of being is involved. That function is *knowing*. (Pp. 2–4)

My thesis is that if we start with the supposition that there is only one primal stuff or material in the world, a stuff of which everything is composed, and if we call that stuff "pure experience," then knowing can easily be explained as a particular sort of relation towards one another into which portions of pure experience may enter. The relation itself is a part of pure experience; one of its "terms" becomes the subject or bearer of the knowledge, the knower, the other becomes the object known. (P. 4)

After explaining the view, which he rejects, that experience contains an essential opposition of subject and object, he proceeds:

Now my contention is exactly the reverse of this. *Experience, I believe, has no such inner duplicity: and the separation of it into con-*

_____

2 This article was first published in 1904.

sciousness and content comes, not by way of subtraction, but by way of addition—the addition, to a given concrete piece of it, of other sets of experiences, in connection with which its use or function may be of two different kinds. The paint will also serve here as an illustration. In a pot in a paint-shop, along with other paints, it serves in its entirety as so much saleable matter. Spread on a canvas, with other paints around it, it represents, on the contrary, a feature in a picture and performs a spiritual function. Just so, I maintain, does a given undivided portion of experience, taken in one context of associates, play the part of a knower, of a state of mind, of "consciousness"; while in a different context the same undivided bit of experience plays the part of a thing known, of an objective "content." In a word, in one group it figures as a thought, in another group as a thing. And, since it can figure in both groups simultaneously, we have every right to speak of it as subjective and objective both at once.   (Pp. 9–10; the italics are in the original)

Consciousness connotes a kind of external relation, and does not denote a special stuff or way of being. *The peculiarity of our experiences, that they not only are, but are known, which their "conscious" quality is invoked to explain, is better explained by their relations—these relations themselves being experiences—to one another*.   (P. 25; the italics are in the original)

James explains, a few pages later, that a vivid image of fire or water is just as truly hot or wet as physical fire or water. The distinction, he says, lies in the fact that the imagined fire and water are not causally operative like the "real" fire and water.

Mental fire is what won't burn real sticks; mental water is what won't necessarily (though of course it may) put out even a mental fire. Mental knives may be sharp, but they won't cut real wood.   (P. 33)

The central point of the pure-experience theory is that "outer" and "inner" are names for two groups into which we sort experiences according to the way in which they act upon their neighbors. Any one "content," such as *hard*, let us say, can be assigned to either group.   (P. 139)

Finally he comes to the alleged introspective certainty of consciousness. But his introspective deliverance is not the usual one. In himself, he says,

the stream of thinking (which I recognize emphatically as a

phenomenon) is only a careless name for what, when scrutinized, reveals itself to consist chiefly of the stream of my breathing. The "I think" which Kant said must be able to accompany all my objects, is the "I breathe" which actually does accompany them. There are other internal facts besides breathing ... and these increase the assets of "consciousness" so far as the latter is subject to immediate perception; but breath, which was ever the original of "spirit," breath moving outwards, between the glottis and the nostrils, is, I am persuaded, the essence out of which philosophers have constructed the entity known to them as consciousness. (P. 37)   10

In order to understand James's theory, it is necessary to consider more in detail his account of "knowing". Mere seeing and hearing, and sensation generally, he does not call "knowing". In all the cases where those who hold a different theory would say we have *direct* knowledge, there is, in James's view, no knowledge at all, but merely the presence of the thing itself as one of the constituents of the mind which is mistakenly supposed to know the thing. Knowing, according to him, is an external relation between two bits of experience, consisting in the fact that one of them leads to the other by means of certain intermediaries. The following illustration aptly introduces his account of knowing: 20

Suppose me to be sitting here in my library at Cambridge, at ten minutes' walk from "Memorial Hall," and to be thinking truly of the latter object. My mind may have before it only the name, or it may have a clear image, or it may have a very dim image of the hall, but such intrinsic differences in the image make no difference in its cognitive function. Certain *extrinsic* phenomena, special experiences of conjunction, are what impart to the image, be it what it may, its knowing office.

For instance, if you ask me what hall I mean by my image, and I can tell you nothing; or if I fail to point or lead you towards the   30 Harvard Delta; or if, being led by you, I am uncertain whether the hall I see be what I had in mind or not; you would rightly deny that I had "meant" that particular hall at all, even though my mental image might to some degree have resembled it. The resemblance would count in that case as coincidental merely, for all sorts of things of a kind resemble one another in this world without being held for that reason to take cognizance of one another.

On the other hand, if I can lead you to the hall, and tell you of its history and present uses; if in its presence I feel my idea, however imperfect it may have been, to have led hither and to be now   40 *terminated*; if the associates of the image and of the felt hall run

parallel, so that each term of the one context corresponds serially, as
I walk, with an answering term of the other; why then my soul was
prophetic, and my idea must be, and by common consent would be,
called cognizant of reality. That percept was what I *meant*....

In this continuing and corroborating, taken in no transcendental
sense, but denoting definitely felt transitions, *lies all that the knowing
of a percept by an idea can possibly contain or signify*.   (Pp. 54–6)

It will be observed that, according to the above account, he usually ceases
to "know" Memorial Hall when he reaches it; he only "knows" it while he
has ideas which lead or enable him to perceive it by taking suitable steps. It
is, however, possible, apparently, to regard an experience as "knowing"
itself in certain circumstances. In an enumeration of cases, James says:

> Either the knower and the known are:
> 1. the self-same piece of experience taken twice over in different
> contexts: or they are
> 2. two pieces of *actual* experience belonging to the same subject,
> with definite tracts of conjunctive transitional experience between
> them; or
> 3. the known is a *possible* experience either of that subject or
> another, to which the said conjunctive transitions *would* lead, if
> sufficiently prolonged.   (P. 53)

In a later illustration, he says:

> To call my present idea of my dog, for example, cognitive of the
> real dog means that, as the actual tissue of experience is constituted,
> the idea is capable of leading into a chain of other experiences on my
> part that go from next to next and terminate at last in vivid sense-
> perceptions of a jumping, barking, hairy body. Those *are* the real
> dog, the dog's full presence, for my common sense.   (P. 198)

And again:

> Should we ever reach absolutely terminal experiences, experiences
> in which we were all agreed, which were superseded by no revised
> continuations, these would not be *true*; they would be *real*, they
> would simply *be*.... Only such *other* things as led to these by satis-
> factory conjunctions would be "true".   (P. 204)

Before proceeding to examine the substantial truth or falsehood of
James's theory, we may observe that his use of the word "experience" is

unfortunate, and points to the lingering taint of an idealistic ancestry. This word is full of ambiguity; it inevitably suggests an experiencing subject; it hints at some common quality, "being experienced", in all the constituents of the world, whereas there is reason to believe that no such common quality is to be found. This word is abandoned by Professor Perry, whose chapters on "A Realistic Theory of Mind" and "A Realistic Theory of Knowledge"[3] give an admirable account of the Mach–James hypothesis. Nevertheless, even in his account, as in the whole doctrine, it seems possible to detect the unconscious influence of an idealistic habit of mind, persisting involuntarily after the opinions upon which it was based have been abandoned. But this can only be made clear by a detailed examination of the grounds for and against the whole theory of neutral monism.

In favour of the theory, we may observe, first and foremost, the very notable simplification which it introduces. That the things given in experience should be of two fundamentally different kinds, mental and physical, is far less satisfactory to our intellectual desires than that the dualism should be merely apparent and superficial. Occam's razor, "*entia non multiplicanda praeter necessitatem*", which I should regard as the supreme methodological maxim in philosophizing, prescribes James's theory as preferable to dualism if it can possibly be made to account for the facts. Again, "matter", which in Descartes's time was supposed to be an obvious datum, has now, under the influence of scientific hypotheses, become a remote supersensuous construction, connected, no doubt, with sense, but only through a long chain of intermediate inferences. What is immediately present in sense, though obviously in some way presupposed in physics, is studied rather in psychology than in physics. Thus we seem to have here, in sense, a neutral ground, a watershed, from which we may pass either to "matter" or to "mind", according to the nature of the problems we choose to raise.[4]

The ambiguous status of what is present in sense is illustrated by the difficulties surrounding the notion of "space". I do not intend now to attempt a solution of these difficulties; I wish only to make them felt, lest it should seem as though space afforded a clear distinction between the

---

3 Chaps. XII and XIII of *Present Philosophical Tendencies*.

4 The neutrality of sensation in orthodox philosophy may be illustrated by the following quotation from Professor Stout's *Manual of Psychology*, p. 133: "If we compare the colour *red* as a quality of a material object with the colour *red* as a quality of the corresponding sensation, we find that redness as immediately perceived is an attribute common to both. The difference lies in the different relations into which it enters in the two cases. As a quality of the thing, it is considered in relation to other qualities of the thing,—its shape, texture, flavour, odour, etc. As a psychical state, it is considered as a peculiar modification of the consciousness of the percipient, in relation to the general flow of his mental life." There seems in this passage an acceptance, as regards sensation, of the doctrines of neutral monism which Professor Stout would be far from adopting generally.

material and the mental. It is still sometimes thought that matter may be defined as "what is in space", but as soon as "space" is examined, it is found to be incredibly ambiguous, shifting and uncertain. Kant's a priori infinite given whole, which merely expresses our natural beliefs whenever the difficult disintegrations of analysis escape from our memories, has suffered a series of shattering blows from the most diverse quarters. The mathematicians have constructed a multiplicity of possible spaces, and have shown that many logical schemes would fit the empirical facts. Logic shows that space is not "*the* subject-matter of geometry", since an infinite number of
10 subject-matters satisfy any given kind of geometry. Psychology disentangles the contributions of various senses to the construction of space, and reveals the all-embracing space of physics as the outcome of many empirically familiar correlations. Thus the space of actual experience is appropriated by psychology, the space of geometry is appropriated by logic, and the space of physics is left halting between them in the humbled garb of a working hypothesis. It is not in "space", therefore, that we can find a criterion to distinguish the mental and the physical.

A large part of the argument in favour of neutral monism, as stated by its advocates, consists in a polemic against the view that we know the external
20 world through the medium of "ideas", which are mental. I shall consider this view in the next chapter; for the present, I wish only to say that, as against this view, I am in agreement with neutral monism. I do not think that, when an object is known to me, there is in my mind something which may be called an "idea" of the object, the possession of which constitutes my knowledge of the object. But when this is granted, neutral monism by no means follows. On the contrary, it is just at this point that neutral monism finds itself in agreement with idealism in making an assumption which I believe to be wholly false. The assumption is that, *if anything is immediately present to me, that thing must be part of my mind*. The upholders of "ideas",
30 since they believe in the duality of the mental and the physical, infer from this assumption that only ideas, not physical things, can be immediately present to me. Neutral monists, perceiving (rightly, as I think) that constituents of the physical world can be immediately present to me, infer that the mental and the physical are composed of the same "stuff", and are merely different arrangements of the same elements. But if the assumption is false, both these opposing theories may be false, as I believe they are.

Before attempting a refutation of neutral monism, we may still further narrow the issue. Non-cognitive mental facts—feeling, emotion, volition—offer *primâ facie* difficulties to which James offers a *primâ facie*
40 answer. His answer might be discussed, and might prove tenable or untenable. But as we are concerned with the theory of *knowledge*, we will ignore the non-cognitive part of the problem, and consider only what is relevant to knowledge. It is in this sphere that his theory is important to us, and in this

sphere that we must make up our minds as to its truth or falsehood.

Apart from objections depending upon argument, there is an initial difficulty in the view that there is nothing cognitive in the mere presence of an object to the mind. If I see a particular patch of colour, and then immediately shut my eyes, it is at least possible to suppose that the patch of colour continues to exist while my eyes are shut; so far, James would agree. But while my eyes are open, the patch of colour is one of the contents of my momentary experience, whereas when my eyes are shut it is not. The difference between being and not being one of the contents of my momentary experience, according to James, consists in experienced relations, chiefly causal, to other contents of my experience. It is here that I feel an insuperable difficulty. I cannot think that the difference between my seeing the patch of red, and the patch of red being there unseen, consists in the presence or absence of relations between the patch of red and other objects of the same kind. It seems to me possible to imagine a mind existing for only a fraction of a second, seeing the red, and ceasing to exist before having any other experience. But such a supposition ought, on James's theory, to be not merely improbable, but meaningless. According to him, things become parts of my experience in virtue of certain relations to each other; if there were not a system of interrelated things experienced by me, there could not be one thing experienced by me. To put the same point otherwise: it seems plain that, without reference to any other content of my experience, at the moment when I see the red I am acquainted with it in some way in which I was not acquainted with it before I saw it, and in which I shall not be acquainted with it when it ceases to be itself present in memory, however much I may be able to recall various facts which would enable me to see it again if I chose. This acquaintance which I have with what is part of my momentary experience seems to deserve to be called cognitive, with a more indefeasible right than any connected ideas such as James describes in speaking of Memorial Hall.

I shall return to the above difficulty, which seems to me the main objection to neutral monism, when I come to consider how the contents of my momentary experience are to be distinguished from other things; in this connection, the difficulty will take a more general form, and will raise questions which can be better considered after various more detailed difficulties have been dealt with.

The first difficulty which seems to require an answer is as to the nature of *judgment* or *belief*, and more particularly of erroneous belief. Belief differs from sensation in regard to the nature of what is before the mind: if I believe, for example, "that to-day is Wednesday", not only no sensation, but no presentation of any kind, can give the same objective content as is involved in my belief. This fact, which is fairly obvious in the above instance, is obscured, I think, by the unconscious habit of dwelling upon existential beliefs. People are said to believe in God, or to disbelieve in Adam and Eve. But in such cases what is believed or disbelieved is that there is an entity answering to a certain description. This, which can be believed or disbelieved, is quite different from the actual entity (if any) which does answer to the description. Thus the matter of belief is, in all cases, different in kind from the matter of sensation or presentation, and error is in no way analogous to hallucination. A hallucination is a fact, not an error; what is erroneous is a judgment based upon it. But if I believe that to-day is Wednesday when in fact to-day is Tuesday, "that to-day is Wednesday" is not a fact. We cannot find anywhere in the physical world any entity corresponding to this belief. What idealists have said about the creative activity of mind, about relations being due to our relating synthesis, and so on, seems to be true in the case of error; to me, at least, it is impossible to account for the occurrence of the false belief that to-day is Wednesday, except by invoking something not to be found in the physical world.

In *The New Realism*[5] there is an essay called "A Realistic Theory of Truth and Error", by W. P. Montague. It will serve to illustrate the argument if we examine what is said on error in the course of this essay.

"The true and the false", says Mr. Montague, "are respectively the real and the unreal, considered as objects of a possible belief or judgment" (p. 252).

There is nothing unusual in this definition, yet it suffers from a defect so simple and so fundamental that it is amazing how so many philosophers can have failed to see it. The defect is that there is no such thing as the unreal, and therefore, by the definition, there can be no such thing as the false; yet it is notorious that false beliefs do occur. It is possible, however, that Mr. Montague might maintain that there are unreal things as well as real ones, for with him "real" is definable. His definition is as follows:

> The real universe consists of the space-time system of existents, together with all that is presupposed by that system.   (P. 255)

He proceeds at once to deduce his view of the unreal:

> And as every reality can be regarded as a true identity-complex or proposition, and as each proposition has one and only one contradictory, we may say that the remainder of the realm of subsistent objects [i.e. the unreal] must consist of the false propositions or unrealities, particular and universal, which contradict the true propositions comprising reality.   (*Ibid.*)

5 By the American Six Realists (New York and London, 1912).

From the above it appears that, according to Mr. Montague, (1) every reality is a proposition; (2) false propositions subsist as well as true ones; (3) the unreal is the class of false propositions. We cannot now pursue these topics, which belong to logic. But for reasons which I have set forth elsewhere, it would appear (1) that *no* reality is a proposition, though some realities are beliefs, (2) that *true* propositions have a certain correspondence with complex facts, while false propositions have a different correspond- ence, (3) that the unreal is simply nothing, and is only identical with the class of false propositions in the same sense in which it is identical with the class of simoniacal unicorns, namely in the sense that both are null. It follows, if it is not otherwise obvious, that belief involves a different kind of relation to objects from any involved in sensation and presentation. The typical error to Mr. Montague, as to neutral monists generally, is the so-called "illusion of sense", which, as I shall try to show fully on another occasion, is no more illusory or erroneous than normal sensation. The kind of error with which we are all familiar in daily life, such as mistaking the day of the week, or thinking that America was discovered in 1066, is forced into the mould of "illusions of sense", at the expense of supposing the world to be full of such entities as "the discovery of America in 1066"—or in any year that the ignorance of schoolboys may suppose possible.

A further difficulty, not wholly unallied to the difficulty about error, concerns the thought of non-temporal entities, or the belief in facts that are independent of time. Whatever may be the right analysis of belief, it is plain that there are times at which I am believing that two and two are four, and other times at which I am not thinking of this fact. Now if we adopt the view that there is no specifically mental element in the universe, we shall have to hold that "$2+2 = 4$" is an entity which exists at those moments of time when some one is believing it, but not at other moments. It is however very difficult to conceive of an abstract fact of this sort actually existing at certain times. No temporal particular is a constituent of this proposition; hence it seems impossible that, except through the intermediary of some extraneous temporal particular, it should acquire that special relation to certain mo- ments which is involved in its being sometimes thought of and sometimes not. It is, of course, merely another form of the same difficulty that we shall be compelled, if we adopt neutral monism, to attribute causal efficacy to this abstract timeless fact at those moments when it is being believed. For these reasons, it seems almost inevitable to hold that my believing that $2+2 = 4$ involves a temporal particular not involved in the object of my belief. And the same argument, word for word, applies also to presentations when their objects are not temporal particulars.

An analogous problem arises in regard to memory. If I remember now something which happened an hour ago, the present event, namely my remembering, cannot be numerically identical with the event of an hour ago. If, then, my present experience involves nothing but the object experienced, the event which I am said to remember cannot itself be the object experienced when I remember. The object experienced must be something which might be called an "idea" of the past event. To this, however, there seem to be the same objections, if taken (as it would have to be) as applying to *all* memory, that there are to the doctrine that all contact with outside objects occurs through the medium of "ideas"—a doctrine against which neutral monism has arisen as a protest. If the past can never be directly experienced in memory, how, we must inquire, can it ever come to be known that the object now experienced in memory is at all similar to the past object? And if this cannot be known, the whole of our supposed knowledge of the past becomes illusory, while it becomes impossible to account for the obvious difference between our knowledge as regards the past and our knowledge as regards the future.

An objection, possibly not unavoidable, applies to James's account of "processes of leading" as constituting knowledge. His definition of the sort of "leading" required is vague, and would include cases which obviously could not be called knowledge. Take, for example, the instance, quoted above, of James's knowledge of his dog, which consists in the fact that "the idea is capable of leading into a chain of other experiences on my part that go from next to next and terminate at last in vivid sense-perceptions of a jumping, barking, hairy body." Obviously a great deal is unexpressed in this account. The original idea must have somehow "intended" the jumping, barking, hairy body: some purpose or desire must be satisfied when the dog appears. Otherwise, an idea which had led to the dog by accident would equally be cognitive of the dog. It is in this way, I suppose, that James was led to the pragmatic theory of truth. Ideas have many effects, some intended, some unintended; they will be cognitive, according to James, when they have *intended* effects, when we have the feeling "yes, that is what I was thinking of". At this point, the need of a neutral theory of desire becomes very urgent; but we will not dwell on this difficulty. The purely cognitive aspect of James's view offers sufficient difficulties, and we will consider them only.

The relations of cause and effect, which James supposes to intervene between the antecedent knowledge of his dog and the dog's actual presence, will require some further definition; for unintended sequences of cause and effect, even if their final outcome were what is intended, could not be said to show that the original idea was cognitive. Suppose, for example, that I wish to be with my dog, and start towards the next street in hopes of finding him there; but on the way I accidentally fall into a coal-cellar which he has also fallen into. Although I find him, it cannot be said that I knew where he was. And apart from this difficulty, the causal relation is an extremely obscure one. I do not believe the received notions on the subject of causality can possibly be defended; yet, apart from them, James's account of the cognitive relation becomes obscure. There is in James and in some of his followers a certain naïveté towards science, a certain uncritical acceptance of what may be called scientific common sense, which seems to me largely to destroy the value of their speculations on fundamental problems. The notion of "a *chain* of experiences that go from next to next", if introduced in the definition of cognition, seems to me to show an insufficiently critical attitude towards the notion of causality. But I am not at all sure that this is a *vital* objection to James's view: it is not unlikely that it could be avoided by a re-statement.

Another difficulty is that, in order to make his account of cognition fit all cases, he has to include *potential* processes of leading as well as actual ones. Of the three kinds of relation which, according to him, may subsist between knower and known, the third, we saw, is described as follows: "The known is a *possible* experience either of that subject or another, to which the said conjunctive transitions *would* lead, if sufficiently prolonged." It is true he says (p. 54): "Type 3 can always formally and hypothetically be reduced to type 2", and in type 2 both experiences are actual. But by the word "hypothetically" he re-introduces the very element of possibility which he is nominally excluding: *if* you did such-and-such things (which perhaps in fact you do not do), your idea *would* verify itself. But this is a wholly different thing from *actual* verification. And the truth of a possible or hypothetical verification involves, necessarily, considerations which must sweep away verification altogether as the *meaning* of truth. It may be laid down generally that *possibility* always marks insufficient analysis: when analysis is completed, only the *actual* can be relevant, for the simple reason that there is only the actual, and that the merely possible is nothing.

The difficulties in the way of introducing precision into the account of James's "processes of leading" arise, if I am not mistaken, from his having omitted to notice that there must be a *logical* relation between what is believed in the earlier stages and what is experienced in the fulfilment. Let us revert to the instance of Memorial Hall. According to James, I should be said to "know" Memorial Hall if, for example, I know that it is reached by taking the first turning on the right and the second on the left and then going on for about 200 yards. Let us analyze this instance. In the case supposed, I know, or at least I believe truly, the following proposition: "Memorial Hall is the building which is reached by taking the first turning on the right and the second on the left, and then going on for 200 yards." For brevity, let us call this proposition *p*. The name "Memorial Hall", in this proposition, may be assumed to occur as a *description*, i.e. to mean "the building called 'Memorial Hall'". It may occur as a proper name, i.e. as a name for an object directly present in experience; but in the case supposed, when it is being questioned whether I know Memorial Hall at all, it is more instructive to consider the occurrence of the name as a description. Thus p asserts that two descriptions apply to the same entity; it says nothing about this entity except that the two descriptions apply to it. A person may know p (for instance, by the help of a map) without ever having seen Memorial Hall, and without Memorial Hall having ever been directly present in his experience. But if I wish to discover whether the belief in p is true or not, two courses are open to me. I may either search for other propositions giving other descriptions of Memorial Hall, such as that it comes at such-and-such a point on the map; or I may proceed to discover the actual entity satisfying one of the descriptions, and then ascertain whether it satisfies the other. The order, as between the two descriptions, is theoretically irrelevant; but it happens that one of the two descriptions, namely the one telling me the way, makes it easy to find the entity described. I may therefore take the first turning on the right and the second on the left and proceed for 200 yards, and then inquire the name of the building in front of me. If the answer is "Memorial Hall", the belief in p is verified. But it seems a misuse of terms to say that belief in p, when p is in fact true, constitutes knowledge of Memorial Hall. Belief in p is belief in a proposition of which Memorial Hall itself is not even a constituent; it may be entertained, on adequate grounds, by a person who has never experienced Memorial Hall; it may be rejected erroneously by a person who vividly remembers Memorial Hall. And when I actually see Memorial Hall, even if I do not know that that is its name, and even if I make no propositions about it, I must be said to know it in some sense more fundamental than any which can be constituted by the belief in true propositions describing it.

If what has been said is correct, certain points emerge as vital. First, that James and his followers, like many other philosophers, unduly assimilate belief to presentation, and thereby obscure the problem of error; secondly, that what they call knowledge of an object is really knowledge of a proposition in which the object itself does not occur, but is replaced by a *description* in terms of images or other constituents of actual present experience; thirdly, that what makes such a proposition true is the relations of the constituents of this actual proposition, relations which *may* be (but need not always be) established by the intermediary of the object described, but even then are not relations into which the actual object described enters as a term or constituent. Thus what James calls knowledge of objects is really knowledge of propositions in which the objects do not occur, but are replaced by descriptions; and the constituents of such propositions are contained in the present experience of the person who is believing them.

This brings us to the last objection which I have to urge against neutral monism, namely the question: How is the group of my present experiences distinguished from other things? Whatever may be meant by "my experience", it is undeniable that, at any given moment, some of the things in the world, but not all, are somehow collected together into a bundle consisting of what now lies within my immediate experience. The question I wish to consider is: Can neutral monism give a tenable account of the bond which unites the parts of this bundle, and the difference which marks them out from the rest of the things in the world?

This problem is incidentally discussed by Professor Perry in his *Present Philosophical Tendencies*, in the chapter called "A Realistic Theory of Mind". He emphasizes first the fact that the same thing may enter into two different people's experience, and that therefore one mind's objects are not necessarily cut off from the direct observation of another mind. So far, I should agree. But it does not follow, unless neutral monism is assumed (if then), that one man can directly know that a certain thing is part of another man's experience. A and B may both know a certain object O, but it does not follow that A knows that B knows O. Thus the fact that two minds may know the same object does not show that they are themselves accessible to each other's direct observation, unless they *are* simply the objects which constitute the contents of their experience. In that case, of course, they must be accessible to each other's direct observation. Professor Perry regards a shrinking from this conclusion as a mere mistake, due to the fact that so many of our objects are internal bodily states which, for physical reasons, are hidden from other observers. I cannot think that he is right in this. Consider something in no way private: suppose I am thinking $3+3 = 6$. I can know directly that I am thinking this, but no other man can. Professor Perry says:

> If you are a psychologist, or an interpreter of dreams, I may "tell" you what is in my mind. Now it is frequently assumed by the sophisticated that when I thus verbally reveal my mind you do not *directly* know it. You are supposed directly to know only my words. But I cannot understand such a supposition, unless it means simply that you know my mind only *after* and *through* hearing my words. (P. 290)

This passage appears to me to embody a logical error, namely a confusion of universals and particulars. The meanings of words, in so far as they are common to two people, are almost all universals. Perhaps the only exception is "now".[6] If I say "this", pointing to some visible object, what another man sees is not exactly the same as what I see, because he looks from a different place. Thus if he takes the word as designating the object which he sees, it has not the same meaning to him as to me. If he attempts to correct this, he will have to replace the immediate datum of his sight by a description, such as "the object which, from the point of view of my friend, corresponds with

6 Even this exception is open to doubt.   40

the object which I see". The words, therefore, in which I try to tell my experience will omit what is particular to it, and convey only what is universal. (I do not mean that it is *logically* impossible for two men to know the same particular, but only that practically it does not occur, owing to difference of point of view.) It may be said, however, that this difficulty does not apply in the case of an abstract thought consisting wholly of universal or logical constituents. In that case, it is true, I can convey wholly the *object* of my thought; but even then, there is something which I cannot convey, namely that something which makes my thought a particular dated event. If I think, at a certain moment, that $3+3 = 6$, that is an event in time; if you think it at the same moment, that is a second event at the same time. There is thus something in my thought over and above the bare logical fact that $3+3 = 6$; and it is just this something which is partly incommunicable. When I tell you that I am thinking that $3+3 = 6$, I give you information even if you are not wholly ignorant of arithmetic. It is this further something, which makes the thought *my* thought, that we have to consider.

On this point, Professor Perry says:

> When I am thinking abstractions, the contents of my mind, namely the abstractions themselves, are such as you also may think. They are not possessed by me in any exclusive sense. And the fact that they are my contents means that they are somehow bound up with the history of my nervous system. The contents, and the linkage which makes them mine, are alike common objects, lying in the field of general observation and study.   (P. 297)

The important sentence here is "the fact that they are my contents means that they are somehow bound up with my nervous system." The same idea is expressed elsewhere in the same chapter. "Elements become mental content", he says, *"when reacted to in the specific manner characteristic of the central nervous system"* (p. 299, his italics). And again, more fully:

> A mind is a complex so organized as to act desideratively or interestedly. I mean here to indicate that character which distinguishes the living organism, having originally the instinct of self-preservation, and acquiring in the course of its development a variety of special interests. I use the term *interest* primarily in its biological rather than its physiological sense. Certain natural processes act consistently in such wise as to isolate, protect, and renew themselves.   (Pp. 303–4)

But such an account of what makes a mind seems impossible to reconcile with obvious facts. In order to know that such-and-such a thing lies within my experience, it is not necessary to know anything about my nervous system: those who have never learned physiology, and are unaware that they possess nerves, are quite competent to know that this or that comes within their experience. It may be—I have no wish either to affirm or deny it—that the things which I experience have some relation to my nervous system which other things do not have; but if so, this must be a late scientific discovery, built up on masses of observation as to the connections of the object of consciousness with the nervous system and with the physical object. The distinction between things of which I am aware—for instance, between the things I see before my eyes and the things behind my back—is 10 not a late, elaborate, scientific distinction, nor is it one depending upon the relations of these things to each other. So much, I think, is clear to inspection; I do not know how to prove it, for I cannot think of anything more evident. But if so, then neutral monism cannot be true, for it is obliged to have recourse to extraneous considerations, such as the nervous system, in order to explain the difference between what I experience and what I do not experience, and this difference is too immediate for any explanation that neutral monism can give.

We may now sum up this long discussion, in the course of which it has been necessary to anticipate many topics to be treated more fully at a later 20 stage. Neutral monism, we saw, maintains that there are not two sorts of entities, mental and physical, but only two sorts of relations between entities, namely those belonging to what is called the mental order and those belonging to what is called the physical order. In favour of the theory, we may admit that what is experienced may itself be part of the physical world, and often is so; that the same thing may be experienced by different minds; that the old distinction of "mind" and "matter", besides ignoring the abstract facts that are neither mental nor physical, errs in regarding "matter", and the "space" in which matter is, as something obvious, given, and unambiguous, and is in hopeless doubt as to whether the facts of sensation 30 are to be called physical or mental. In emphasizing all this, we must acknowledge that neutral monism has performed an important service to philosophy. Nevertheless, if I am not mistaken, there are problems which this theory cannot solve, and there are facts which it cannot account for. The theory has arisen chiefly as a protest against the view that external objects are known through the medium of subjective "ideas" or "images", not directly. But it shares with this view the doctrine that whatever I experience must be part of my mind; and when this doctrine is rejected, much of its plausibility ceases.

The first and chief objection against the theory is based on inspection. 40 Between (say) a colour seen and the same colour not seen, there seems to be a difference not consisting in relations to other colours, or to other objects of experience, or to the nervous system, but in some way more immediate, more intimate, more intuitively evident. If neutral monism were true, a mind which had only one experience would be a logical impossibility, since a thing is only mental in virtue of its external relations; and correspondingly, it is difficult for this philosophy to define the respect in which the whole of my experience is different from the things that lie outside my experience.

A second difficulty is derived from *belief* or *judgment*, which James and his followers unduly assimilate to sensation and presentation, with fatal results as regards the theory of error. Error is defined as "belief in the
10 unreal", which compels the admission that there actually are unreal things.

A third difficulty is that the thought of what is not in time, or a belief in a non-temporal fact, is an event in time with a definite date, which seems impossible unless it contains some constituent over and above the timeless thing thought of or believed. The same point arises in regard to memory; for if what is remembered actually exists in the remembering mind, its position in the time-series becomes ambiguous, and the essential pastness of the remembered object disappears.

A fourth difficulty arises in regard to the definition of knowledge offered by James, though here it is hard to say how far this definition is essential to
20 neutral monism. James considers throughout rather knowledge of things than knowledge of truths, and he regards it as consisting in the presence of other things capable of leading to the thing which these other things are said to know. Immediate experience, which I should regard as the only real knowledge of things, he refuses to regard as knowledge at all; and it would seem that what he calls knowledge of a thing is really knowledge of a proposition of which the thing is not even a constituent.

In addition to the above difficulties, there is a fifth, more fatal, I think, than any of them, which is derived from considerations of "this" and "now" and "I". But this difficulty demands considerable discussion, and is there-
30 fore reserved for the next chapter.

For these reasons—some of which, it must be confessed, assume the results of future discussions—I conclude that neutral monism, though largely right in its polemic against previous theories, cannot be regarded as able to deal with all the facts, and must be replaced by a theory in which the difference between what is experienced and what is not experienced by a given subject at a given moment is made simpler and more prominent than it can be in a theory which wholly denies the existence of specifically mental entities.

Chapter III
Analysis of Experience

IN OUR FIRST chapter, we took a preliminary survey of the objects experienced. In the second chapter, we considered the theory that experience is merely a certain interrelation of these objects, involving no particular existent in addition to what is experienced. Having found this theory unsatisfactory, we have now to seek out the additional constituent of experience, and to consider the nature of its relation to the objects experienced.

Before embarking upon our analysis, let us again take stock of those 10 relevant facts which are least open to doubt. From the diversity of philosophical theories on the subject, it is evident that the true analysis, whatever it may be, cannot itself be among the facts that are evident at once, but must be reached, like a scientific hypothesis, as the theoretic residue left by the comparison of data. Here, as in philosophy generally, it is not the few logically simplest facts that form our data, but a large mass of complex every-day facts, of which the analysis offers fresh difficulties and doubts at every step. For this reason, if we wish to start with what is undeniable, we have to use words, at first, which, though familiar, stand in need of a dissection and definition only possible at a later stage. 20

The most obvious fact, in our present inquiry, is that, whatever may be the definition of "experience", some objects undoubtedly fall within my present experience, and of these objects some at least did not fall within my experience at earlier times which I can still remember. What is only slightly less obvious is that remembered objects sometimes—at least in the case of the immediate past—are still experienced, so that the objects experienced are not necessarily contemporaneous with the experiencing. It is obvious also that we can think of abstract facts, such as those of logic and mathematics; but in this case some argument is needed to discover what we experience when we think of them. If it were not for the fact that neutral monism 30 has been believed, I should have said it was obvious that we can experience our own experiencing, and that this is different from experiencing the object of our experiencing; and in spite of neutral monism, I think a place must be found for what appears as an experience of our experiencing, since it is hard to see how otherwise we should have arrived at the notion that we have experiences.

At an earlier stage, we decided that our present experience can be known not to be all-embracing. It is sometimes maintained that this cannot be known, on the ground that if a thing lies outside our experience we cannot know that there is such a thing. At the risk of repetition, it may be worth while to repeat the reasons (belonging to logic rather than to theory of knowledge) which show that this argument is fallacious. An object may be *described* by means of terms which lie within our experience, and the proposition that there is an object answering to this description is then one composed wholly of experienced constituents. It is therefore possible to know the truth of this proposition without passing outside experience. If it appears on examination that no *experienced* object answers to this description, the conclusion follows that there are objects not experienced. For example, we may know Jones and paternity and the fact that every man has a father. Then we know there is "the father of Jones", although we may never have experienced him. To consider this case more fully would demand a discussion of knowledge by description. For the present, it is only necessary to remove a possible objection to the view, which I shall henceforth assume, that what is experienced at any moment is known not to be the sum total of the things in the world. At the same time, it is important to remember that I can never give an actual instance of a thing not now within my experience, for everything that I can mention otherwise than by a description must lie within my present experience. This is involved in the very nature of experience, and is one of the most important of the obvious facts about it.

Experiencing is only one, though perhaps the most characteristic and comprehensive, of the things that happen in the mental world. Judging, feeling, desiring, willing, though they presuppose experiencing, are themselves different from it; they may be themselves experienced, and they doubtless require that we should experience the objects with which they are concerned, but they do not themselves consist *merely* in experiencing objects.

It is important to be clear as to the extent to which the experience of one mind may overlap that of another. Neutral monists have done a service to philosophy in pointing out that the same object may be experienced by two minds. This certainly applies, as a matter of fact, to all experiencing of universals and abstracts; it applies also, though I think only as a theoretic possibility, to the things of sense. But there remain a large number of things which only one mind can experience. First and foremost, an experiencing, as opposed to the mere object experienced, seems, empirically, not as a matter of a priori necessity, to be only capable of being experienced by one person. I can know by immediate experience what I am seeing at this moment; but another person, though it is theoretically possible for him to see the same object, cannot, as a matter of empirical fact, know by immediate experience that I am seeing it. Exactly the same is true of other mental facts, such as judging, feeling, desiring, willing. All these can only be experienced by one person.

Thus when an object O is experienced by two different persons A and B, the experiencing of O by A is one fact, and the experiencing of O by B is another. The experiencing of O by A may be experienced by A, and the experiencing of O by B may be experienced by B, but neither can experience the other's experiencing. A can experience his experiencing of O without logically requiring any other experience; hence the fact that he experiences O cannot consist in a relation to other objects of experience, as neutral monism supposes. From these characteristics of experience, it seems an unavoidable inference that A's experiencing of O is different from O, and is in fact a complex, of which A himself, or some simpler entity bound up with A, is a constituent as well as O. Hence experiencing must be a relation, in which one term is the object experienced, while the other term is that which experiences. We might continue to call this relation "experience", but we have employed the word "experience" hitherto because it is a non-committal word, which seemed not to prejudge the issue of our analysis. Now, since we have decided that experience is constituted by a relation, it will be better to employ a less neutral word; we shall employ synonymously the two words "acquaintance" and "awareness", generally the former. Thus when A experiences an object O, we shall say that A is acquainted with O.

We will define a "subject" as any entity which is acquainted with something, i.e. "subjects" are the domain of the relation "acquaintance". Conversely, any entity with which something is acquainted will be called an "object", i.e. "objects" are the converse domain of the relation "acquaintance". An entity with which nothing is acquainted will not be called an object. A fact will be called "mental" if it contains either acquaintance or some relation presupposing acquaintance as a component. Thus any instance of acquaintance is mental, since it is a complex in which a subject and an object are united by the relation of acquaintance. The object by itself need not be mental. We will call a fact "physical" when some particular, but no relation presupposing acquaintance, is a constituent of it. The reason for defining mental *facts* rather than mental *entities* is that we reach subjects only by description, and cannot know whether they are among objects or not.

It is to be observed that we do not identify a mind with a subject. A mind is something which persists through a certain period of time, but it must not be assumed that the subject persists. So far as our arguments have hitherto carried us, they give no evidence as to whether the subject of one experience is the same as the subject of another experience or not. For the present, nothing is to be assumed as to the identity of the subjects of different experiences belonging to the same person.

The strongest objection which can be urged against the above analysis of experience into a dual relation of subject and object is derived from the elusiveness of the subject in introspection. We can easily become aware of our own experiences, but we seem never to become aware of the subject itself. This argument tends, of course, to support neutral monism. It is a serious argument, and deserves careful consideration. We may attempt to meet it in either of two ways, namely by maintaining that we do have acquaintance with the subject, or by maintaining that there is no reason why, even if the theory is true, we should have acquaintance with the
10 subject.

Let us consider first the theory that we have acquaintance with the subject.[1] It is obvious that the question is bound up with that of the meaning of the word "I". This is a question in which confusions are very hard to avoid, but very fatal if they are not avoided. In the first place, the meaning of the word "I" must not be confused with the meaning of "the ego". "The ego" has a meaning which is a universal: it does not mean one person more than another, but rather that general characteristic, whatever it is, which makes each one of us call himself "I". But "I" itself is not a universal: on each occasion of its use, there is only one person who is I, though this person
20 differs according to the speaker. It is more nearly correct to describe "I" as an ambiguous proper name than to describe it as a universal. But when used, "I" is not in the least ambiguous: it means the person using it, and no one else. In order, however, to obtain a clear statement of our problem, it is necessary to pare away from "I" a great deal that is usually included—not only the body, but also the past and future in so far as they may possibly not belong to the subject of the present experience. It is obvious that all these are obtained by an extension from the present subject, and that the essential problem is concerned with our consciousness of the present subject. Let it therefore be assumed, in this discussion, that "I" means the subject of the
30 experience which I am now having (the vicious circle here is important to observe), and that we have to ask ourselves whether "I" in this sense is something with which we are acquainted.

On this question, it must be confessed that introspection does not give a favourable answer. Hume's inability to perceive himself was not peculiar, and I think most unprejudiced observers would agree with him. Even if by great exertion some rare person could catch a glimpse of himself, this would not suffice; for "I" is a term which we all know how to use, and which must therefore have some easily accessible meaning. It follows that the word "I", as commonly employed, must stand for a description; it cannot be a true

40 1 In a former discussion of this point, I maintained tentatively that we have such acquaint-
ance. Cf. "Knowledge by Acquaintance and Knowledge by Description", *Proceedings of the Aristotelian Society*, 1910–11, esp. pp. 110, 127.

proper name in the logical sense, since true proper names can only be conferred on objects with which we are acquainted.

We are thus forced to investigate the second answer suggested above, and to ask ourselves whether our theory of acquaintance in any way implies a direct consciousness of the bare subject. If it does, it would seem that it must be false; but I think we can show that it does not. Our theory maintains that the datum when we are aware of experiencing an object O is the fact "something is acquainted with O". The subject appears here, not in its individual capacity, but as an "apparent variable"; thus such a fact may be a datum in spite of incapacity for acquaintance with the subject.

If it is true, as it seems to be, that subjects are not given in acquaintance, it follows that nothing can be known as to their intrinsic nature. We cannot know, for example, that they differ from matter, nor yet that they do not differ. They are known merely as referents for the relation of acquaintance, and for those other psychical relations—judging, desiring, etc.—which imply acquaintance. It follows that psychical data—at any rate those that are cognitive—consist not of particulars, but of certain *facts* (i.e. of *what certain propositions assert*), and of *relations*, namely acquaintance and certain others which presuppose acquaintance. We may distinguish sensation from perception by saying that the former gives *particulars* while the latter gives *facts*; in this case, introspection consists wholly of perceptions, not of sensations.

The definition of what is "mental" as what involves subjects is inadmissible, in view of the fact that we do not know what subjects are. We may define a mental fact as one involving acquaintance or one of those other relations—judging, desiring, etc.—which presuppose acquaintance. It *may* be that subjects are constituents of other facts of the kind we should call physical, and therefore a fact which involves a subject may not be always a mental fact.

When two objects O and O' are given as parts of one experience, we perceive the fact "something is acquainted with both O and O'". Thus two instances of acquaintance can be given as having a common subject, even when the subject is not given. It is in this way, I think, that "I" comes to be popularly intelligible. When we have recognized that an experience is constituted by the relation of acquaintance, we may define "I" as the subject of the present experience, and we can see that, so defined, it denotes the same entity as is denoted by our former more popular definition. But in neither form does it require us to assume that we are ever acquainted with the bare subject of an acquaintance.

One very interesting and important point, however, remains to be investigated in the above definition of "I", and that is, what is meant by the "present" experience. If "I" is to be defined as we have suggested, it seems evident that the "present" experience must be known by acquaintance.

There are here several points to be brought out. First, it is necessary to consider the connection (if any) between psychological presence and the present time. Secondly, it is necessary to consider what is psychologically involved in our acquaintance with the present experience. Thirdly, it is necessary to consider the logical difficulty of the vicious circle in which any definition of the present experience appears to be entangled.

(1). Whatever I experience is, in one sense, "present" to me at the time when I experience it, but in the temporal sense it need not be present—for example, if it is something remembered, or something abstract which is not in time at all. The sense in which everything experienced is "present" may be disregarded, the rather as we already have three words—experience, acquaintance, and awareness—to describe what is meant by this sense. There is, however, another sense in which objects given in *sensation* are "present". As we shall find later, there is reason to suppose that there are several species of the general relation "acquaintance", and it would seem that one of these species is "presence" in the sense in which objects are present in sensation and perception but not in memory. The relation of "presence" in this sense is, I think, one of the ultimate constituents out of which our knowledge of time is built, and the "present" time may be defined as the time of those things which have to me the relation of "presence". But remembering what has been said about "I", we see that, when we speak of things which have the relation of presence to "me", we mean things which have the relation of presence to the subject of the present experience. Thus "the present experience" is a more fundamental notion than "the present time": the latter can be defined in terms of the former, but not vice versa.

(2). What is psychologically involved in our acquaintance with the present experience? The least that is possible is obviously that there should be an experience of an object O, and another experience of experiencing O. This second experience must involve presence in the sense in which objects of sensation and perception are present and objects of memory are not present. Let us call this sense P. Then it is necessary that a subject should have the relation P to an object which is itself an experience, which we may symbolize by S—A—O. Thus we require an experience which might be symbolized by

$$S'—P—(S—A—O).*$$

When such an experience occurs, we may say that we have an instance of "self-consciousness", or "experience of a present experience". It is to be observed that there is no good reason why the two subjects S and S' should be numerically the same: the one "self" or "mind" which embraces both

---

* Or rather, $S'—P—[(\exists S).(S—A—O)]$.

may be a construction, and need not, so far as the logical necessities of our problem are concerned, involve any identity of the two subjects. Thus "present experiences" are those experiences that have the relation of presence to the subject using the phrase.

(3). But there remains a logical difficulty, of which the solution is both interesting and important. In order to know a present experience, it is not necessary that I should perceive the fact

$$S'—P—(S—A—O),$$

and it must be possible to pick out an experience as present without having perception of this fact. If it were necessary to perceive this fact, it is fairly 10 evident that we should be embarked upon an endless regress. It is in fact obvious that "the present experience", or "the present object", or some phrase fulfilling a similar purpose, must be capable of being used as a proper name; all manner of objects are present on different occasions to different subjects, and we have already seen that the subject concerned in presence to "me" must be defined by means of presence.

The main consideration is undoubtedly to be derived from remembering what "presence" actually is. When an object is in my present experience, then I am acquainted with it; it is not necessary for me to reflect upon my experience, or to observe that the object has the property of belonging to my 20 experience, in order to be acquainted with it, but, on the contrary, the object itself is known to me without the need of any reflection on my part as to its properties or relations. This point may perhaps be made clearer by an illustrative hypothesis. Suppose I were occupied, like Adam, in bestowing names upon various objects. The objects upon which I should bestow names would all be objects with which I was acquainted, but it would not be necessary for me to reflect that I was acquainted with them, or to realize that they all shared a certain relation to myself. What distinguishes the objects to which I can give names from other things is the fact that these objects are within my experience, that I am acquainted with them, but it is only 30 subsequent reflection that proves that they all have this distinguishing characteristic; during the process of naming they appear merely as this, that, and the other.

Further consideration of the word "this" will help to make the point clear. The word "this" is always a proper name, in the sense that it applies directly to just one object, and does not in any way *describe* the object to which it applies. But on different occasions it applies to different objects. For the purposes of our present problem, we may say that "this" is the name of the object attended to at the moment by the person using the word. The relation of attention, here introduced, is of course different from that of 40 acquaintance, and one point in which it differs is that a subject can only attend to one object, or at least a very small number, at a time. (This may of

course be disputed, but for our purposes it may be assumed.) Thus we may
speak of "*the* object of attention of a given subject at a given moment". The
object so described is the object which that subject at that moment will call
"this". But it would be an error to suppose that "this" *means* "the object to
which I am now attending". "This" is a proper name applied to the object to
which I am now attending. If it be asked how I come to select this object, the
answer is that, by hypothesis, I am selecting it, since it is the object of my
attention. "This" is not waiting to be defined by the property of being
given, but is given; first it is actually given, and then reflection shows that it
is "that which is given".

We may now retrace our steps in the opposite order. At any moment of
my conscious life, there is one object (or at most some very small number of
objects) to which I am attending. All knowledge of particulars radiates out
from this object. This object is not intrinsically distinguishable from other
objects—it just happens (owing to causes which do not concern us) that I am
attending to it. Since I am attending to it, I can name it; I may give it any
name I choose, but when inventiveness gives out, I am apt to name it "this".
By the help of reflection and special experiences, it becomes evident that
there is such a relation as "attention", and that there is always a subject
attending to the object called "this". The subject attending to "this" is
called "I", and the time of the things which have to "I" the relation of
presence is called the present time. "This" is the point from which the
whole process starts, and "this" itself is not defined, but simply given. The
confusions and difficulties arise from regarding "this" as *defined by the fact
of being given*, rather than simply as given.

The objection to our theory of acquaintance which was derived from the
absence of acquaintance with the subject is thus capable of being answered,
while admitting that the objectors are in the right in maintaining that we are
not acquainted with the subject. Having answered the objection, we can
now retort on neutral monism with the demand that it should produce an
account of "this" and "I" and "now". I do not mean merely that it should
produce an account of particularity and selfhood and moments of time; all
this it might accomplish without in any way touching the problem. What I
demand is an account of that principle of selection which, to a given person
at a given moment, makes one object, one subject and one time intimate and
near and immediate, as no other object or subject or time can be to that
subject at that time, though the same intimacy and nearness and immediacy
will belong to these others in relation to other subjects and other times. In a
world where there were no specifically mental facts, is it not plain that there
would be a complete impartiality, an evenly diffused light, not the central
illumination fading away into outer darkness, which is characteristic of
objects in relation to a mind? It may be that some answer can be found to
these queries without admitting specifically mental facts; but to me it seems
obvious that such "emphatic particulars" as "this" and "I" and "now"

would be impossible without the selectiveness of mind. I conclude, therefore, that the consideration of emphatic particulars affords a new refutation,
and the most conclusive one, of neutral monism.

Before leaving the analysis of experience, we must take account of a
widely held theory according to which our acquaintance with objects involves not only subject and object, but also what is called "content". The
distinction between content and object is set forth very explicitly by
Meinong, for instance in his article "Über Gegenstände höherer Ordnung
und deren Verhältniss zur inneren Wahrnehmung".[2] The following quotations from this article may serve to make the theory plain.   10

> That it is essential to everything psychical to have an object, will
> presumably be admitted without reserve at least in regard to that
> psychical material which will here exclusively concern us. For no
> one doubts that one cannot have a presentation[3] without having a
> presentation of *something*, and also that one cannot judge without
> judging about *something*. People will probably also concede just as
> willingly that there is no presentation or judgment without content;
> but for not a few this readiness comes from the assumption that
> content and object are pretty much the same thing. I also long
> believed that the two expressions could be used indifferently, and   20
> that therefore one of them could be dispensed with. To-day I regard
> this as a mistake.   (P. 185)

He proceeds at once to give his grounds. The chief ground, he says, is that
we may have a presentation or judgment whose object is non-existent,
whether because it is self-contradictory, like the round square, or because,
like the golden mountain, there happens to be no such thing, or because,
like the difference between red and green, it is not the kind of thing which
can exist, although it may "subsist", or because, though now presented, its
existence belongs to the past or the future. He concludes:

> Thus the presentation exists: but who, except in the interests of a   30
> theoretical preconception, will be willing to assume that the presen-
> tation exists, but not its content?   (P. 186)

Thus the first difference between object and content is that the object may
be something non-existent, but the content must exist when the presentation exists. A second difference is that the object may be not psychical,
whereas the content must be psychical. The object may be blue or warm or

---

2 *Zeitschrift für Psychologie und Physiologie der Sinnesorgane*, Vol. XXI, 1899, pp. 182ff.
3 I think the relation of subject and object in presentation may be identified with the relation
  which I call "acquaintance".

heavy, but the content cannot have attributes of this kind (pp. 187–8). All presentations, however different their objects, have in common, he says, just what makes them presentations, namely "das Vorstellen oder den Vorstellungsact"; but two presentations of different objects cannot be completely similar to each other, and therefore the difference in the objects must point to some difference in the presentations. Now that in which two presentations may differ in spite of the identity of the "act" is what is to be called the "content". This exists now and is psychical, even when the object does not exist, or is past or future, or is not psychical (p. 188).

10   Before deciding whether in fact there are "contents" as well as objects of presentations, let us examine Meinong's arguments in the above. The instances of non-existent objects quoted by Meinong are largely disposed of by the theory of incomplete symbols—the round square and the golden mountain, at any rate, are not objects. (I do *not* mean that they are objects which do not exist.) The other instances are less intractable. The difference between red and green, for example, has the kind of subsistence appropriate to objects of this kind; and future things are not presented, although they may be known by description. Nevertheless, it remains the case that we can have a presentation of an abstract (which has no position in time), or of a
20 remembered object which exists no longer. The case of memory suffices to illustrate Meinong's difficulty in the supposition that a presentation can exist when its content does not exist. We should say that we remember now, and in popular language we should say that we are in a different "state of mind" when we remember from that in which we should be if we were not remembering. Meinong's "content" is in fact what would commonly be called a "state of mind". Thus the question is: Are there "states of mind", as opposed to objects cognized in various ways? We are told that it is impossible the presentation should exist now, if its content does not exist now. But if presentation consists wholly and solely, as we have contended, in a
30 relation of subject and object, then a memory-presentation is a complex of which one constituent is present while the other is past. It is not clear that such a complex has any definite position in the time-series: the fact that the remembering subject is in the present is no sufficient reason for regarding the whole complex as present. And similar remarks apply to the case of presentations whose objects are not in time at all. Thus the question "who will be willing to assume that the presentation exists but not its content?" loses its force: the word "exist" is very ambiguous, but if it means "being at some part of the time-series", then it is not at all clear that the presentation does exist; and if it means any other legitimate meaning, it is not clear that
40 the object does not exist.

The arguments that the content but not the object must be psychical, and that the object but not the content may have such attributes as blue or warm or heavy, may be passed by, since they do not afford any independent ground for believing that there are such things as contents.

The argument which has probably done most to produce a belief in "contents" as opposed to objects is the last of those adduced by Meinong, namely that there must be some difference between a presentation of one object and a presentation of another, and this difference is not to be found in the "act" of presentation. At first sight, it seems obvious that my mind is in different "states" when I am thinking of one thing and when I am thinking of another. But in fact the difference of object supplies all the difference required. There seems to be, in the hypothesis of "states" of mind, an operation (generally unconscious) of the "internal" theory of relations: it is 10 thought that some intrinsic difference in the subject must correspond to the difference in the objects to which it has the relation of presentation. I have argued this question at length elsewhere, and shall therefore now assume the "external" theory of relations, according to which difference of relations affords no evidence for difference of intrinsic predicates. It follows that, from the fact that the complex "my awareness of A" is different from the complex "my awareness of B", it does not follow that when I am aware of A I have some intrinsic quality which I do not have when I am aware of B but not of A. There is therefore no reason for assuming a difference in the subject corresponding to the difference between two presented objects. 20

It remains to inquire whether there are any other reasons for assuming "contents". I think perhaps belief in them has been encouraged by a careless use of such words as "image" and "idea". It may be thought that, when a given physical object is seen from many different points of view, the physical object itself is the object of many presentations, and that the different images are the different contents. Meinong himself is far from any such confusion, but language tends to encourage it. In fact, of course, the one physical object which is supposed to be seen from different points of view is a theoretical construction, and is not the object of any presentation. The objects of the various presentations concerned are the immediate visual 30 data from the different points of view. The change in the visual data, combined with the belief that the physical object is unchanged, tends to generate the belief that the visual data are "subjective modifications", and thus to obscure their character as objects. I shall not enlarge on this subject now, as I have dealt with it at length in an article in *Scientia* for July 1914.

It may be urged that different people can know the same object, but cannot have the same presentation, and that this points to something other than the object as a constituent of a presentation. As against neutral monism, the argument is valid if its premiss is granted; but in our theory, the difference between the subjects suffices to distinguish the two presenta- 40 tions, and therefore no problem arises.

The chief argument *against* contents is the difficulty of discovering them introspectively. It may be said that this difficulty—which is admitted—

applies equally to the subject in our theory of acquaintance. This is true; but our theory is based on inference from the nature of experience, not on any supposed introspective perception of the subject. If the arguments by which Meinong supports his belief in contents had appeared to us valid, we should have admitted contents; but in the absence of valid arguments introspective evidence alone could lead us to admit contents. Since such evidence is lacking, we may therefore conclude that there is no reason to admit contents.

The belief in "contents" as subjective modifications is often held in a
10 more extreme form than that advocated by Meinong. It is thought that whatever can be immediately known must be "in the mind", and that it can only be by inference that we arrive at a knowledge of anything external to ourselves. This view may be combated in many ways. It would be well to know, first of all, what is meant by "my mind", and what really is being debated when it is asked whether this or that is "in my mind". We might next point out that abstract facts and universals may be known to many people, and that therefore, if they are "in my mind", the same thing may be in two minds at once. But I think the main source of subjective theories has always been the supposed illusions of sense. The sun, as it appears in
20 astronomical theory, is not immediately given: what is immediately given is a certain visible bright patch, which according to physics depends upon the intervening medium and our sense-organs. Hence if we suppose that the astronomer's sun is the object when we "see the sun", then what is actually given has to be degraded to the level of something subjective. But in fact, the physical object which the astronomer deals with is an inference, and the bright patch that we see, in spite of its variability, is only thought to be illusory as the result of fallacious arguments.

To sum up: The obvious characteristics of experience seem to show that experiencing is a two-term relation; we call the relation *acquaintance*, and we
30 give the name *subject* to anything which has acquaintance with objects. The subject itself appears to be not acquainted with itself; but this does not prevent our theory from explaining the meaning of the word "I" by the help of the meaning of the word "this", which is the proper name of the object of attention. In this respect, especially, we found our theory superior to neutral monism, which seems unable to explain the selectiveness of experience. Finally we considered and rejected the opinion that experience involves mental modifications called "contents", having a diversity which reproduces that of objects—an opinion which appeared to rest upon the internal theory of relations; and along with this opinion we rejected—
40 though partly by arguments which await amplification on another occasion—the doctrine that all immediate knowledge is confined to knowledge of ourselves.

Chapter IV
Definitions and Methodological
Principles in Theory of Knowledge

IN THE FOLLOWING chapter, I propose to suggest some definitions resulting from the analysis of experience suggested in previous chapters, and some methodological precepts which I believe to be useful in the later portions of theory of knowledge. It was scarcely possible to state either the definitions or the precepts until we had decided that the relation of acquaintance is fundamental to experience, for almost all definitions and principles that we can adopt will presuppose this theory. 10

Subjects have been already defined in a previous chapter as entities which are acquainted with something, and *objects* as entities with which something is acquainted. In other words, subjects are the domain, and objects are the converse domain, of the relation *acquaintance*. It is not necessary to assume that acquaintance is unanalyzable, or that subjects must be simple; it may be found that a further analysis of both is possible. But I have no analysis to suggest, and therefore formally both will appear as if they were simple, though nothing will be falsified if they are found to be not simple.

Cognitive facts will be defined as facts involving acquaintance or some relation which presupposes acquaintance. 20

It is to be observed that we can define cognitive *facts*, not mental *particulars*, since we have no reason to assume that subjects are in fact always or ever of a different kind from other particulars. The distinguishing mark of what is mental, or at any rate of what is cognitive, is not to be found in the particulars involved, but only in the nature of the relations between them. Of these relations acquaintance appears to be the most comprehensive and therefore the most suitable for the definition of cognitive facts.

There is, however, a certain difficulty in defining the word "presuppose" which occurs in the above definition. What is intended is to include such relations as (e.g.) attention and judgment, which seem plainly to involve 30 acquaintance with the object attended to or the objects entering into the judgment. But it is not intended to include relations which merely *happen*, as an empirical fact, to occur only where there is acquaintance. In the cases which it is intended to include, the fact that acquaintance is involved seems a priori evident, and not merely a statistical occurrence. I do not know what, precisely, is the logical difference between these two kinds of connection, but it seems plain that there is a difference. The kind of connection intended in the definition is what we may call the a priori kind; and since the difficulties of the distinction belong solely to logic, we need not investigate them further at present.

Theory of knowledge, or epistemology, is more difficult to define. To begin with, no definition can be satisfactory which introduces the word "knowledge", both because this word is highly ambiguous, and because every one of its possible meanings can only be made clear after much epistemological discussion. Then again, difficulties arise as regards the relations of epistemology to psychology and to logic respectively. It is obvious that much of
10 epistemology is included in psychology. The analysis of experience, the distinctions between sensation, imagination, memory, attention, etc., the nature of belief or judgment, in short all the analytic portion of the subject, in so far as it does not introduce the distinction between truth and falsehood, must, I think, be regarded as strictly part of psychology. On the other hand, the distinction between truth and falsehood, which is plainly relevant to the theory of knowledge, would seem to belong to logic, though this is open to some degree of doubt. And in any case, as soon as we reach the theory of judgment, even apart from truth and falsehood, the difficulties encountered are almost entirely logical, and logical discoveries are what are most re-
20 quired for the progress of the subject. It can be shown[1] that a judgment, and generally all thought whose expression involves propositions, must be a fact of a different logical form from any of the series: subject–predicate facts, dual relations, triple relations, etc. In this way, a difficult and interesting problem of pure logic arises, namely the problem of enlarging the inventory of logical forms so as to include forms appropriate to the facts of epistemology. It would seem, therefore, that it is impossible to assign to the theory of knowledge a province distinct from that of logic and psychology. Any attempt to mark out such a province must, I believe, be artificial and therefore harmful.

30   The central problem of epistemology is the problem of distinguishing between true and false beliefs, and of finding, in as many regions as possible, criteria of true belief within those regions. This problem takes us, through the analysis of belief and its presuppositions, into psychology and the enumeration of cognitive relations, while it takes us into logic through the distinction of truth and falsehood, which is irrelevant in a merely psychological discussion of belief. We may define epistemology in terms of this problem, as: *The analysis of true and false belief and their presuppositions, together with the search for criteria of true belief.* But *practically* this definition is somewhat wide, since it will include parts of psychology and logic whose
40 importance is not mainly epistemological; and for this reason, the definition must not be interpreted quite strictly.

---

1 As I have come to know through unpublished work of my friend Mr. Ludwig Wittgenstein.

Data are by no means easy to define, since there are various logically different kinds of data. The simplest kind will be *objects*: in this sense, a given person's data are those *particulars* with which he is acquainted. Even in this very narrow sense, there are, as I shall try to show in subsequent chapters, still at least three ways in which data may be given, namely in sense, in memory, or in imagination; but these different ways of being given do not involve corresponding differences in the objects given. On the other hand, we can understand universals, and any primitive understanding of a universal (i.e. any understanding not derived from some other understanding) is in a sense a case of acquaintance, and is certainly sufficient 10 ground for calling the universal in question a datum. What is the correct analysis of the understanding of universals is a difficult question, but such understanding must certainly be included among the data of knowledge. Again, *perceptions of facts* (as opposed to the corresponding judgments) must be included among data; if I see that one thing is to the left of another, or if I observe that the thunder is later than the lightning in a particular case, these perceived facts are certainly among my data. And perceived facts are not always thus particular: general logical facts, for example, are often such as can be perceived. I do not know whether any *judgments* (as opposed to perceptions) are to be included among the data of knowledge: arguments 20 may be adduced on either side in this question. But certainly all epistemologically legitimate inference demands that both the premiss and the connection of premiss and conclusion should be data, either for perception or for judgment.

I think we may say broadly that *data* include all particulars, universals, and facts, which are cognized otherwise than by inference or by belief not derived from analysis of a perceived fact. Thus the only cognitions which do not give data are (a) beliefs obtained by inference, and (b) beliefs not obtained either by inference or by analysis of perceived facts. Beliefs of the second kind might be fitly called *prejudices*: it will be a mere accident 30 whether they are true or false. Inferred beliefs, on the other hand, if derived from data and not from prejudices, will be true. But in these remarks we are anticipating the outcome of lengthy discussions which cannot be undertaken at present.

There is another, somewhat vaguer, sense in which the word "data" may be used in epistemology. If we are analyzing some body of knowledge, say physics, with a view to disentangling its truth and falsehood, we may give the name "data" to all the beliefs which we entertain when we enter on the inquiry. In this sense, "data" will be opposed to "premisses", and what we have hitherto called data will be more fitly called premisses. This usage is 40 convenient in some discussions, but for our present purposes it seems not desirable.

It is a common error to suppose that it must be obvious what are our data in any subject-matter to which we turn our attention. This need by no means be the case, since something may quite well be a datum without the fact of its being a datum being also a datum. There is therefore nothing surprising in the fact that it is often very difficult to discover what our data really are.

I pass now to some methodological principles which may be useful in our subsequent inquiries.

(1). *The objects of acquaintance cannot be "illusory" or "unreal".* It is customary to speak of dreams and hallucinations as illusory, and to regard images as unreal in some sense not applicable to the objects of normal sensations. No doubt there are important differences between the objects commonly considered "real" and the objects commonly considered "unreal". But for purely logical reasons, these differences demand some entirely different analysis. If an object is given in acquaintance, then that object has a certain relation to the subject which is acquainted with it. But this would be meaningless if there were no such object. An object of acquaintance is an object to which it is possible to give a proper name, as opposed to a description; it may become the "this" of attention. Of such an object, it is meaningless to suppose it unreal. A proper name which names nothing is not a proper name, but a meaningless noise. An acquaintance which is acquainted with nothing is not an acquaintance, but a mere absurdity. The conception "unreal" is not applicable to such immediate data, but only to *described* entities. We may say "the present king of France is unreal", meaning that there is no present king of France, but not meaning "there is an entity which is at present king of France and which is unreal". Unreality, in fact, is a notion which owes its origin to grammatical forms. These forms make it possible for the grammatical subject of a sentence to be a description, which is not the name of any constituent of the proposition expressed by the sentence. In such a case, if the description applies to nothing, we may say that the subject is unreal; and if we fail to realize that the unreal subject is merely grammatical, we may come to think that there are entities which are unreal. This, however, is a plain absurdity: given an entity, it is absurd to inquire whether it is real or unreal: there the entity is, and there is no more to be said. Thus the supposition that some objects with which we are acquainted are unreal is one which logic shows to be untenable.

The conclusion that no object of acquaintance can be "unreal" forces upon us a certain attitude of respect towards dreams, hallucinations, and images. There are, of course, important epistemological differences between such objects and the objects of normal sensation, but these differences belong to a much later and more complex part of the subject. Their *likeness* to the objects of normal sensation is much less realized, but is far more important for our present purpose. Mankind has gradually selected a kind of aristocracy among entities, which it calls the "real" world. But, as Parmenides told Socrates, in philosophy we must not despise even the meanest things; and the entities which mankind has condemned as "unreal" are full of interest and importance. It will be said: "No doubt the things we see in dreams exist in a sense, but it is a purely subjective sense: they exist only because we are dreaming, and are merely parts of our mind." This may or may not be true. I am not concerned at present with the question whether it is true or false. I wish merely to point out the great complexity of what is asserted, and the immense system of knowledge which it presupposes. It is asserted that the objects of dreams exist only because we are dreaming; this means, I suppose, that there is some essential impossibility in such objects existing except when some subject is aware of them. It is asserted that they exist only in our mind; this means, I suppose, that not more than one subject can possibly be aware of them. But to know all this is to have an enormous knowledge of the external world, and to see that it cannot harbour anywhere such objects as I saw in my dream. And there is always the fear that the same proposition might be maintained regarding the things seen in waking life. If dreams are to be given a lower status than waking life, as a source of knowledge concerning the external world, this must be done, not by condemning them *ab initio*, but by showing that the world which is constructed on the assumption that they and waking life have exactly the same *immediate* reality is one in which dream-objects are less intimately related to *other* entities than are the objects of our waking sensations. In fact, what is *called* the unreality of an immediate object must always be really the unreality of some other object inferred from the immediate object and described by reference to it. This conclusion, we shall find, is of great importance in all problems concerning our knowledge of the external world.

(2). *The possibility of error in any cognitive occurrence shows that the occurrence is not an instance of a dual relation.* This maxim is closely connected with our first maxim, and equally has a purely logical origin. We saw that when we are acquainted with an object, there certainly is such an object, and the possibility of error is logically excluded. Exactly the same argument would apply to any two-term relation. But when the occurrence is one which unites the subject with several objects in a single fact, the situation is different. In this case, the several objects may or may not be themselves the constituents of a certain related fact; thus a certain described fact, namely the fact composed, in some specified manner, of the objects of the occurrence in question, may occur in certain cases and not in others. The further explanation and exemplification of this maxim will come better in the account of belief. For the present, its chief importance is negative: where error is possible, something not acquaintance or attention or any other two-term relation is involved. This applies, for instance, to the case of memory, in so far as memory is fallible.

(3). *The epistemological order of deduction involves both logical and psychological considerations.* It is obvious that any order of valid deduction must involve *logical* considerations, since the propositions deduced must follow logically from their premisses. But given a certain body of propositions of which some are deducible from others, there will be many ways of selecting some among them as the premisses from which the others are to be inferred. Any such set of premisses may be called a set of *logical premisses* for that body of propositions. In a purely logical problem, in which we do not consider the question whether any of the body of propositions are *known to be true*, conditions of elegance suggest that a set of logical premisses should be such that no one follows from the others, and should consist of the smallest possible number of the simplest possible propositions. In epistemology, however, our premisses have to fulfil other requisites. We are concerned not merely with truth, but with knowledge; hence our premisses should be such as can be known to be true without being deduced from any others of the body of propositions in question. For this reason, a certain artificial naïveté is required in beginning epistemology: we must avoid assuming many things which we firmly believe to be true, but which can only be reached by a process of inference. On the other hand, in order to minimize the risk of error, which always exists in regard to premisses, it is wise to include whatever appears to be known without proof, even if it could be deduced from other propositions so known. Thus the set of *epistemological premisses* for any body of propositions consists of all those relevant propositions which appear to be known otherwise than by inference, and from which the given body of propositions can be deduced. If some of the epistemological premisses can be deduced from others, that tends to confirm our belief in the premisses, and does not afford a reason for excluding those that can be deduced. We may call a body of propositions *epistemologically self-contained* when it contains all its own epistemological premisses. The propositions constituting our epistemology must, of course, be epistemologically self-contained—except that some of its premisses belong to logic; but those that belong to logic ought to be stated. Since the question as to what appears to be known without inference involves psychology, the epistemological order is partly determined by psychological considerations. The real business of epistemology is largely the discovery of its own epistemological premisses; the deductions from them will of course proceed according to the rules of logic, and may therefore be left to the logician.

(4). *A knowledge of physics and physiology must not be assumed in theory of knowledge.* This maxim follows from the preceding account of the epistemological order. Physics and physiology belong to our knowledge of what is called the external world; our knowledge of them is obviously dependent upon sensation, and is obtained by methods which the theory of knowledge must investigate. Thus however firmly we may be convinced of the truth of physics and physiology, we must only use this conviction as a means of *testing* our epistemology, not as affording premises upon which our epistemology may build from the start. To take a crude illustration: if we are considering whether or how the sense of sight gives knowledge of physical objects, we must not assume that we know all about the retina, for the retina is a physical object of which we obtain knowledge by seeing it. Thus to assume that we know this or that about the retina is to assume that we have already solved the epistemological problem of the physical knowledge to be derived through sight.   10

It is to be observed, however, that it would not be a logical fallacy to assume knowledge of the organs of sense for a purely sceptical purpose, i.e. in order to show that no knowledge of physical objects is to be derived from the senses. If it could be shown that the hypothesis that we obtain such knowledge through the senses leads to a theory of the sense-organs which shows that they cannot give such knowledge, then the hypothesis with which we started would have refuted itself, and would therefore be false. But although some such position is sometimes advanced, and is not *logically* unsound, it is hardly possible that it should be true in substance. The hypothesis that we obtain knowledge of physical objects through the senses   20 is one which is capable of a multitude of forms, according to the view we adopt as to the nature of physical objects. If one view on this point is self-refuting, another may not be, and we can never be sure that we have tried all possible views. Thus a dogmatic scepticism as to the knowledge of physical objects derived from the senses can never be warranted by such arguments as we have been considering. Nevertheless, the possibility is one which it is important to remember, since it affords a test to which any theory as to our knowledge of the external world may be submitted.

It is no doubt the case that our sensations are functions of the sense-organs and the nervous system, but this is not the *primitive* knowledge—it is   30 a scientific inference, and cannot form part of the epistemological premises of epistemology. In epistemology, it is important to reduce our problems to what is actually experienced. Take, for example, such a simple fact as that we no longer see objects when we shut our eyes. A number of immediate experiences have to be combined in order to reach this result. We can know from our own experience that visual objects disappear when we have certain muscular and tactile sensations, which we learn to locate in our eyelids. By shutting one eye in front of a looking-glass we may learn (assuming what we know of looking-glasses) what is the visual appearance of the eyelid when we have the muscular sensation in question. By seeing others shut their eyes,   40 and learning that then they no longer see, we can learn without looking-glasses what shutting the eyes looks like. But all this is a complicated process, learned, no doubt, at an early age, but not known without learning.

Thus the dependence of sight upon the eyes is not the sort of thing to be *assumed* in epistemology. And what is true of this very simple physiological fact is true *a fortiori* of the complicated and difficult knowledge concerning the brain which is sometimes thought relevant to the foundations of epistemology. All such knowledge is excluded by the rule which must guide us throughout our investigation: Seek always for what is obvious, and accept nothing else except as the result of an inference from something obvious which has been found previously. With this rule, a great simplification is effected, and vast masses of erudition can be swept aside as irrelevant.

Chapter V
Sensation and Imagination

O F ALL THE direct two-term relations which can subsist between subjects and other entities, of the kind with which theory of knowledge is concerned, *acquaintance* is the most comprehensive. I do not mean that this is a priori necessary, but that, so far as can be seen by observation, it is in fact true. If an instance to the contrary could be established, no prejudice ought to prevent us from admitting the instance; in the absence of such an instance, however, I shall assume that all direct two-term relations of a subject to other entities, in so far as such relations can be directly 10 experienced by the subject in question, imply acquaintance with those other entities. There are various words, such as sensation, imagination, conception, immediate memory, which denote two-term relations of subject and object, and we have to inquire whether these are distinguished by the nature of the relation or only by the nature of the object. Differences in the object (except when the object is mental) do not directly concern theory of knowledge, at any rate in its analytical portion; but differences in the *relation* to the object do directly concern the analytical portion of theory of knowledge. In the present chapter, we have to consider whether the difference between sensation and imagination is a difference in the object or in the relation. 20

The epistemological importance and difficulty of this inquiry have not, I think, been sufficiently appreciated by any writer except Hume; and even Hume, though aware of the problem, offers a quite unduly simple solution. What is required is to find a tenable interpretation of the feeling that objects of sense are "real" while objects of imagination are "imaginary" or "unreal". In accordance with the maxim explained in our last chapter, it is not open to us to say that the objects of imagination are "unreal"; the whole conception of "reality" or "unreality", "existence" or "non-existence", as applied to particulars, is a result of logical confusion between names and descriptions. A colour visualized, or a sound heard in imagination, must be 30 just on the same level as regards "reality" as a colour seen or a sound heard in sensation: it must be equally one of the particulars which would have to be enumerated in an inventory of the universe. Nevertheless, there is undoubtedly *some* important difference between sense-data and imagination-data, which is confusedly indicated by calling the former "real" and the latter "unreal". One outcome of this difference is that sense-data, but not imagination-data, are relevant to physics, being in fact that part of the material world which is immediately given. It is therefore of the utmost importance to epistemology to decide both how imagination and sense are distinguished, and what is the basis for the difference which we feel as regards their power of giving information about the material world.

In the first half of this inquiry, the following criterion will be useful. If we can find a case where the object is the same in two experiences which yet differ intrinsically, then the two experiences must involve different relations to the object. Thus if an object O can be given either in sensation or in
10 imagination, and if the two experiences can be seen to be different by mere inspection, without taking account of their relations to other experiences, then we must conclude that sensation is a different relation from imagination. For two complexes which involve the same related terms can only differ if the relations differ in the two complexes. If, on the other hand, it should appear that, whenever the object is given, sensation and imagination become intrinsically indistinguishable, we shall conclude that the relation involved is the same in both. If, lastly, we find that the object of sensation is never identical with the object of imagination, then our criterion fails; but in this case we at least know that the difference in their objects is quite enough
20 to account for the fact that sensation and imagination are distinguished, and that there is no logical necessity to suppose the relations different.

The use of the above criterion may be made clearer by considering the difference between belief and doubt on the one hand, and the difference between true and false belief on the other hand. If I first doubt a given proposition, and then believe it, the two experiences are quite different intrinsically, and therefore the relation involved must be different in the two cases. In the case of true and false belief, on the contrary, the objects must be different when the belief is true and when it is false; moreover inspection shows no other intrinsic difference between true and false beliefs except the
30 difference of their objects. Hence we may conclude that belief is one relation to objects, which is the same in the case of true beliefs as in the case of false beliefs. We cannot, by the nature of the case, find a true belief and a false belief which have the same objects in the same order, and therefore the more stringent form of our test is inapplicable; but it is sufficiently nearly applicable to make it practically certain that true and false beliefs differ only as regards their objects.

In the case of sensation and imagination, I believe that sometimes, though rarely, their objects may be identical, and that then they are still intrinsically distinguishable. I conclude that different relations to objects are involved in
40 the two cases, although the distinction is facilitated partly by differences in their usual objects, and partly also by means of their external relations to other things. This is the proposition which I wish to establish in the present chapter.

Before we can advance, it is necessary to have a definition of sensation and imagination respectively. In this, the usual psychological accounts are not of much use to us, because, in the first place, they do not regard either sensation or imagination as involving a relation of subject and object, and in the second place, they assume, as a rule, a knowledge of physiology which, as explained in the preceding chapter, we must at our present stage do our best to ignore.

Thus Stout says:[1] "One characteristic mark of what we agree in calling sensation is its mode of production. It is caused by what we call a *stimulus*. A stimulus is always some condition, external to the nervous system itself and operating upon it." He proceeds to explain the importance of distinguishing the stimulus from the object of sense-perception. Thus the stimulus and its causal connection with the sensation are only known by means of a body of knowledge not derivable without much inference. The connection with a stimulus will not appear necessarily in any intrinsic quality of a sensation; and so far as I can discover, no intrinsic quality distinguishing sensations from other experiences is given by Stout.

What James says about sensation comes much nearer to giving us what we require. He says: "Its [sensation's] function is that of mere *acquaintance* with a fact. Perception's function, on the other hand, is knowledge *about* a fact" (*Psychology*, II, p. 2). Again:

> As we can only think or talk about the relations of objects with which we have *acquaintance* already, we are forced to postulate a function in our thought whereby we first become aware of the *bare immediate natures* by which our several objects are distinguished. This function is sensation. (*Ibid.*, p. 3)

He does not discuss "acquaintance", and it would be unfair to assume that he means by it what we mean. Nevertheless, if we take him to mean what we mean, his statement is one which we can in a great measure accept, and which at least has the merit of giving an *intrinsic* character of sensation. But although sensation has the characteristic which he mentions, it would seem that other experiences also have this characteristic; for he identifies sensation with acquaintance, and we are in fact acquainted with objects logically similar to those of sensation in imagination and immediate memory, and with objects of another kind in conception and abstract thought. Thus some further characteristic is required to distinguish sensation from other kinds of acquaintance.

One obvious characteristic, which distinguishes sensation from conception and abstract thought, is that its objects are *particulars*. A particular is

defined as an entity which can only enter into complexes as the subject of a
predicate or as one of the terms of a relation, never as itself a predicate or a
relation. This definition is purely logical, and introduces nothing belonging
to theory of knowledge. Thus we may say that sensations are always cases of
acquaintance with particulars. But this is still not a definition, since it fails to
exclude imagination and immediate memory.

In the analysis of memory there are special difficulties, which make it
doubtful how far it is to be included under acquaintance. But assuming that
there is a kind of memory which involves acquaintance with its object, such
10 memory may be distinguished from sensation and imagination by the fact
that its object is given as in the past: there is a temporal relation of subject
and object which is involved in the actual experience of memory. Being in
the past is not an intrinsic property of the object, but a relation to the subject; thus memory will have to be distinguished from sense and imagination
as a different relation to objects, not as the same relation to different objects.
This topic will be resumed in the next chapter; for the present, it is enough
to observe that memory is excluded if we say that the acquaintance we are
concerned with must not be with an object given as past.

Sensation and imagination together, therefore, may be defined as "ac-
20 quaintance with particulars not given as earlier than the subject". What is
meant by "given as earlier" is a question requiring discussion; for the present, we may say that we mean "having an immediately experienced relation
to the subject of that kind which underlies our knowledge of the past". The
further definition of this relation must be reserved for the next chapter.

Since no acquaintance with particulars given as future occurs, it might be
thought that "particulars not given as earlier than the subject" might be
identified with "particulars given as simultaneous with the subject". But
such identification presupposes, what must not be assumed without discussion, that an experienced particular must be given as in some temporal rela-
30 tion with the subject. If this can be denied, we may find here an intrinsic
difference between sense and imagination. It may be that in sense the object
is given as "now", i.e. as simultaneous with the subject, whereas in imagination the object is given without any temporal relation to the subject, i.e. to
the present time. It is difficult even to discuss this question without an
analysis of our perception of time, but let us make the attempt.

The theory I wish to examine will maintain that, whatever time-relation
may in fact subsist between the subject and an object which is imagined, no
time-relation is implied by the mere fact that the imagining occurs. I do not
know whether this theory is tenable or not, but I think there is more to be
40 said in its favour than might be thought at first sight. I propose, therefore, to
do what I can to make the theory seem *possible*, without coming to a decision
as to its truth or falsehood.

It may be said that, while we are imagining, the object imagined may undergo processes of change—for example when we imagine a tune or when we mentally recite a poem. This of course is true, and might be thought to imply that the object must be contemporaneous with the imagining subject. But such an inference would be erroneous, as may be seen by the analogy of abstract thought. I may reflect that twice two are four, and then that twice three are six, and so on throughout the multiplication-table. In this case, I have different objects before my mind at different times, but none of the objects are themselves in time at all. In like manner, I may at one time imagine one object, at another time another object, or even at a continuous series of times a continuous series of objects—for example, the sound of a violin-string running down—while yet the objects imagined may be destitute of temporal position, or may have a temporal position which cannot be inferred from the fact that they are now imagined. An object imagined at one moment but not at another need not itself undergo any intrinsic change during the time between the two moments: it may merely cease to have that relation to the subject which consists in its being imagined. But such cessation may easily produce the belief that the object itself was at the time when it was imagined, though, as is clear in the case of abstract objects, this is in no way implied by the change that has occurred.

Consider, again, the kind of imagination which is connected with memory. In remembering, say, my breakfast this morning, I shall normally use images which are called up at will and are said to be "of" my breakfast. It might be thought that in this case the object is in the past. But this would involve confusing the image with true memory. The image is not *identical* with the past sense-datum which it helps me to remember; and it is only when there is such identity that the object is in the past. I think in the case of *immediate* memory there is such identity, but in this case the object is not an image. When we use images as an aid in remembering, we judge that the images have a resemblance, of a certain sort, to certain past sense-data, enabling us to have knowledge by description concerning those sense-data, through acquaintance with the corresponding images together with a knowledge of the correspondence. The knowledge of the correspondence is obviously only possible through some knowledge, concerning the past, which is not dependent upon the images we now call up. This, however, belongs to the analysis of memory, which is not our present problem; for the present, all that is necessary to observe is that the images which are said to be "of" past sensible objects are not themselves in the past, and therefore form no objection to the hypothesis that images are not given in such a way as to enable us to assign a date to them.

One merit of the above theory is that it accounts, in a manner consistent with logic, for what is called the "unreality" of things merely imagined. This "unreality" will consist in their absence of date, which will also explain fully their irrelevance to physics.

If the above hypothesis is adopted, we can lay down the following definitions:

"Imagination" is acquaintance with particulars which are not given as having any temporal relation to the subject.

"Sensation" is acquaintance with particulars given as simultaneous with the subject.

It is to be observed that, in the above definition, it is not asserted that an object imagined has in actual fact no temporal relation to the subject, but merely that this temporal relation, if it exists, forms no part of the experience of imagining. The question whether this is the case or not must be capable of being decided by introspection, but introspection is difficult, and I cannot myself arrive at any certain conclusion in this way. We may observe, however, that "imagining" must not be held to include after-images, which, from our present point of view, belong rather to sensation; from the physiological point of view, also, they differ wholly from imagination, since they depend upon the recent stimulation of the sense-organ.

Leaving, for the present, this possible method of distinguishing sensation and imagination, let us consider other alleged differences, namely:

(1) the physiological difference, in relation to stimulus,
(2) the different relation to the will,
(3) the less degree of vividness in images,
(4) the different relation to belief and "physical reality".

We will consider these alleged differences successively.

(1). The difference in causal relation to stimulus, as already pointed out, is one which is not relevant at our present stage; that is to say, if this were the only difference between sense and imagination, we should have to construct our theory of the knowledge of external reality before distinguishing between sense and imagination, since a knowledge of external reality is presupposed in the recognition of a different relation to stimulus. Now theories of our knowledge of external reality generally rely on sensation to the exclusion of imagination; hence unless we can invent a theory which uses both equally, we must not rest content with the proposed method of distinguishing between them. For this reason, it is important to examine other proposed distinctions.

(2). It may be said that images are capable of being called up at will, in a way in which objects of sense are not. This, if true at all, is only true when stated with very careful limitations. We have at most times considerable choice as to what we shall see or touch, though of course we are limited to what is visible or palpable from where we are. As to what we shall imagine, we are limited by our imaginative powers, and though the field of choice is different, it is just as truly limited as in the case of sense. It is true that we can, more or less at will, call up images of past events, whereas in sense we are confined to what is at the present time. But this is a difference in the area of choice, not in the relation to the will. Moreover images may appear with just as little cooperation of the will as in the case of sensations. Stout, after explaining the sudden shock of a flash of lightning or a steam-whistle, says "no mere image ever does strike the mind in this manner" (*Manual*, p. 417). Macbeth speaks of

> that suggestion
> Whose horrid image doth unfix my hair
> And make my seated heart knock at my ribs
> Against the use of nature.

10

The whistle of a railway engine could hardly have a stronger effect than this; and in morbid and insane states of mind images must frequently have the violence of sensations, with the same independence of the will. This distinction, therefore, cannot be accepted as adequate.

(3). The view that images can be distinguished from objects of sense by their smaller degree of vividness has already been partly answered by anticipation under our previous heading. Stout sums up as follows:

> Our conclusion is that at bottom the distinction between image and percept, as respecting faint and vivid states, is based on a difference of quality. The percept has an aggressiveness which does not belong to the image. It strikes the mind with varying degrees of force or liveliness according to the varying intensity of the stimulus. This degree of force or liveliness is part of what we ordinarily mean by the intensity of a sensation. But this constituent of the intensity of sensations is absent in mental imagery. (*Manual*, p. 419)

20

I believe this, however true as a general rule, to be liable to exceptions which make it quite useless as a test. A very strong emotion will often bring with it—especially where some future action or some undecided issue is involved—powerful, compelling images which may determine the whole course of life, sweeping aside all contrary solicitations to the will by their capacity for exclusively possessing the mind. And in all cases where images, originally recognized as such, gradually pass into hallucinations, there must be just that "force or liveliness" which is supposed to be always absent in imagination.

30

(4). We may attempt to distinguish sensations from images by the belief in their "reality", in their power of giving knowledge of the "external world". This difference is hard to analyze or to state correctly, but in some sense it has plainly a large element of truth. Images are "imaginary"; in *some* sense, they are "unreal". They cannot be employed to give knowledge of physics. They are destitute of causal efficacy, they are not impenetrable, and altogether they fail to compel respect. But however true it may be that images differ from objects of sense in these respects, it is impossible that these differences should be the ultimate source of the difference between imagination and sense. The "unreality" of images requires interpretation: it cannot mean what we should express by "there's no such thing", for this phrase is only applicable to a thing described, not to a thing immediately given. The word "unreal", as applied to something immediately given, has always some rather complicated meaning. A visual object, such as Macbeth's dagger or a reflection in a looking-glass, is "unreal" if it is not correlated with the usual tactile sensations; and the "unreality" of images might consist only in their not obeying the laws of motion and in their being generally unconventional in their behaviour. But in any case, "unreality", as applied to objects of acquaintance, is some complicated conception, always derivative from some other difference between the objects so condemned and the objects recognized as "real". The difference, therefore, which undoubtedly exists between images and objects of sensation, in respect of our belief in their "reality", must be derivative from some other and simpler difference. If it be the case, as was suggested earlier, that images are not given as simultaneous or in any other time-relation with the subject, then an image need not exist at the moment when it is imagined, nor indeed at any other moment; such a difference as this, between images and objects of sense, would, it seems to me, amply account for the feeling that images are "unreal". This feeling, therefore, on examination, is found to afford a confirmation of our theory.

The case of dreams demands discussion: is dreaming sensation or imagination? The four differences which we have considered leave the matter doubtful. (1) Physiologically, in relation to stimulus, dreams cannot count as sensations, except in certain cases, e.g. where a door banging makes us dream of some noisy event such as a naval battle. In this case, the noise in the dream may be considered sensation, while the rest of the dream is taken as imagination together with false interpretation. But as a rule, for example with all the objects we see in dreams while our eyes are shut, the relation to stimulus which is supposed to be characteristic of sensation is absent. Thus as regards this criterion, the greater part of the objects in dreams would count as images. (2) As regards the relation to the will, dreams belong rather with sensation. The procession of objects in a dream is received by us passively, in the same sense and to the same degree as the objects of waking sensation are received passively. But this difference between sense and imagination, we found, is by no means absolute: some images seem to come in just the way in which sensations come. Thus although, under this head, it would be more natural to put dreams with sensations, yet we cannot lay very

much stress on this fact. (3) As regards the less degree of vividness of images, it would seem that dreams on the whole belong with images rather
than with objects of sense. People, for example, whose visual images are not
brightly coloured, but are all of some dim shade of grey, are likely to see a
similarly colourless world in their dreams, though often the power of vis-
ualizing in dreams will be more nearly that which the dreamer possessed in
youth than that which he possesses now. Most people, I think, would say
that the world of dreams has the fragmentary indistinctness of the world of
images: it is fairly finished in the parts that specially interest the dreamer,
but creation has been scamped elsewhere and it remains very much in the   10
rough. It may be doubted, however, whether this is not equally true of the
world of sense, and only seems untrue because we always pass away from
sense to "physical reality" by an unconscious inference. What we see out of
the corners of our eyes is very dim, but we do not feel it so, because as soon
as we look at it straight we find it is distinct. Nevertheless, it must be admitted, I think, that as a general rule sensations have a vividness and dis-
tinctness which is lacking in imagination, and that in this respect dreams
resemble imagination rather than sense. (4) What makes dreams really
puzzling is their relation to belief and "physical reality". While they last,
their relation to belief appears to be precisely that of sensation: they never   20
seem, at the moment, to be our own invention. Yet, when we wake, they are
dismissed from belief on the ground that they do not fit in with our constructions of "physical reality". There is thus a conflict between belief
(while we are dreaming) and "physical reality" (after we wake). As regards
the belief, dreams belong with sense, while as regards the "physical reality"
they belong with imagination. In this, dreams resemble hallucinations; they
also resemble what we are told of the imagination of children, who sometimes, as Galton states,[2] "seem to spend years of difficulty distinguishing
between the subjective and objective world".

   The conclusion which is *suggested* by these considerations is that dreams   30
belong mainly, but not wholly, to imagination, but are mistakenly supposed
by the subject to belong to sensation even in their imagined parts. I do not
mean that the subject, as a rule, definitely *judges* that they belong to sensation, but that his feelings towards them, while he is dreaming, are such as he
would usually only have towards objects of sense, and such as he would
cease to have if he recognized that the objects in question were mere images.
In order that this theory may be tenable, it is not necessary to suppose that
there is no intrinsic difference between imagining and sensation, but only
that the difference is one which sometimes remains unfelt. If it is the case, as
it seems to be, that a great majority of imagined objects differ in recogniza-   40
ble ways from sensible objects—by greater dimness, vagueness, subjection

2 Quoted by James, *Psychology*, II, p. 55.

to our will, etc.—then it would be surprising if, when an imagined object fails to differ in these ways from an object of sense, the subject is mistakenly led to regard it as an object of sense, overlooking the less easily detected difference of relation which, if we are right, constitutes the true *differentia* of imagination. The way in which hallucinations and delusions often begin as mere vivid images, recognized as such, and only gradually acquire a hold on belief, suggests that, to the end, they remain different from sensations. Dreams will then be, in the main, identical in nature with hallucinations, and will be accounted for by the fact that in sleep our imagination is unusu-
10 ally active and our critical faculties unusually slight. All such experiences, which, if accompanied by belief, are recognized as sources of error, will be classed with imagination. With this conclusion, a great simplification will be introduced, at a later stage, into the problem of our knowledge of the external world.

If the hypothesis that images are not given in any time-relation to the subject is rejected, as perhaps it may have to be, it will be necessary to find some other way of explaining what is meant when images are said to be "unreal". We must in any case, I think, allow that imagination and sensation are different relations to objects, since, in spite of the differences usu-
20 ally to be found between images and sense-data, the difference between the two experiences of imagining and sensation seems too clear and profound to be accounted for by such differences alone. It seems evident that, if images have any given time-relation to the subject, it must be that of simultaneity; hence in this respect they will be indistinguishable from sense-data. We cannot hope, therefore, in this case, to explain the "unreality" of images by the nature of the relation of imagining; and I do not think that there is anything in the *intrinsic* character of images by which we can explain it. We must, therefore, if we allow images to be simultaneous with the subject, define their "unreality" by means of their behaviour and relations.

30 The "unreality" of images may, on our present hypothesis, be defined as consisting merely in their failure to fulfil the correlations which are fulfilled by sense-data. An imagined visual object cannot be touched, that is to say, if we perform those movements which, in the case of a visual sense-datum, would procure a sensation of touch, we shall not have a sensation of touch, nor, as a rule, an image of touch. Again, images change in ways which are wholly contrary to the laws of physics; the laws of their changes seem, in fact, to be psychological rather than physical, involving reference to such matters as the subject's thoughts and desires. This would, I think, sufficiently explain what is meant by the "unreality" of images. I do not,
40 therefore, know how to decide between our present and our former hypothesis as to the nature of imagination.

We may now sum up the above discussion. In spite of certain differences usually to be found between images and sense-data, we decided that there is also a difference, usually recognizable introspectively, between the relation of imagining and the relation of sensation. We failed to find any way of deciding between the view that an image is given as simultaneous with the subject and the view that it is not given as in any time-relation to the subject. If it is given as simultaneous with the subject, its "unreality" must consist merely in its failure to obey the laws of correlation and change which are obeyed by sense-data and which form the empirical basis of physics. If, on the other hand, imagination involves no time-relation of subject and object, then it is a simpler relation than sensation, being, in fact, merely *acquaintance with particulars*. The object imagined may, on this view, have any position in time or none, so far as the mere fact of its being imagined is concerned. *Sensation*, on the other hand, is a relation to a particular which involves simultaneity between subject and object. Sensation *implies* acquaintance with the object, but is not identical with acquaintance. It is not a definition of sensation to say that it is acquaintance with an object which is in fact simultaneous with the subject: the simultaneity must be not merely a fact, but must be deducible from the nature of the experience involved in sensation. We might take sensation as indefinable, and define simultaneity by its means; but whether this is really feasible is a question which must be postponed until we come to consider our experience of time-relations. The "unreality" of images, which cannot be taken in a strict sense, may, we found, on this theory, be interpreted as expressing the fact that they are not given with any definite position in time. Dreams and hallucinations, we found, are to be classed, mainly, though not wholly, with images, and the mistaken view that they are sensations, which is normally held by the experiencing subject, may be accounted for by the fact that their objects have characteristics generally associated with objects of sense.

The next problem which must occupy us is a problem raised by our definition of sensation, and involved in any theory of memory, namely the problem of our acquaintance with time-relations. This problem will occupy us in the next chapter.

Chapter VI
On the Experience of Time

IN THE PRESENT chapter, we shall be concerned with all those immediate experiences upon which our knowledge of time is based. Broadly speaking, two pairs of relations have to be considered, namely (a) sensation and memory, which give time-relations between object and subject, (b) simultaneity and succession, which give time-relations among objects. It is of the utmost importance not to confuse time-relations of subject and object with time-relations of object and object; in fact, many of the worst difficulties in the psychology and metaphysics of time have arisen from this confusion. It will be seen that past, present, and future arise from time-relations of subject and object, while earlier and later arise from time-relations of object and object. In a world in which there was no experience there would be no past, present, or future, but there might well be earlier and later. Let us give the name of *mental time* to the time which arises through relations of subject and object, and the name *physical time* to the time which arises through relations of object and object. We have to consider what are the elements in immediate experience which lead to our knowledge of these two sorts of time, or rather of time-relations.

Although, in the finished logical theory of time, physical time is simpler than mental time, yet in the analysis of experience it would seem that mental time must come first. The essence of physical time is succession; but the experience of succession will be very different according as the objects concerned are both remembered, one remembered and one given in sense, or both given in sense. Thus the analysis of sensation and memory must precede the discussion of physical time.

Before entering upon any detail, it may be well to state in summary form the theory which is to be advocated.

(1). *Sensation* (including the apprehension of present mental facts by introspection) is a certain relation of subject and object, involving acquaintance, but recognizably different from any other experienced relation of subject and object.

(2). Objects of sensation are said to be *present* to their subject in the experience in which they are objects.

(3). Simultaneity is a relation among entities, which is given in experience as sometimes holding between objects present to a given subject in a

64

single experience.

(4). An entity is said to be *now* if it is simultaneous with what is present to me, i.e. with *this*, where "this" is the proper name of an object of sensation of which I am aware.

(5). *The present time* may be defined as a class of all entities that are *now*. [This definition may require modification; it will be discussed later.]

(6). *Immediate Memory* is a certain relation of subject and object, involving acquaintance, but recognizably different from any other experienced relation of subject and object.

(7). *Succession* is a relation which may hold between two parts of one sensation, for instance between parts of a swift movement which is the object of one sensation; it may then, and perhaps also when one or both objects are objects of immediate memory, be immediately experienced, and extended by inference to cases where one or both of the terms of the relation are not present.

(8). When one event is succeeded by another, the first is called *earlier* and the second *later*.

(9). An event which is earlier than the whole of the present is called *past*, and an event which is later than the whole of the present is called *future*.

This ends our definitions, but we still need certain propositions constituting and connecting the mental and physical time-series. The chief of these are:

(a). Simultaneity and succession both give rise to transitive relations; simultaneity is symmetrical, while succession is asymmetrical, or at least gives rise to an asymmetrical relation defined in terms of it.

(b). What is remembered is past.

(c). Whenever a change is immediately experienced in sensation, parts of the present are earlier than other parts. (This follows logically from the definitions.)

(d). It may happen that *A* and *B* form part of one sensation, and likewise *B* and *C*, but when *C* is an object of sensation *A* is an object of memory. Thus the relation "belonging to the same present" is not transitive, and two presents may overlap without coinciding.

The above definitions and propositions must now be explained and amplified.

(1). *Sensation*, from the point of view of psychophysics, will be concerned only with objects not involving introspection. But from the point of view of theory of knowledge, all acquaintance with the present may advantageously be combined under one head, and therefore, if there is introspective knowledge of the present, we will include this with sensation. It is sometimes said that all introspective knowledge is of the nature of memory; we will not now consider this opinion, but will merely say that *if* introspection ever gives acquaintance with present mental entities in the way in which the senses give acquaintance with present physical entities, then such acquaintance with mental entities is, *for our purposes*, to be included under the head of sensation. Sensation, then, is that kind of acquaintance with particulars which enables us to know that they are at the present time. The object of a sensation we will call a *sense-datum*. Thus to a given subject sense-data are those of its objects which can be known, from the nature of their relation to the subject, to be at the present time.

The question naturally arises: how do we know whether an object is present or past or without position in time? Mere acquaintance, as we
10 decided in considering imagination, does not necessarily involve any given temporal relation to the subject. How, then, is the temporal relation given? Since there can be no *intrinsic* difference between present and past objects, and yet we can distinguish by inspection between objects given as present and those given as past, it follows from the criterion set forth at the beginning of the preceding chapter that the relation of subject to object must be different, and recognizably different, according as the object is present or past. Thus sensation must be a special relation of subject and object, different from any relation which does not show that the object is at the present time. Having come to this result, it is natural to accept "sensa-
20 tion" as an ultimate, and define the present time in terms of it; for otherwise we should have to use some such phrase as "given as at the present time", which would demand further analysis, and would almost inevitably lead us back to the relation of sensation as what is meant by the phrase "given as at the present time". For this reason, we accept sensation as one of the ultimates by means of which time-relations are to be defined.

(2). Our theory of time requires a definition, without presupposing time, of what is meant by "one (momentary) total experience". This question has been already considered in a previous chapter, where we decided that "being experienced together" is an ultimate relation among objects, which
30 is itself sometimes immediately experienced as holding between two objects. We cannot analyze this into "being experienced by the same subject", because A and B may be experienced together, and likewise B and C, while A and C are not experienced together: this will happen if A and B form part of one "specious present", and likewise B and C, but A is already past when C is experienced. Thus "being experienced together" is best taken as a simple relation. Although this relation is sometimes perceived, it may of course also hold when it is not perceived. Thus "one (momentary) total experience" will be the experience of all that group of objects which are experienced together with a given object. This, however, still contains a
40 difficulty, when viewed as a definition, namely that it assumes that no object is experienced twice, or throughout a longer time than one specious present. This difficulty must be solved before we can proceed.

Two opposite dangers confront any theory on this point. (a). If we say that no one object can be experienced twice, or rather, to avoid what would be *obviously* false, that no one object can be twice an object of sense, we have to ask what is meant by "twice". If a time intervenes between the two occasions, we can say that the object is not numerically the same on the two occasions; or, if that is thought false, we can say at least that the experience is not numerically the same on the two occasions. We can then define "one (momentary) total experience" as everything experienced together with "this", where "this" is an experience, not merely the object of an experience. By this means, we shall avoid the difficulty in the case when "twice" means "at two times separated by an interval when the experience in question is absent". But when what seems to be the same experience persists through a longer continuous period than one specious present, the overlapping of successive specious presents introduces a new difficulty. Suppose, to fix our ideas, that I look steadily at a motionless object while I hear a succession of sounds. The sounds A and B, though successive, may be experienced together, and therefore my seeing of the object while I hear these sounds need not be supposed to constitute two different experiences. But the same applies to what I see while I hear the sounds B and C. Thus the experience of seeing the given object will be the same at the time of the sound A and at the time of the sound C, although these two times may well not be parts of one specious present. Thus our definition will show that the hearing of A and the hearing of C form parts of one experience, which is plainly contrary to what we mean by one experience. Suppose, to escape this conclusion, we say that my seeing the object is a different experience while I am hearing A from what it is while I am hearing B. Then we shall be forced to deny that the hearing of A and the hearing of B form parts of one experience. In that case, the perception of change will become inexplicable, and we shall be driven to greater and greater sub-division, owing to the fact that changes are constantly occurring. We shall thus be forced to conclude that one experience cannot last for more than one mathematical instant, which is absurd.

(b). Having been thus forced to reject the view that the existence of one experience must be confined within one specious present, we have now to consider how we can define "one (momentary) total experience" on the hypothesis that a numerically identical experience may persist throughout a longer period than one specious present. It is obvious that no one experience will now suffice for definition. All that falls within one (momentary) total experience must belong to one specious present, but what is experienced together with a given experience need not, on our present hypothesis, fall within one specious present. We can, however, avoid all difficulties by defining "one (momentary) total experience" as a group of objects such that *any two* are experienced together, and nothing outside the group is experienced together with all of them. Thus, for example, if A and B, though not

simultaneous, are experienced together, and if B and C likewise are experienced together, C will not belong to one experience with A and B unless A and C also are experienced together. And given any larger group of objects, any two of which are experienced together, there is some one (momentary) total experience to which they all belong; but a new object x cannot be pronounced a member of this total experience until it has been found to be experienced together with all the members of the group. A given object will, in general, belong to many different (momentary) total experiences. Suppose, for example, the sounds A, B, C, D, E occur in succession, and three
10 of them can be experienced together. Then C will belong to a total experience containing A, B, C, to one containing B, C, D, and to one containing C, D, E. In this way, in spite of the fact that the specious present lasts for a certain length of time, experience permits us to assign the temporal position of an object much more accurately than merely within one specious present. In the above instance, C is at the end of the specious present of A, B, C, in the middle of that of B, C, D, and at the beginning of that of C, D, E. And by introducing less discrete changes the temporal position of C can be assigned even more accurately.

We may thus make the following definitions:
20 "One (momentary) total experience", is a group of experiences such that the objects of any two of them are experienced together, and anything experienced together with all members of the group is a member of the group.

The "specious present" of a momentary total experience is the period of time within which an object must lie in order to be a sense-datum in that experience.

This second definition needs some amplification. If an object has ceased to exist just before a given instant,[1] it may still be an object of sense at that instant. We may suppose that, of all the present objects of sense which have
30 already ceased to exist, there is one which ceased to exist longest ago; at any rate a certain stretch of time is defined from the present instant back through the various moments when present objects of sense ceased to exist. This stretch is the "specious present". It will be observed that this is a complicated notion, involving mathematical time as well as psychological presence. The purely psychological notion which underlies it is the notion of one (momentary) total experience.

Sense-data belonging to one (momentary) total experience are said to be *present* in that experience. This is a merely verbal definition.

The above definitions still involve a certain difficulty, though perhaps not
40 an insuperable one. We have admitted provisionally that a given particular may exist at different times. If it should happen that the whole group of

---

1 The word "instant" has a meaning defined later in the present chapter.

particulars constituting one (momentary) total experience should recur, all
our definitions of "the present time" and allied notions would become
ambiguous. It is no answer to say that such recurrence is improbable: "the
present time" is plainly not ambiguous, and would not be so if such
recurrence took place. In order to avoid the difficulty, one of two things is
necessary. Either we must show that such complete recurrence is *impossible*,
not merely improbable; or we must admit absolute time, i.e. admit that
there is an entity called a "moment" (or a "period of time" possibly) which
is not a mere relation between events, and is involved in assigning the
temporal position of an object. The problem thus raised is serious; but it
belongs rather to the physical than to the psychological analysis of time.
Within our experience, complete recurrence does not occur. So long,
therefore, as we are considering merely the psychological genesis of our
knowledge of time, objections derived from the possibility of recurrence
may be temporarily put aside. We shall return to this question at a later stage
of this chapter.

(3). *Simultaneity*. This is a relation belonging to "physical" time, i.e. it is
a relation between objects primarily, rather than between object and subject. By inference, we may conclude that sense-data are simultaneous with
their subjects, i.e. that when an object is present to a subject, it is simultaneous with it. But the relation of simultaneity which is here intended is one
which is primarily given in experience only as holding among objects. It
does not mean simply "both present together". There are two reasons
against such a definition. First, we wish to be able to speak of two entities as
simultaneous when they are not both parts of one experience, i.e. when one
or both are only known by description; thus we must have a meaning of
simultaneity which does not introduce a subject. Secondly, in all cases
where there is a change within what is present in one experience, there will
be succession, and therefore absence of simultaneity, between two objects
which are both present. When two objects form part of one present, they
may be simultaneous, and their simultaneity *may* be immediately experienced. It is however by no means necessary that they should be simultaneous in this case, nor that, if they are in fact simultaneous, they should form
part of what is present in one experience. The only point of connection, so
far as knowledge is concerned, between simultaneity and presence, is that
simultaneity can only be *experienced* between objects which are both present
in one experience.

(4). *The definition of "now"*. We saw that both "I" and "now" are to be
defined in terms of "this", where "this" is the object of attention. In order to
define "now", it is necessary that "this" should be a sense-datum. Then
"now" means "simultaneous with this". Since the sense-datum may lie
anywhere within the specious present, "now" is to that extent ambiguous;
to avoid this ambiguity, we may define "now" as meaning "simultaneous

with some part of the specious present". This definition avoids ambiguity, but loses the essential simplicity which makes "now" important. When nothing is said to be contrary, we shall adopt the first definition; thus "now" will mean "simultaneous with this", where "this" is a sense-datum.

(5). *The present time* is the time of entities which are present, i.e. of all entities simultaneous with some part of the specious present, i.e. of all entities which are "now" in our second, unambiguous sense. If we adopt a relational theory of time, we may define a time simply as the class of all entities which are commonly said to be at that time, i.e. of all entities simultaneous with a given entity, or with a given set of entities if we do not wish to define a mathematical instant. Thus with a relational theory of time, "the present time" will be simply all entities simultaneous with some part of the specious present. With an absolute theory of time, "the present time" will be the time occupied by the specious present. We shall not at present attempt to decide between the absolute and relative theories of time.

This completes our theory of the knowledge of the present. Although knowledge of *succession* is possible without passing outside the present, because the present is a finite interval of time within which changes can occur, yet knowledge of the *past* is not thus obtainable. For this purpose, we have to consider a new relation to objects, namely *memory*. The analysis of memory is a difficult problem, to which we must now turn our attention.

(6). *Immediate memory*. Without, as yet, asserting that there is such a thing as immediate memory, we may define it as "a two-term relation of subject and object, involving acquaintance, and such as to give rise to the knowledge that the object is in the past". This is not intended as a satisfactory definition, but merely as a means of pointing out what is to be discussed. It is indubitable that we have knowledge of the past, and it would seem, although this is not logically demonstrable, that such knowledge arises from acquaintance with past objects in a way enabling us to know that they are past. The existence, extent, and nature of such immediate knowledge of the past is now to be investigated.

There are two questions to be considered, here as in theory of knowledge generally. First, there is the question: What sort of data would be logically capable of giving rise to the knowledge we possess? And secondly, there is the question: How far does introspection or other observation decide which of the logically possible systems of data is actually realized? We will deal with the first question first.

We certainly know what we mean by saying "such-and-such an event occurred in the past". I do not mean that we know this *analytically*, because that will only be the case with those (if any) who have an adequate philosophy of time; I mean only that we know it in the sense that the phrase expresses a thought recognizably different from other thoughts. Thus we must understand complexes into which "past", or whatever is the essential constituent of "past", enters as a constituent. Again it is obvious that "past" expresses a relation to "present", i.e. a thing is "past" when it has a certain relation to the present, or to a constituent of the present. At first sight, we should naturally say that what is past cannot also be present; but this would be to assume that no particular can exist at two different times, or endure throughout a finite period of time. It would be a mistake to make such an assumption, and therefore we shall not say that what is past cannot also be present. If there is a sense in which this is true, it will emerge later, but ought not to be part of what is originally taken as obvious.

The question now arises whether "past" can be defined by relation to 10 some one constituent of the present, or whether it involves the whole present experience. This question is bound up with another question, namely can "past" be defined as "earlier than the present"? We have seen that *succession* may occur within the present; and when A is succeeded by B, we say that A is earlier than B. Thus "earlier" can be understood without passing outside the present. We cannot say, however, that the past is whatever is earlier than this or that constituent of the present, because the present has no sharp boundaries, and no constituent of it can be picked out as certainly the earliest. Thus if we choose any one constituent of the present, there may be earlier entities which are present and not past. If, 20 therefore, "past" is to be defined in terms of "earlier", it must be defined as "earlier than the whole of the present". This definition would not be open to any *logical* objection, but I think it cannot represent the epistemological analysis of our knowledge of the past, since it is quite obvious that, in order to know that a given entity is in the past, it is not necessary to review the whole present and find that it is all later than the given entity. This argument seems to show that the past must be definable without explicit reference to the whole present, and must therefore not be defined in terms of "earlier".

Another question, by no means easy to answer, is this: Does our knowl- 30 edge of the past involve *acquaintance* with past objects, or can it be accounted for on the supposition that only knowledge by description is involved in our knowledge of the past? That is, must our knowledge of the past be derived from such propositions as "*This* is past", where *this* is an object of present acquaintance, or can it be wholly derived from propositions of the form: "An entity with such-and-such characteristics existed in the past"? The latter view might be maintained, for example, by introducing images: it might be said that we have images which we know to be more or less like objects of past experience, but that the simplest knowledge we have concerning such objects is their resemblance to images. In this case, 40 the simplest *cognition* upon which our knowledge of the past is built will be perception of the fact "this-resembles-something-in-the-past", where *this* is an image, and "something" is an "apparent variable". I do not believe that such a view is tenable. No doubt, in cases of remembering something not very recent, we have often only acquaintance with an image, combined with the *judgment* that something like the image occurred in the past. But such memory is liable to error, and therefore does not involve *perception* of a fact of which "past" is a constituent. Since, however, the word "past" has significance for us, there must be perception of facts in which it occurs, and in such cases memory must be not liable to error. I conclude that, though other complications are logically possible, there must, in some cases, be immediate acquaintance with past objects given in a way which enables us to know that they are past, though such acquaintance may be confined to the very recent past.

Coming now to what psychology has to say as to the empirical facts, we find three phenomena which it is important to distinguish. There is first what may be called "physiological" memory, which is simply the persistence of a sensation for a short time after the stimulus is removed. The time during which we see a flash of lightning is longer than the time during which the flash of lightning, as a physical object, exists. This fact is irrelevant to us, since it has nothing to do with anything discoverable by introspection alone. Throughout the period of "physiological memory", the sense-datum is actually *present*; it is only the inferred physical object which has ceased.

Secondly, there is our awareness of the *immediate* past, the short period during which the warmth of sensation gradually dies out of receding objects, as if we saw them under a fading light. The sound we heard a few seconds ago, but are not hearing now, may still be an object of acquaintance, but is given in a different way from that in which it was given when it was a sense-datum. James[2] seems to include what is thus still given in the "specious present", but however we may choose to define the "specious present", it is certain that the object thus given, but not given in sense, is given in the way which makes us call it *past*; and James[3] rightly states that it is this experience which is "the *original* of our experience of pastness, from whence we get the meaning of the term".

Thirdly, there is our knowledge concerning more remote portions of the past. Such knowledge is more difficult to analyze, and is no doubt derivative and complicated, as well as liable to error. It does not, therefore, belong to the elementary constituents of our acquaintance with the world, which are what concern us at present. Or, if it does contain some elementary constituent, it must be one which is not essential to our having a knowledge of time, though it may increase the extent of our knowledge concerning past events.

Thus of the three phenomena which we have been considering, only the

2 *Cf.*, e.g., *Psychology*, Vol. I, p. 630.
3 *Loc. cit.*, p. 605.

second seems directly relevant to our present problem. We will give the name "immediate memory" to the relation which we have to an object which has recently been a sense-datum, but is now felt as past, though still given in acquaintance. It is essential that the object of immediate memory should be, at least in part, identical with the object previously given in sense, since otherwise immediate memory would not give acquaintance with what is past, and would not serve to account for our knowledge of the past. Hence, by our usual criterion, since immediate memory is intrinsically distinguishable from sensation, it follows that it is a different relation between subject and object. We shall take it as a primitive constituent of experience. We may define one entity as "past" with respect to another when it has to the other that relation which is experienced, in the consciousness of immediate memory, as existing between object and subject. This relation, of course, will come to be known to hold in a vast number of cases in which it is not experienced; the epistemological need of the immediate experience is to make us know what is meant by "past", and to give us data upon which our subsequent knowledge can be built. It will be observed that in order to know a past object we only need immediate memory, but in order to know what is meant by "past", an immediate remembering must be itself made an object of experience. Thus introspection is necessary in order to understand the meaning of "past", because the only cases in which this relation is immediately given are cases in which one term is the subject. Thus "past", like "present", is a notion derived from psychology, whereas "earlier" and "later" can be known by an experience of non-mental objects.

The extent of immediate memory, important as it is for other problems, need not now concern us; nor is it necessary to discuss what is meant by memory of objects with which we are no longer acquainted. The bare materials for the knowledge that there is a time-series can, I think, be provided without considering any form of memory beyond immediate memory.

(7). *Succession* is a relation which is given between objects, and belongs to physical time, where it plays a part analogous to that played by memory in the construction of mental time. Succession may be immediately experienced between parts of one sense-datum, for example in the case of a swift movement; in this case, the two objects of which one is succeeded by the other are both parts of the present. It would seem that succession may also be immediately experienced between an object of immediate memory and a sense-datum, or between two objects of immediate memory. The extensions of our knowledge of succession by inference need not now concern us.

(8). We say that A is *earlier* than B if A is succeeded by B; and in the same case we say B is *later* than A. These are purely verbal definitions. It should be observed that *earlier* and *later* are relations given as between objects, and not in any way implying past and present. There is no logical reason why the relations of earlier and later should not subsist in a world wholly devoid of consciousness.

(9). An event is said to be *past* when it is earlier than the whole of the present, and is said to be *future* when it is later than the whole of the present. It is necessary to include the *whole* of the present, since an event may be earlier than *part* of the present and yet be itself present, in cases where there is succession within the present. It is also necessary to define the past by means of *earlier* rather than by means of memory, since there may be things in the past which are neither themselves remembered nor simultaneous with anything remembered. It should be noted that there is no experience of the future. I do not mean that no particulars which are future are or have been experienced, because if a particular recurs or endures it may be experienced at the earlier time. What I mean is that there is no experience of anything *as* future, in the way in which sensation experiences a thing as present and memory experiences it as past. Thus the future is only known by inference, and is only known *descriptively*, as "what succeeds the present".

Having now ended our definitions, we must proceed to the propositions constructing and connecting the physical and mental time-series.

(a). Simultaneity and succession both give rise to transitive relations, while simultaneity is symmetrical, and succession asymmetrical, or at least gives rise to an asymmetrical relation defined in terms of it.

This proposition is required for the construction of the physical time-series. At first sight, it might seem to raise no difficulties, but as a matter of fact it raises great difficulties, if we admit the possibility of recurrence. These difficulties are so great that they seem to make either the denial of recurrence of particulars or the admission of absolute time almost unavoidable.

Let us begin with simultaneity. Suppose that I see a given object A continuously while I am hearing two successive sounds B and C. Then B is simultaneous with A and A with C, but B is not simultaneous with C. Thus it would seem to follow that simultaneity, in the sense in which we have been using the word, is not transitive. We might escape this conclusion by denying that any numerically identical particular ever exists at two different instants: thus instead of the one A, we shall have a series of A's, not differing as to predicates, one for each instant during which we had thought that A endures. Such a view would not be logically untenable, but it seems incredible, and almost any other tenable theory would seem preferable.

In the same way as we defined one (momentary) total experience, we may, if we wish to avoid absolute time, define an "instant" as a group of events any two of which are simultaneous with each other, and not all of which are simultaneous with anything outside the group. Then an event is "at" an instant when it is a member of the class which is that instant. When a number of events are all at the same instant, they are related in the way which we have in mind when we think that simultaneity is transitive. It must be observed that we do not thus obtain a transitive two-term relation unless the instant is *specified*: "*A* and *B* are at the instant *t*" is transitive, but "there is an instant at which *A* and *B* are" holds whenever *A* and *B* are simultaneous, and is thus not transitive. In spite of this, however, the above definition of an "instant" provides formally what is required, so far as simultaneity is concerned. It is only so far as succession is concerned that this definition will be found inadequate.

Succession, if the time-series is to be constituted, must give rise to an asymmetrical transitive relation. Now if recurrence or persistence is possi- 10 ble, succession itself will have neither of these properties. If *A* occurs before *B*, and again after *B*, we have a case where succession is not asymmetrical. If *B* occurs both before *A* and after *C*, while *A* occurs before *C* but never occurs after *C*, *A* will succeed *B* and *B* will succeed *C*, but *A* will not succeed *C*; thus succession will not be transitive. Let us consider how this is affected if we pass on to "instants" in the sense above defined. We may say that one instant is *posterior* to another, and the other *anterior* to the one, if every member of the one succeeds every member of the other. But now we are faced with the possibility of *repetition*, i.e. of an instant being posterior to itself. If everything in the universe at one instant were to occur again after a 20 certain interval, so as again to constitute an instant, the anterior and posterior instants would be *identical* according to our present definition. This result cannot be avoided by altering the definition of *anterior* and *posterior*. It can only be avoided by finding some set of entities of which we know that they cannot recur. If we took Bergson's view, according to which our mental life at each moment is intrinsically different, owing to memory, from that of a moment preceded by different experiences, then the experience of each moment of life is unique, and can be used to define an instant. In this way, if the whole universe may be taken as one experience, the time-series can be constructed by means of memory. There is no *logical* 30 error in such a procedure, but there is a greater accumulation of questionable metaphysics than is suitable for our purposes. We must, therefore, seek for some other way of constructing the time-series.

It is no answer to our difficulty to reply that the complete recurrence of the whole momentary state of the universe is *improbable*. The point of our difficulty is this: If the whole state of the universe did recur, it is obvious that there would be *something* not numerically identical in the two occurrences, something, in fact, which leads us to speak of "two occurrences". It would be contrary to what is self-evident to say that there was strictly *one* occurrence, which was anterior and posterior to itself. Without taking 40 account of the whole universe, if a thing *A* exists at one time, then ceases, and then exists again at a later time, it seems obvious that there is *some* numerical diversity involved, even if *A* is numerically the same. In this case, in fact, where *A* reappears after an absence, it would seem strained to say that the *same* particular had reappeared: we should more naturally say that a new precisely similar particular had appeared. This is by no means so obvious in the case of a thing which persists unchanged throughout a continuous period. Before going further, we must consider whether there can be any substantial difference between persistence and recurrence.

The view which I wish to advocate is the following. An entity may persist unchanged throughout a continuous portion of time, without any numerical diversity corresponding to the different instants during which it exists; but
10 if an entity ceases to exist, any entity existing at a subsequent time must be numerically diverse from the one that has ceased. The object of this hypothesis is to preserve, if possible, a relational theory of time; therefore the first thing to be done is to re-state it in terms which do not even verbally imply absolute time. For this purpose, we may adopt the following defini-tions. We shall say that a thing *exists at several times* if it is simultaneous with things which are not simultaneous with each other. We shall say that it *exists throughout a continuous time* when, if it is simultaneous with two things which are not simultaneous with each other, it is also simultaneous with any thing which comes after the earlier and before the later of the two things. The
20 assumption that two things which are separated by an interval of time cannot be numerically identical is presupposed in the above definition. This assumption, in relational language, may be stated as follows: *If* A *precedes* B *and is not simultaneous with it, while* B *precedes* C *and is not simultaneous with it, then* A *and* C *are numerically diverse.*[4] We have to inquire whether a logically tenable theory of the time-series can be constructed on this basis.

The difficulty of possible recurrence of the whole state of the universe, which troubled us before, is now obviated. It is now possible to define an *instant* as a class of entities of which any two are simultaneous with each other and not all are simultaneous with any entity outside the class. It will
30 follow that it is meaningless to suppose the universe to persist unchanged throughout a finite time. This is perhaps an objection; on the other hand, it may be said that, when we suppose that such persistence is possible, we are imagining ourselves as spectators watching the unusual immobility with continually increasing astonishment; and in this case, our own feelings, at least, are in a state of change. Let us, then, suppose that it is logically impossible, as our present theory requires, for the universe to persist unchanged throughout a finite time. Then if two times are different, some-thing must have changed meanwhile; and if this something has changed back so far as its character goes, yet what has reappeared is, in virtue of our
40 assumption, numerically different from what has disappeared. Thus it is impossible that the world should be composed of numerically the same

---

4 Another form of the same axiom is : *If* A *both precedes and succeeds* B, *then* A *is simultaneous with* B.

particulars at two different times.

We may now define an *instant* as a class which is identical with all the terms that are simultaneous with every member of itself. We will say that one event "wholly precedes" another when it precedes it without being simultaneous with it; and we will say that one instant is "anterior" to another when there is at least one member of the one instant which wholly precedes at least one member of the other instant. We shall assume that simultaneity is symmetrical, and that every event is simultaneous with itself, so that nothing can wholly precede itself. We will also assume that "wholly preceding" is transitive. These two assumptions together imply our previous assumption, which was that "wholly preceding" is asymmetrical, i.e. that if A wholly precedes B, then B does not wholly *precede* A. Finally, we will assume that of any two events which are not simultaneous one must wholly precede the other. Then we can prove that "anterior" is a serial relation, so that the instants of time form a series. The only remaining thing that needs to be proved is that there are instants, and that every event belongs to some instant. For this purpose let us call one event an "early part" of another when everything simultaneous with the one is simultaneous with the other, and nothing wholly preceding the one is simultaneous with the other. Let us define the "beginning" of an event as the class of events simultaneous with all its early parts. Then it will be found that, if we assume that any event wholly after something simultaneous with a given event is wholly after some early part of the given event, then the beginning of an event is an instant of which the event in question is a member.[5]

It would seem, therefore, that the physical time-series can be constructed by means of the relations considered in the earlier part of this chapter. Our few remaining propositions, which are chiefly concerned with mental time, offer less difficulty.

(b). What is remembered is past. It should be noted that the past was defined as "what is earlier than the whole of the present", so that it cannot be supposed that whatever is past is remembered, nor does memory enter into the *definition* of the past.

(c). When a change is immediately experienced in sensation, parts of the present are earlier than other parts. This follows, because, since the change, by hypothesis, lies within sensation, it follows that the earlier and the later state of things are both present according to the definition.

(d). If A, B, and C succeed each other rapidly, A and B may be parts of one sensation, and likewise B and C, while A and C are not parts of one sensation, but A is remembered when C is present in sensation. In such a

5 In symbols, the above theory, with certain logical simplifications, has been set forth by Dr. Norbert Wiener in his "Contribution to the Theory of Relative Position", *Proceedings of the Cambridge Philosophical Society*, Vol. XVII, Part 5 (1914).

case, A and B belong to the same present, and likewise B and C, but not A and C; thus the relation "belonging to the same present" is not transitive. This has nothing to do with the question of persistence or recurrence which we considered under (a), but is an independent fact concerned with mental time, and due to the fact that the present is not an instant. It follows that, apart from any question of duration in objects, two presents may overlap without coinciding.

Chapter VII
On the Acquaintance Involved in
Our Knowledge of Relations

WE HAVE NOW considered the various kinds of acquaintance upon which our knowledge of particulars appears to be based. We have seen that, within the general relation of acquaintance, there are various recognizably different ways of experiencing particular objects. There is *attention*, which selects what is in some sense *one* object. There is *sensation*, which serves to define "the present time", as the time of objects of sensation. There is *memory*, which applies only to past objects; and there is imagination, which gives objects without any temporal relation to the subject. All these are different relations to objects, such that, even when the object is the same, the experience can be distinguished owing to the difference of relation. We have also considered two special kinds of *objects* of acquaintance, namely (1) mental objects, which are those of which a subject is a constituent; and here, in particular, we have had to consider the relation of "being experienced together", which we found necessary in defining the unity of one experience; (2) simultaneity and succession among objects, which it was necessary to consider in order to avoid confusing the relations involved with the relations involved in sensation and memory. But the consideration of these two special kinds of objects has been more or less incidental; our main purpose has been to consider, not kinds of *objects*, but kinds of *relations* to objects. We have, however, confined our attention to such objects as are *particulars*. It is now time to pass to the consideration of the objects with which we are acquainted when we "understand" universals.

Before embarking upon our epistemological inquiry, a few logical preliminaries are indispensable. I shall, however, state these briefly and dogmatically, since I have discussed the problems involved at length elsewhere.

A "complex" is anything analyzable, anything which has *constituents*. When, for example, two things are related in any way, there seems to be a "whole" consisting of the two things so related; if, say, *A* and *B* are similar, "the similarity of *A* to *B*" will be such a whole; and such a whole will be a "complex". It may be questioned whether a complex is or is not the same as a "fact", where a "fact" may be described as what there is when a judgment is true, but not when it is false. (I do not suggest that this is a proper definition of a "fact", but merely that it serves to point out what sort of object is in question.) However this may be, there is certainly a one-one correspondence of complexes and facts, and for our present purposes we shall assume that they are identical.

Complexes are of two kinds, which we may distinguish as "atomic" and "molecular". The former must be explained first. A criterion by which, before they have been discussed, the two kinds can be distinguished, is the following: In the verbal expression of an atomic complex, only one *proposition*[1] is involved, whereas a molecular complex involves several propositions, with such words as "and" or "or" or "not". For the moment we will
10 ignore molecular complexes.

In any complex, there are at least two kinds of constituents, namely the terms related, and the relation which unites them. What precisely the difference is between these two kinds of constituents, is a difficult logical question, which need not now concern us. All that now concerns us is to observe that the difference between the two sorts of constituents is unmistakable. In (say) "*A* precedes *B*", *A* and *B* occur differently from the way in which "precedes" occurs. On the other hand, in "preceding is the converse of succeeding", "preceding" occurs, *primâ facie*, in the same way in which *A* and *B* occur in "*A* precedes *B*". The difference in the manner of occurrence
20 is indicated by the use of the verbal noun "preceding" instead of the indicative "precedes". An entity which *can* occur in a complex as "precedes" occurs in "*A* precedes *B*" will be called a *relation*. When it *does* occur in this way in a given complex, it will be called a "relating relation" in that complex. In "*A* precedes *B* or *A* is simultaneous with *B*", there appear to be *two* relating relations; in such a case, the complex concerned is *molecular*. An *atomic* complex is one in which there is only one relating relation. But this definition is merely provisional; it is not to be assumed that it will be found ultimately satisfactory.

Atomic complexes may be classified according to the number of terms
30 other than the relating relation that they contain; we will call them *dual* complexes if they contain two terms, and so on. Relations may be similarly classified: relations which can be relating in dual complexes will be called *dual* relations, and so on. Many problems in philosophy require the consideration of triple, quadruple ... relations, which have in general been unduly neglected.

It may be that there are complexes in which there is only one term and one predicate, where the predicate occurs as relations occur in other complexes. In that case, predicates will be defined as entities occurring in this manner in complexes containing only one other entity. It is, however, doubtful

40 1 By a "proposition", here, I mean a phrase which is grammatically capable of expressing a judgment; or one which, so far as form goes, might express a fact, though it may fail to do so owing to falsehood.

whether there are such complexes, whereas it seems certain that there is a relation of *predication*; thus predicates may be defined as terms which have the relation of predication to other terms. "Whiteness" will be a predicate of a particular white patch, "roundness" of a particular round patch, and so on.

Relations and predicates together will be called "universals". All the constituents of a complex are either particular or universal, and at least one must be universal.

But not even an atomic complex is determinate when its constituents, particular and universal, are given. "*A* precedes *B*" is a different complex from "*B* precedes *A*", though it consists of the same constituents. A complex has a property which we may call its "form", and the constituents must have what we call determinate "position" in this form. "*A* precedes *B*" and "*B* precedes *A*" have the same form as well as the same constituents; they differ only as regards the "position" of the constituents. Questions concerning form and position are very difficult; but we need not deal with them until we come to consider our knowledge of logic. For the present, we are concerned only with universals; and since predicates involve special difficulties, we shall confine ourselves, in this chapter, to relations. It is obvious that we possess some kind of acquaintance out of which our knowledge of relations is derived, but it is not obvious whether this is acquaintance with relations themselves, or with other entities from which relations can be inferred. It is this question that we have now to examine.

It is clear, to begin with, that we "understand" the words which stand for relations, whatever that may mean. Some relations, no doubt, like some particulars, are only known by description, i.e. as the relations having some known relation to something known. But other relations are known in a more immediate way. All descriptions contain universals, and therefore nothing can be known by description unless some universals can be understood otherwise. To fix our ideas, let us take a relation which is certainly as much "given" as any relation can be, namely the relation "preceding". Whenever we have an immediate experience of sequence in time, for example in hearing the words of a spoken sentence, we have an experience which in some way involves the relation "preceding". We "understand" the word "before", in the sense that we know what is meant when we are told that (say) lightning comes before thunder. And we understand this, not merely through a description, but through something which may be described as immediate acquaintance with time-sequence. We have to ask ourselves what, exactly, is the object with which we are acquainted when we understand the word "before". There are several possibilities, between which I do not know how to choose; but something can be done in the way of showing the conditions which must be fulfilled in order to account for the facts.

The first point to notice is a very obvious one. In order to understand the word "before", it is not enough to be acquainted with complexes which consist of one thing before another. We may be acquainted with innumerable instances of succession, without being aware that they are instances of succession, or that they have anything whatever in common. We may see movements or hear sentences, which strike us as perfectly familiar, but would seem extraordinary if we saw them reversed on a cinematograph, or heard them reversed on a phonograph. In such cases, we have certainly been acquainted with a complex constituted by temporal succession, but we have
10 not necessarily had that more abstract acquaintance which would enable us to understand the word "before". Thus acquaintance with a complex does not necessarily involve acquaintance with its relating relation. It seems plain that acquaintance with a complex may occur at a lower stage of mental development than acquaintance with its relating relation, or whatever other acquaintance it is that enables us to "understand" the name of the relation.

A plausible view, though not, I think, an ultimately tenable one, is that we need only be acquainted with similarities between complexes which contain the same relation, and need not be acquainted ever with the bare relation itself. Our first task must be to endeavour to state this view in its
20 least untenable forms, and to show that even in these forms it cannot account for the knowledge which we obviously possess concerning relations.

The first step towards understanding the relation, on the view in question, would seem to consist in noticing a similarity between a number of complexes which in fact all involve the same relating relation. To continue the illustration of time-sequence, let us suppose that a number of complexes, A-before-B, C-before-D, etc., are all experienced by one person, and that he observes that they have a certain similarity. We suppose these complexes given as wholes; thus they are not experienced in the analyzed
30 form implied when they are called "A-before-B" and so on. To avoid confusion, let us call "A-before-B" α, and "C-before-D" γ. Then we suppose that the subject which experiences α and γ becomes aware of a certain resemblance between them, that is to say, he experiences the complex "α-resembling-γ". In this complex, we must not suppose that "resembling" is separately noticed, since that would presuppose acquaintance with relations, which we are assuming to be not yet attained. But α and γ, ex $hypothesi$, are already given in experience; thus we may assume that they are known as constituents of the complex "α-resembling-γ". Thus we may denote this complex by the symbol "$(\alpha\gamma)$", without implying more knowl-
40 edge than actually belongs to the experience supposed.

But before going further, we must particularize the nature of the resemblance which is supposed to be experienced between α and γ. Two dual complexes may have their first terms identical, or their second, or both. We have thus three ways in which two dual complexes may resemble each other without involving the same relation. The third of these ways is the combination of the other two, and need not therefore be further considered; but the other two, we may suppose, can each be experienced in cases where the identical constituents involved are not experienced. For example, we may suppose that two experiences can be seen to have a certain resemblance which in fact consists in their having the same subject, even if the subject itself is not given in acquaintance. (I am not asserting that this *is* the case, but only that it may be.) If, then, an experience of similarity between complexes is to be a source of our knowledge of relations, we must suppose that there are three recognizably different kinds of resemblance between two dual complexes, arising from identity in their first terms, or their second terms, or their relations. Let us denote these three respectively by $(\alpha\beta)_1, (\alpha\beta)_2$, and $(\alpha\beta)_R$. But if these three are to be *recognizably different*, as the theory requires, it is not sufficient that $(\alpha\beta)_1, (\alpha\beta)_2$, and $(\alpha\beta)_R$ should each be immediately experienced, but we must also have knowledge corresponding to the difference in the suffixes. But this would be knowledge involving much more difficult universals than the kind that was to be explained; thus on this line we become involved in a vicious endless regress.

It would seem, however, that the discovery of the *terms* of a complex is easier, psychologically, than the discovery of the relation; thus it is probably a mistake to treat the two kinds of analysis as on a level. If we experience the complex A-before-B, it seems to require a less effort of analysis, and therefore probably a different kind of mental operation, to discover that A and B are constituents of this complex than to discover that "before" is a constituent. That is, using α again to denote the unanalyzed given complex A-before-B, the two propositions "A is part of α" and "B is part of α" seem easier to discover than the proposition "*before* is part of α". (It may be doubted whether "part" has quite the same meaning in the last proposition as in the two others, but this question need not now concern us.) We will therefore adopt the hypothesis that the two complexes "A-part-of-α" and "B-part-of-α" must be experienced before we can isolate the relating relation in α, and on this basis we will attempt again to deduce our knowledge of relations from acquaintance with similarity between complexes.

Let us suppose that a number of time-sequences are given as complexes, and that analysis has proceeded to the point of knowing what events are concerned in these sequences. We are given, say, α and γ, and we know that A and B are parts of α, while C and D are parts of γ; all this, we assume, is matter of experience, i.e. we are acquainted with the complexes concerned. This is not yet enough even to enable us to know that α and γ have no common *terms*; in order to know this, we must know that A and B are the only terms in α, while C and D are the only terms in γ. This is a much more serious matter than any knowledge we have hitherto assumed, since it demands a known exhaustiveness of analysis so far as the *terms* of our complexes are concerned. Yet, if we do not know this, any resemblance we may find between α and γ may be supposed due to identity of terms, and cannot be a ground for inferring identity of relation. Let us, therefore, suppose this known, in order to discover whether, even then, the knowledge we possess concerning relations can be explained by observed similarities between complexes.

We assume, now, that between the complexes (AB), (CD) we perceive a certain similarity, which does not depend upon any identity of terms, and is
10 found to subsist between *some* dual complexes, but not between others. We can then *define* the relation of all these complexes as the class of them. In other words, given a certain complex whose terms are A and B, and to which we give the name "A-before-B", the complex "C-before-D" will be defined as "the complex of which C and D are the terms, and which has relation-similarity to A-before-B". This definition, however, is illusory. To begin with, it will not distinguish between C-before-D and D-before-C. This might perhaps be got over, though I doubt it; but even if it could, there is a second objection which could not be got over, and that is, that "relation-similarity" enters into the above definition, and is plainly a relation, de-
20 manding the same treatment as any other relation. Hence it would be a vicious circle to define relations in general by means of it.

Of course if we chose we could substitute for similarity of complexes a common predicate, which would be perceived as belonging to those complexes that in fact contained a given relating relation. But the same objections would recur. The predicate would have to be a perceived universal, on pain of a vicious regress; and there would still be the difficulty of distinguishing C-before-D from D-before-C.[2] Thus the attempt to deduce our knowledge of relations from knowledge of complexes alone must be abandoned.

30   We are thus forced to the conclusion that the knowledge which we indubitably possess concerning relations involves acquaintance, either with the bare relations themselves, or at least with something equally abstract; and by "something equally abstract" I mean something which is determinate when the relation is given, and does not, like a complex, demand some further datum. It is not, of course, necessary that we should have such acquaintance in the case of *all* relations concerning which we can make true propositions, for, when some relations are given, others can be defined by description. For example, it would be logically possible, as we have just seen, to define all other relations by means of the relation which we called
40 "relation-similarity" between complexes, though few would pretend that this relation is to be singled out from all others as the only one with which we

2 *Cf. Principles of Mathematics*, §215.

have acquaintance as a matter of psychological fact. What is essential is that we should *sometimes* be acquainted with a relation or with some corresponding equally abstract entity. This conclusion is important, in view of the objection often felt to what is abstract. It only remains to discover what precisely the abstract entity is which gives us knowledge of a relation.

The difficulties in framing a correct theory as to our acquaintance with relations are rather logical than psychological. Two closely connected questions at once arise: (1) Is the acquaintance from which we derive our knowledge of "before" the same as or different from that from which we derive our knowledge of "after"? (2) Does this abstract acquaintance take account of the fact that "before" needs terms between which it is to hold? These two questions may be used to illustrate the difficulties besetting any theory of relations.

(1). As regards the difference between "before" and "after", it is plain, of course, that they are different in the sense that one cannot be substituted for another in a true statement: if A is before B, it must not be inferred that A is after B. But it may be inferred that B is after A, and it would seem that this is absolutely the same "fact" as is expressed by saying that A is before B. Looking away from everything psychological, and considering only the external fact in virtue of which it is true to say that A is before B, it seems plain that this fact consists of two events A and B in succession, and that whether we choose to describe it by saying "A is before B" or by saying "B is after A" is a mere matter of language. Owing to the fact that speech is in time and writing in space, we must mention A before mentioning B, or B before mentioning A, and if we are to write along a line, rather than in two dimensions like Frege, we must put A to the left of B or B to the left of A. Let us ignore writing, and only consider speech. Then what happens is this: Given two things in a time-sequence, if we wish to express their time-sequence in words, we may do it in two ways, namely by mentioning their two names successively and indicating whether the order of the names is the same as that of the things, or the opposite. When it is the same, we use the word "before" in addition to the names; when different, we use the word "after". In other languages, of course other plans may be used; for instance, difference of case may perform the same function as difference in the time-order of the names performs in an uninflected language like English. But whatever method is adopted, it remains obvious that the difference between "before" and "after" is purely linguistic: there is no fact (except linguistic facts) which cannot be described without using both words. If, for example, the word "before" alone existed, all facts of time-sequence could be just as fully stated as they can by the help of the two words. There cannot, therefore, be two acquaintances, one for "before" and one for "after", but there must be only one, from which both are derived. This conclusion may seem to have been unduly laboured, but it is very important.

(2). Thus the difference which demands elucidation is not that between "A is before B" and "B is after A", but that between "A is before B" and "B is before A". Whatever exactly may be meant by "understanding" the word "before", it is plain that such understanding enables us to distinguish between the two propositions "A is before B" and "B is before A". This fact shows that, in the understanding of the abstract "before", which is what we are trying to isolate, there must be some kind of reference to terms, something, in fact, which we call "sense" or "direction". The two propositions "A is before B" and "B is before A" contain the same constituents, and they are put together according to the same form; thus the difference is neither in the form nor in the constituents. It would thus seem that a relation must have essentially some "from-and-to" character, even in its most abstract form, like a goods-truck which has a hook in front and an eye behind. The hook and eye are of course merely symbolic; but they have the merit of illustrating the main fact about relations, which is that there is something in their nature that cries out for terms, some sort of grappling apparatus which is always looking out for things to grapple on to.

But all this is pictorial, and in one respect it is positively misleading. We decided that "before" and "after" only differ linguistically; hence whatever a relation is, it must be symmetrical with respect to its two ends. It must not be pictured as having a hook in front and an eye behind, but as having a hook at each end, and as equally adapted for travelling in either direction. This fact must not be lost sight of in the endeavour to explain difference of sense.

The subject of "sense" in relations is rendered difficult by the fact that the words or symbols by which we express a dual complex always have a time-order or a space-order, and that this order is an essential element in their meaning. When we point out, for example, that "x precedes y" is different from "y precedes x", we are making use of the order of x and y in the two complex symbols by which we symbolize our two complexes. By thus utilizing order among symbols, we can content ourselves with one name for a relation, instead of requiring two, one for each sense. But if we eliminate the symbolizing properties of order among symbols by deciding in advance which of our terms we are going to mention first, we can no longer dispense with two names for the two senses of a relation, except when the relation is symmetrical. Suppose, for example, we decide beforehand that x is to be mentioned first. Then one complex is "x is before y" while the other is "x is after y"; here the *two* words "before" and "after" are both indispensable. Nevertheless, we decided that there are not two different relations, one called *before* and the other called *after*, but only one relation, for which two words are required because it gives rise to two possible complexes with the same terms.

It might perhaps be supposed that every relation has one proper sense, i.e. that it goes essentially *from* one term *to* another. In the case of time-relations, it might be thought that it is more proper to go from the earlier to the later term than from the later to the earlier. And in many relations it might be thought that one term is *active* while the other is *passive*; thus "*A* loves *B*" seems more natural than "*B* is loved by *A*". But this is a peculiarity of certain relations, of which others show no trace. Right and left, up and down, greater and less, for example, have obviously no peculiarly "natural" direction. And in the cases where there seemed to be a "natural" direction, this will be found to have no logical foundation. In a dual complex, there is no essential order as between the terms. The order is introduced by the words or symbols used in naming the complex, and does not exist in the complex itself. Our problem arises from the fact that, although this is the case, a different complex results from interchanging the terms, and that such interchange *looks* like a change of order.

The whole puzzle would be avoided if we could deny the result we reached at the beginning of this discussion, to the effect that "*x* is before *y*" and "*y* is after *x*" are two different symbols for the same fact. If we could say that these two symbols represent two different facts, which merely imply one another, we could then say that there are two different correlated relations, *before* and *after*, each of which goes essentially *from* one term *to* another.[3] But tempting as such a theory is, in view of the difficulties which arise from rejecting it, it seems nevertheless so obvious as to be undeniable that, when we think of what actually takes place rather than of its verbal expression, we cannot find a vestige of difference between *x* preceding *y* and *y* succeeding *x*. The two are merely different names for one and the same time-sequence. No doubt there is a difference in the order of our thoughts while we hear the two sentences spoken, but this difference is quite irrelevant. We must therefore explain the sense of a relation without assuming that a relation and its converse are different entities.

In order to avoid confusions due to the symbolizing properties of order among our symbols, we must arbitrarily decide which of two terms is to be mentioned first in naming a dual complex. Instead of speaking of "*x* before *y*" and "*y* before *x*", we must speak of "*x* before *y*" and "*x* after *y*". These two are both logically possible complexes, which are immediately distinguishable although the terms and the relation and the form of the complex are the same in both. Let us suppose an *a* and a *b* given, and let us suppose it known that *a* is before *b*. Of the two possible complexes, one is realized in this case. Given another case of sequence, between *x* and *y*, how are we to know whether *x* and *y* have the same time-order as *a* and *b*, or the opposite time-order?

---

3 Arguments in favour of this view, with which I no longer agree, will be found in *Principles of Mathematics*, §219.

To solve this problem, we require the notion of *position* in a complex with respect to the relating relation. With respect to time-sequence, for example, two terms which have the relation of sequence have recognizably two different positions, in the way that makes us call one of them *before* and the other *after*. Thus if, starting from a given sequence, we have recognized the two positions, we can recognize them again in another case of sequence, and say again that the term in one position is *before* while the term in the other position is *after*. That is, generalizing, if we are given any relation R, there are two relations, both functions of R, such that, if x and y are terms in a
10 dual complex whose relating relation is R, x will have one of these relations to the complex, while y will have the other. The other complex with the same constituents reverses these relations. Let us call these relations A_R and B_R. Then if we decide to mention first the term which has the relation A_R to the complex, we get one sense of the relation, while if we decide to mention first the other, we get the other sense. Thus the sense of a relation is derived from the two different relations which the terms of a dual complex have to the complex. Sense is not in the relation alone, or in the complex alone, but in the relations of the constituents to the complex which constitute "position" in the complex. But these relations do not essentially put one term
20 *before* the other, as though the relation went *from* one term *to* another; this only appears to be the case owing to the misleading suggestions of the order of words in speech or writing.

From what has been said, it follows that such words as *before* and *after*, *greater* and *less*, and so on, are not the names of relations: they always involve, in addition to the relation, an indication as to "sense". For any such pair of correlative terms, there is only one relation, which is neutral as regards sense. The word "sequence" would be better than "before" or "after" as the name of the relation involved. I think—though this may be doubted—that the apparent incapacity of relations for subsisting without
30 terms is partly due to the fact that our words for relations are nearly all such as involve a definite sense, and that sense is only explicable by means of terms. The difference between "before" and "after" is not explicable except by reference to the fact that two complexes can be made out of two given terms and a given relation. But "sequence" (if we take this as neutral with regard to sense) does not require this reference to complexes. Hence it would seem that, when the relation is pure, it ceases to demand terms in order to be intelligible.

The conclusion to be drawn is, if I am not mistaken, that no difficulty stands in the way of admitting acquaintance with the bare abstract relation
40 itself. When we perceive, as we easily can, that the same relation is involved in "x is before y" and in "x is after y", it seems as though we must be having or have had acquaintance with the relation of sequence itself. This view is by far the simplest of those that are compatible with the facts, and it explains all

the facts adequately. I shall therefore henceforth assume that we have, in some cases, direct acquaintance with relations, in the abstract signification which does not distinguish between the two "senses" of a relation.

There are, it is true, other theories which would also account for the data. It may be said, for example, that what we are acquainted with is the fact "something has the relation in question to something". Such facts have a one-one correlation with the relations with which they are concerned, except when the relation is one which never holds between any pair of terms. If it could be shown that we have the most direct knowledge possible of relations of which there is no instance, or even of which no instance is known to us, that would decide against the theory we are considering. The question is analogous to Hume's question concerning the shade of colour that we have never seen. It might happen that a number of relations could be arranged in a scale by degrees of similarity, and that we could find parts of the scale where the dissimilarity between consecutive relations would be greater than usual, if we confined ourselves to relations of which we had instances. If, then, we found ourselves able to imagine intermediate relations, so as to be acquainted with them as directly as with the relations of which we knew instances, that would decide the question. But I know of no reason to suppose that, as a matter of actual fact, any such method of decision is possible.

The possible theories, however, which remain as to our acquaintance with relations, do not differ in any epistemologically important respect. If we have been right in our discussions in this chapter, we must have acquaintance either with bare relations, or with something equally abstract, and standing in some one-one correlation with bare relations. And if this is so, it can make very little difference whether it is the relations themselves that we are acquainted with or not. We shall therefore run only a very small risk of substantial error if we assume, as we shall do henceforth, that direct acquaintance with bare relations does occur. With this result, we can pass on to consider our acquaintance with predicates.

Chapter VIII
Acquaintance with Predicates

THE STUDY OF predicates is more interesting from a logical than from an epistemological point of view. In logic, many interesting questions arise, such as: Whether there are complexes having only two constituents, a subject and a predicate, or whether, in all cases of predication, subject and predicate are the terms of a dual relation; whether predicates are altogether illusory, and can be replaced by symmetrical transitive relations; whether, assuming there are predicates, two numerically diverse entities can have exactly the same predicates; and what is the connection (if any) between predication and the common-sense relation of thing and attribute. These questions demand, in logic, a lengthy discussion. For our present purposes, it will be sufficient to give a summary statement of results.

We saw, in the last chapter, that the way in which a relating relation occurs in an atomic complex is quite different from the way in which its terms occur. An atomic complex may have any number of terms, and relations differ according to the number of terms which they relate in an atomic complex; but in spite of this difference, there is something in common among all relations, which makes us consider that they all occur in one way, while their terms all occur in another. The first of the above logical questions is: Are there universals which occur as relating relations occur, but in complexes which have only one other constituent? If so, such universals may be defined as "predicates". If there are specific subject–predicate propositions, it would seem that the above question must be answered in the affirmative, though no quite conclusive reasons are known to me. The grounds would be: first, that subject and predicate obviously differ *logically*, and not merely as two particulars differ, so that, if predication were primarily a dual relation, it would have to be a very strange one; secondly, that it would seem very odd if there were no complexes of two constituents, though there were complexes with three, four, five ... constituents; thirdly, that such terms as *white*, *painful*, etc., seem to demand subjects in just the same sort of way as relations demand terms. For these reasons, we shall assume that, if there are predicates at all, they can occur in complexes which have only one other constituent, and not *only* in complexes in which they have a dual relation, called "predication", to their subjects.

The next question is whether predicates are altogether illusory, and should be replaced by transitive symmetrical relations, which we may call "specific similarities". Given any transitive symmetrical relation, the terms which have this relation to a given term form a group. The group of terms having this relation to *a* and the group having the relation to *b* are either identical or mutually exclusive. Thus the relation gives rise to a number of mutually exclusive groups. Membership of a given group has all the formal logical properties of possession of a given predicate. Hence so far as formal arguments go, there can be nothing to show, in a given case, whether what combines certain terms into one group is a common predicate or a transitive symmetrical relation.

The case of colours will illustrate this point. We may suppose that all the things which are of a given shade of colour are defined as having a certain transitive symmetrical relation, which we may call "colour-similarity", to a certain given example of the shade in question. This is the view adopted by Berkeley and Hume, who fondly imagined that in abolishing predicates they were abolishing all "abstract ideas". Whether true or false, it certainly accounts for the *logical* aspects of the data. Probably in some cases what appear to be predicates are generated in this way, but I cannot see any reason to think that there are *no* genuine predicates.

There is, however, another quite different set of considerations by which doubt may be thrown on the subsistence of predicates. It may be said, for example, that "white" is not a predicate, but is what actually exists wherever there is anything white. According to this view, two different patches of white will be absolutely numerically identical so far as colour goes: what makes them two and not one must be something else. Instead of saying "this is white" and "that is white", we ought to say, on this theory, "whiteness is here" and "whiteness is there". To go into this subject fully would demand a longer discussion of space than is appropriate at this point. We may observe, however, that two things in different places are at once recognized as numerically diverse, without any need of diversification by difference of qualities. It follows that either two patches of white in different places are numerically diverse, and therefore neither is whiteness itself; or the "places" must be absolute, not merely relative. In that case, the "places" (or "points", or whatever their ultimate constituents may be) are particulars which have something in common, distinguishing them, for example, from times; and it is hard to believe that this something will not be a predicate.

The common-sense "thing" (generally an orange), which can be seen and touched and smelled and eaten, is not the subject of such predicates as "yellow" or "hard". The common-sense thing will have to be conceived as a bundle of particulars—how united, we need not now inquire—each of which severally has its appropriate predicate, "yellow" or "hard" or what not. The subject of such predicates will be not the "thing", but a single sense-datum. Of a visual sense-datum we may say that it is yellow and bright, but it cannot be hard; what is hard is the tactile sense-datum which is associated with the visual one in making up our notion of the "thing". From the "thing" to the general attribute "yellow", we have to pass through two stages, owing to the fact that it is logically possible for things in different places to differ numerically though their attributes are precisely the same. The intermediate stage may be constituted by position in space, if we are willing to admit absolute space; but if not, it must be constituted by particulars which are "instances" of the general attributes. The general attributes are then either predicates of these particulars, or derivative from symmetrical transitive relations of specific similarity among the particulars.

The connection of predicates with ancient controversies is interesting, but confusing unless the differences from traditional opinions are realized. Predicates are the only universals much recognized or discussed until very recent times, although, as we have seen, they are much less indubitable than relations. We will, however, to avoid circumlocution, assume, throughout the rest of this chapter, that there are predicates. If there are not, a little change of wording will make our remarks applicable to the specific similarities by which we shall have to replace them.

A predicate is obviously akin to a Platonic idea. But it would be a mistake to suppose that a particular which has a predicate in any way resembles it or is an imperfect copy of it or has a "reality" in any way derivative from that of the predicate. Nobody supposes, for example, that an event which is before some other event resembles the relation "before" or is a "copy" of it or derives "reality" from it. And what is obvious in the case of relations must be equally admitted in the case of predicates. Subjects and predicates belong to different logical divisions, and cannot properly be said to be either like or unlike, because that would give them similar "positions" in one complex, whereas, if both occur in one complex, they must have differences of "position" corresponding to the fact that they can form a subject–predicate complex. Moreover the Platonic view seems to presuppose that no particular has more than one predicate. Now although it may well be maintained that in general a simple particular has very few predicates, it cannot, I think, be maintained that it never has more than one; a uniform visible patch, for example, will have both a shade of colour and a degree of brightness.

A predicate, again, is akin to a scholastic universal, and in maintaining that there are predicates we are classing ourselves with scholastic realists. But in saying that "there are" predicates, we are not necessarily saying that they have the same sort of "reality" as particulars have. The word "reality" is one which seems better avoided altogether, since it is difficult to give any precise meaning to it. What we affirm is that there are complexes of which predicates are constituents, and that predicates occur in the logical inventory of the world. But when we say "there are" predicates, it is rash to affirm that these words have precisely the same meaning as when we say "there are" particulars. This whole subject, however, bristles with difficulties, which ought to be solved in logic, but which, in theory of knowledge, need not be explicitly discussed.

One confusion, which runs through a great deal of philosophy, and still unconsciously inspires much fallacious reasoning, is the notion that a predicate is an actual constituent of its subject. It is supposed that the subject, when it is particular, and not general like "all men", is actually a certain collection of predicates, and that predication consists merely in singling out one predicate and asserting that it belongs to the collection. This view is very seldom explicit or fully self-conscious, yet it is astonishing how much philosophizing really assumes it. The old view that subject–predicate propositions are analytic obviously involves it. The polemic of the English empiricists against "substance" as the unknown substratum of the predicates really agrees with its opponents as to the logical nature of subject–predicate propositions. This view is also involved in the belief, very widely entertained, that particulars can be constituted by means of universals alone, which in turn is responsible for much of the metaphysical dislike of space and time, because they render impossible the specification of particulars by universals alone. And even in the most modern doctrines—for example, the neutral monism which we examined in Chapter II—the influence of this same logical error is still traceable. It is, therefore, of the highest importance to dispel this error.

The error has, I think, two different sources. One of these is a mistaken view as to the nature of a "thing"; the other is the mistaken identification, in formal logic, of such propositions as "Socrates is mortal" with such propositions as "all men are mortal". Let us begin with the "thing".

The grammatical prominence of the subject–predicate form presumably arose through the importance and frequency of such questions as "what is that?", where "that" is some given "thing". We can then proceed to investigate and describe "that"—"that" is round and hard and yellow and good to eat and so on. It is felt that when we have made all such statements about "that", we shall have exhausted its nature, and have learnt all there is to know about it. We may therefore simply identify the thing with the collection of its qualities. If there were anything else, it could be of no importance, since it would make no difference; and it would be unknowable, since we can make no propositions about a thing except such as assign properties to it. Gross and crude as such a view is, there can be no doubt that it is at the bottom of much metaphysics, and that, by its consonance with grammar, it has a hold on the imagination hardly to be shaken except by learning some symbolic language specially designed to correct the misleading logic suggested by common speech.

The "thing", as we have already pointed out, is a complicated inference from correlated sense-data. The true particular, in our experience, is not the

thing, but the single sense-datum. It is absurd to speak of this as "unknow-able", since it is given in acquaintance. It is erroneous to regard its identity as constituted by its predicates, because a precisely similar sense-datum may exist in another place. (By "precisely similar" I mean "having the same predicates".) Hence its predicates are not its parts, and predication is not analytic. On the other hand, it and various other sense-data *are* parts of the "thing". Hence, by confusing the sense-datum with its predicates, it comes to appear as if the predicates were parts of the thing. The particular instance of whiteness in a particular place is part of the "thing" associated with that
10 place; and it is easy to confuse the particular example of whiteness with whiteness in general. Hence it is supposed that whiteness in general is part of the "thing". This is one line of argument by which philosophers have been led to the view that predication is analytic and that the subject is a mere bundle of predicates.

The other line of argument is less popular, and has doubtless had a less wide-spread influence. Nevertheless, with those to whom the traditional logic was familiar, it must have very considerably reinforced the line of argument derived from "things". In the traditional logic, the two proposi-tions "All men are mortal" and "Socrates is mortal" are treated as though
20 they were of the same form: they both count as universal. Now "all men are mortal" may, rightly or wrongly, be taken as expressing a relation of predi-cates, "humanity implies mortality"; and it is natural to suppose that this implication is known through mortality being actually *part* of humanity. For example, we may say "human = animal and rational"; hence humanity contains rationality, and all men are rational. Proceeding to add more and more predicates in addition to "human", we increase the intension and di-minish the extension, until at last the class of terms possessing all our predi-cates is reduced to Socrates alone. Of this class, we can predicate analytically all the predicates used in defining it; and since this class consists of Socrates
30 alone, it would seem natural to suppose that it *is* Socrates. Hence predica-tion concerning Socrates is analytic, like predication concerning "all men".

We cannot here explain all the logical errors involved in such an argu-ment. We will merely assert dogmatically (1) that "all men are mortal" is not the same proposition as "humanity contains mortality"; (2) that it is a fun-damental and fatal error in logic to identify a class containing only one term with that one term; (3) that a proposition containing a subject *named*, like "Socrates", is vitally different in form from one containing a subject *de-scribed*, like "all men". The two first points need not be amplified here, but the third is so important that it must be briefly explained. When a subject
40 like "all men" occurs, we are not told what are the actual particulars that come under it, but we are told a certain universal which applies to them, whichever they may be. Hence what is required for a knowledge of this proposition concerns rather the universal than the particulars under it. If we

know enough about the universal "man", we can know things about "all men" without examining men individually. But it does not follow that what we know about "all men" we shall know about this or that particular which is in fact a man, because we may not know that it is a man. But when the subject is simply named, like "Socrates", assuming that we are acquainted with Socrates and thus know who is named by the name, we may understand the name without (theoretically) needing to know *any* of the properties of Socrates: he is simply a given *this*. When he is so given, obviously any proposition about his properties is synthetic, i.e. no predicate is actually *part* of the given particular. Thus by realizing the difference between a subject named and a subject described, we come to see the confusion involved in regarding true subject–predicate propositions as analytic.

After our long excursion into logic, we can now return to the epistemological question, namely: Do we ever have acquaintance with bare predicates, or are they merely an inferred residuum in complexes with which we are acquainted?

The arguments used in the preceding chapter are now not fully available, for all that we obviously know concerning predicates can be accounted for by supposing that we have acquaintance with relations of specific similarity. Since acquaintance with relations has been already admitted, we derive no new kind of objects of acquaintance in this way. If, then, our question is to be decided, it must be by direct inspection of data.

The strongest case in favour of acquaintance with predicates is derived, I think, from the qualities of sense-data. The theory of Berkeley and Hume, that we are not acquainted with white or yellow or any other universal colour, but only with similarities to various particular patches of white or yellow or some other colour, does not seem introspectively plausible, and would not, I fancy, have been maintained if they had realized that it did not dispense with the necessity of "abstract ideas", but merely transferred this necessity from predicates to relations. It would seem, too, that the different senses are distinguished by different predicates common to all the data of one sense. All visible things, for example, seem to have something in common with which we are acquainted. Obviously it is not merely the physiological connection with the eye that they have in common: it is not a tautology to say that it is through the eye that we become acquainted with visual sense-data. And the same applies to sounds, or to data of touch. Take again the localization of bodily sensations. All feelings in the great toe have something in common, however they may differ otherwise; it is in virtue of this common quality that we learn to locate them all in the great toe. It is difficult not to believe that this common quality is a predicate with which we are acquainted. There is, so far as I can see, no absolutely conclusive way of showing that we are acquainted with some predicates. But having admitted acquaintance with universals when they are relations, we have now no theoretic motive for denying acquaintance with universals which are predicates.

The conclusion of our discussion would seem to be, therefore, that, although less certainty is attainable than in the case of relations, yet there is good reason to believe that there are predicates, and that we are acquainted with certain of them. To inquire in detail what the predicates are with which we are acquainted is matter rather for psychology than for theory of knowledge. For our purposes, it is enough to know that such acquaintance probably occurs, and that no theoretic obstacle stands in the way of our assuming 10 it where it serves to explain the data.

Chapter IX
Logical Data

IN THE PRESENT chapter, we shall be concerned with the basis of acquaintance that must underlie our knowledge of logic. It should be said, to begin with, that "acquaintance" has, perhaps, a somewhat different meaning, where logical objects are concerned, from that which it has when particulars are concerned. Whether this is the case or not, it is impossible to decide without more knowledge concerning the nature of logical objects than I possess. It would seem that logical objects cannot be regarded as "entities", and that, therefore, what we shall call "acquaint- 10 ance" with them cannot really be a dual relation. The difficulties which result are very formidable, but their solution must be sought in logic. For the present, I am content to point out that there certainly is such a thing as "logical experience", by which I mean that kind of immediate knowledge, other than judgment, which is what enables us to understand logical terms. Many such terms have occurred in the last two chapters, for instance, particulars, universals, relations, dual complexes, predicates. Such words are, no doubt, somewhat difficult, and are only understood by people who have reached a certain level of mental development. Still, they are understood, and this shows that those who understand them possess something 20 which seems fitly described as "acquaintance with logical objects". It is this that I now wish to investigate.

In spite of the antiquity of logic, the peculiarity of the objects with which it deals has not been adequately realized; it has not been realized, for example, what a much higher degree and kind of abstraction is involved in understanding the word "relation" than in understanding the name of this or that relation. A given dual relation is still one of a class of more or less similar entities, namely dual relations; but "dual relation" itself, although it might *seem* to be one of a class whose other members would be "triple relation", etc., is really, in a very important sense, unique, and not a 30 member of any class containing any terms other than itself. Every logical notion, in a very important sense, is or involves a *summum genus*, and results from a process of generalization which has been carried to its utmost limit. This is a peculiarity of logic, and a touchstone by which logical propositions may be distinguished from all others. A proposition which mentions any definite entity, whether universal or particular, is not logical: no one definite entity, of any sort or kind, is ever a constituent of any truly logical proposition. "Logical constants", which might seem to be entities occurring in logical propositions, are really concerned with pure *form*, and are not actually constituents of the propositions in the verbal expression of which their names occur. The way in which this comes about must be briefly explained.

The proposition "if Socrates is human, and whatever is human is mortal, then Socrates is mortal" might be thought, at first, to be a proposition of logic. But it is obvious that its truth is in no way dependent on any
10 peculiarity of Socrates or humanity or mortality, but only on the *form* of the proposition; that is to say, Socrates, humanity, and mortality may be varied as we please without the proposition ceasing to be true. Thus we arrive at the pure logical proposition: "Whatever x and α and β may be, if x is α and whatever is α is β, then x is β". Here there is no longer any constituent corresponding to Socrates and humanity and mortality: the only thing that has been preserved is the pure *form* of the proposition, and the form is not a "thing", not another constituent along with the objects that were previously related in that form. Take, for example, "x is α", which is a constituent phrase in the above proposition. It might be thought that "is", here, is a
20 constant constituent. But this would be a mistake: "x is α" is obtained by generalization from "Socrates is human", which is to be regarded as a subject–predicate proposition, and such propositions, we said, have only two constituents. Thus "is" represents merely the way in which the constituents are put together. This cannot be a new constituent, for if it were, there would have to be a new way in which it and the two other constituents are put together, and if we take this way as again a constituent, we find ourselves embarked on an endless regress.

It is obvious, in fact, that when *all* the constituents of a complex have been enumerated, there remains something which may be called the "form"
30 of the complex, which is the way in which the constituents are combined in the complex. It is such pure "forms" that occur in logic. The natural way to symbolize a form is to take some phrase in which actual entities are put together in that form, and replace all these entities by "variables", i.e. by letters having no meaning. Take, for example, the proposition "Socrates precedes Plato". This has the form of a dual complex: we may naturally symbolize the form by "xRy", where we use a different sort of letter for the relation, because the difference between a relation and its terms is a *logical* difference. When we have reached the form "xRy", we have effected the utmost generalization which is possible starting from "Socrates precedes
40 Plato". In order to understand the phrase "dual complex" or the phrase "dual relation", we must be capable of the degree of abstraction involved in reaching the pure form. It is not at all clear what is the right logical account of "form", but whatever this account may be, it is clear that we have

acquaintance (possibly in an extended sense of the word "acquaintance") with something as abstract as the pure form, since otherwise we could not use intelligently such a word as "relation".

I think it may be shown that acquaintance with logical form is involved before explicit thought about logic begins, in fact as soon as we can understand a sentence. Let us suppose that we are acquainted with Socrates and with Plato and with the relation "precedes", but not with the complex "Socrates precedes Plato". Suppose now that some one tells us that Socrates precedes Plato. How do we know what he means? It is plain that his statement does not give us *acquaintance* with the complex "Socrates pre- 10 cedes Plato". What we understand is that Socrates and Plato and "precedes" are united in a complex of the form "xRy", where Socrates has the x-place and Plato has the y-place. It is difficult to see how we could possibly understand how Socrates and Plato and "precedes" are to be combined unless we had acquaintance with the form of the complex. As a matter of introspection, it may often be hard to detect such acquaintance; but there is no doubt that, especially where very abstract matters are concerned, we often have an acquaintance which we find it difficult to isolate or to become acquainted with. The introspective difficulty, therefore, cannot be regarded as fatal, or as outweighing a logical argument of which the data and the 20 inference seem to allow little risk of error.

Besides the forms of atomic complexes, there are many other logical objects which are involved in the formation of non-atomic complexes. Such words as *or*, *not*, *all*, *some*, plainly involve logical notions; and since we can use such words intelligently, we must be acquainted with the logical objects involved. But the difficulty of isolation is here very great, and I do not know what the logical objects involved really are.

In the present chaotic state of our knowledge concerning the primitive ideas of logic, it is impossible to pursue this topic further. Enough has been said, I hope, to show that acquaintance with logical form, whatever its 30 ultimate analysis may be, is a primitive constituent of our experience, and is presupposed, not only in explicit knowledge of logic, but in any understanding of a proposition otherwise than by actual acquaintance with the complex whose existence it asserts.

Before embarking on the study of judgment, it will be advisable to review our survey of acquaintance. We found, to begin with, that there is such a fact as "experiencing", and that this fact itself may be experienced. Starting from one momentary experience, which we found to be constituted by the relation of "being experienced together" which holds between any two objects belonging to one momentary experience, we found that there was 40 reason to regard this as not all-embracing, even when extended by successive links of memory to include the whole experience of one "person". The theory that experience does not involve any special kind of entity, such as we should naturally call "mental", was found to be unable to explain many of the obvious facts, such as memory, error, and above all "I" and "now" and "this", which involve a selectiveness not possible in a purely material world. All the facts, we found, could be explained by assuming that experiencing is a dual relation of a subject to an object, though it is not necessary to assume that we experience either the subject or the relation, but only the object and (sometimes) the complex subject-experiencing-object. Assuming that this analysis is correct, we called the dual relation in question "acquaintance".

We then considered various kinds of acquaintance. The first classification is according to the logical character of the object, namely according as it is (a) particular, (b) universal, or (c) formal, i.e. purely logical. Relations to objects differing in logical character must themselves differ in logical character; hence there is a certain looseness in using the one word "acquaintance" for immediate experience of these three kinds of objects. But from the point of view of epistemology, as opposed to logic, this looseness is somewhat immaterial, since all three kinds of acquaintance fulfil the same function of providing the data for judgment and inference.

Towards particulars with which we are acquainted, three subordinate dual relations were considered, namely sensation, memory, and imagination. These, we found, though their objects are usually somewhat different, are not essentially distinguished by their objects, but by the relations of subject and object. In sensation, subject and object are simultaneous; in memory, the subject is later than the object; while imagination does not essentially involve any time-relation of subject and object, though all time-relations are compatible with it. We considered also, though briefly, a fourth relation of subject and object, namely attention, which, however, does not require that the object should be particular.

Acquaintance with universals must be sub-divided according to the logical character of the universals involved. We considered specially acquaintance with dual relations and with predicates. Dual relations, we decided, must, in their abstraction, be objects of acquaintance, and cannot only be known by inference from the complexes in which they occur. In order to account for the "sense" of a relation, we pointed out that two complexes are logically possible with the same relation and the same terms, and that we must be acquainted with the two different "positions" which a term may occupy in a complex having a given relating relation. As regards predicates, we found that it is logically possible to doubt whether there are such entities, and also whether, if there are, they are objects of acquaintance. But we found no reason to attach much weight to either of these doubts, and we found further that, as regards consequences, no very great importance attached to the questions which were doubtful. We therefore proceeded on the assumption that there are predicates, and that we have acquaintance with them, since it seemed highly probable that this assumption is true, and highly improbable that it is gravely misleading if it is false. Acquaintance with universals may be called "conception", and universals with which we are acquainted may be called "concepts".

Finally, in the present chapter, we considered acquaintance with logical form, which may perhaps be called "logical intuition". This sort of acquaintance, we found, is required to account for our understanding such words as "predicate", "relation", "dual complex", as well as for such words as "or", "not", "all", and "some". But it is also required in all cases where we understand a statement without having acquaintance with the complex whose existence would insure the truth of the statement. If we are acquainted with a and with similarity and with b, we can understand the statement "a is similar to b", even if we cannot directly compare them and "see" their similarity. But this would not be possible unless we knew how they are to be put together, i.e. unless we were acquainted with the form of a dual complex. Thus all "mental synthesis", as it may be called, involves acquaintance with logical form. But this topic raises questions which will be more naturally discussed in connection with *belief*, to which we must now turn our attention.

Part II
Atomic Propositional Thought

Chapter I
The Understanding of Propositions

THE TRADITIONAL DIVISION of logic into the three heads of terms, propositions, and inference was not a happy one. The study of "terms" hardly touches logic at any point, since no particular terms ever occur in a logical proposition. The study of "propositions" also is very largely extra-logical, since the definite propositions that occur in logic are of a very peculiar kind. And as for "inference", it is almost unavoidably taken in a more or less psychological sense, as the passage from one belief to another in virtue of some relation between the propositions believed. But in 10 theory of knowledge, the traditional division is far more appropriate. Knowledge of terms, knowledge of atomic propositions, and knowledge of molecular propositions, raise different problems and demand separate treatment. Knowledge of terms is what we have called "acquaintance". Knowledge of propositions is a more complicated matter, and has forms which differ both according to the relation of the subject to the objects involved, and also according to the nature of the objects themselves. One very important relation which comes under the head of knowledge of propositions is *belief* or *judgment*; but this relation requires different treatment according as the proposition concerned is atomic or molecular. Belief 20 in a molecular proposition gives what is most distinctive in the process of inferring; thus the epistemological problems connected with inference arise naturally in connection with molecular propositions, while problems which exclusively concern belief may be studied in their simplest form in connection with atomic propositions. Hence the threefold division which we have adopted corresponds roughly with the traditional threefold division of logic.

Before proceeding further, it is necessary to define atomic and molecular propositions; and it is obviously desirable that our definitions should be such as to facilitate the discussion of the various problems involved, without assuming in advance any particular opinion on any of these problems. One 30 way in which this might be thought possible, is to give purely linguistic definitions. Let us, to begin with, define a *proposition* as any complete sentence capable of expressing a statement. When I say that it is capable of expressing a statement, I mean that it contains at least one verb, and is not the expression of a question or a command. It may be that questions and commands can also be regarded as statements, but if so, they can be

expressed in terms which are no longer grammatically questions or commands; thus this problem need not concern us. We may then define an
atomic proposition as one of which no part is a proposition, while a *molecular*
proposition is one of which at least one part is a proposition.

But the above definitions, though they may serve to indicate what is
meant, will not bear scrutiny. In the first place, the grammatical element
needs to be softened down. We want to regard the negation of a proposition
as molecular, on the ground that the proposition negated is contained in it.
But this will not always be *verbally* the case. Again, take such a proposition
10 as "If wishes were horses, beggars would be riders". We wish to regard this
as molecular, and as containing the two propositions "wishes are horses"
and "beggars are riders". Thus if our definition is to be applicable, we must
be allowed to ignore the mood of the verb. But it is obvious that we are
governed, in all this, by considerations which are not linguistic. Such
considerations obtrude themselves even more obviously when we ask what
is meant by a "statement". We defined a "sentence expressing a statement",
above, as a "sentence not expressing a question or command". But it is at
least as easy to know what a statement is as to know what is a question or a
command. Such a definition, therefore, is foolish. It follows that we must
20 seek some other definition of a "proposition".

It is obvious, to begin with, that a number of phrases may "have the same
meaning". It must not be inferred that there is an obvious meaning which
they all have: to find out what is meant by "the meaning of a phrase" is very
difficult, even when it is quite easy to see that two phrases have the same
meaning. We therefore take "having the same meaning" as a transitive
symmetrical relation between phrases, which can be known to subsist when
no entity is known which is their common meaning. Now it is plain that, in
theory of knowledge as in logic, it is unnecessary to distinguish between two
phrases that have the same meaning: the distinction between them, however
30 interesting linguistically, may be wholly ignored for our purposes. If we
cannot isolate anything which is their common meaning, we shall have to
take the whole group of phrases having the same meaning, and define this as
the proposition, for otherwise trivial linguistic considerations will perpetu-
ally obtrude themselves.

But now we come to a somewhat more difficult and important point. A
sentence, even when it is apparently concerned only with objects, very often
also expresses some fact about our relation to those objects. This is most
obvious in the case of time. "There *was* an eclipse of the sun on April 17,
1912" expresses now exactly the same objective fact as was expressed before
40 that date by "There *will be* an eclipse of the sun on April 17, 1912." The
difference between these two sentences lies solely in the time-relation
asserted to hold between the subject and the event concerned. (The difference does not lie in what the time-relation *is*, but in what it is *asserted to be*:

the past tense will be used by a person who mistakenly believes that the date is past.) European languages are absolutely destitute of means of speaking of an event without indicating its temporal relation to the speaker; I believe Hebrew and Chinese are preferable in this respect, but unfortunately I was never taught either. There can be no doubt that the philosophy of time has suffered very seriously from this gross incapacity of the languages spoken by western philosophers, since there is no way of expressing the eternity of the *fact* as opposed to the transiency of the *event*. This, however, is not the point that concerns us at present. What concerns us at present is the sort of difference between two phrases which is not concerned with the objects in themselves, but only with their relation to the subject. And since, in our present discussions, time-relations are not directly relevant, we shall not now consider them further.

Take our previous illustration, of the difference between "beggars are riders" and "beggars would be riders". We may now add the question and the imperative, "are beggars riders?" and "beggars shall be riders". In all these, the relation between beggars and riders is the same; but in the first it is asserted, in the second suggested as a consequence of a hypothesis, in the third the object of a doubt, and in the fourth the object of a volition. We should not say that these four phrases "have the same meaning", yet they all have something very important in common. The word "proposition" is a natural one to use for expressing what they all have in common: we may say that they express different attitudes towards the same "proposition". This is not to be regarded as a *definition* of the word "proposition", since a host of problems must be solved before we can disentangle the common element which we feel. But it will serve to indicate what the problem is, and in what region we have to look for something which can be called a "proposition".

In order to avoid the suggestion of assertion, we may express the proposition by the phrase "beggars being riders". It is clear that there is something which we may call "understanding the proposition", which is presupposed equally by assertion, suggestion, doubt and volition. This has some affinity to acquaintance, though it is really much more complicated. It is perhaps easier to discover what is meant by "understanding a proposition" than to discover what is meant by a "proposition". In the present chapter, we wish to discover what is meant by "understanding" when the proposition concerned is atomic.

What I mean by "understanding a proposition" is apparently not quite the same as what Meinong means by an "Annahme". There are, according to him, two marks of beliefs, namely (1) conviction, (2) affirmation or negation; of these the second, but not the first, belongs to "Annahmen". It is the possession of this affirmative or negative character which, according to him, chiefly distinguishes assumptions (as I shall call them) from presentations; while the absence of conviction suffices to distinguish them from judgments. Now when I speak of "understanding a proposition", I am speaking of a state of mind from which both affirmation and negation are wholly absent. The state of mind in question would not be regarded by Meinong as merely the presentation of the proposition, because he holds that there can be no such thing as the presentation of a proposition (i.e. of what he calls an "Objektiv"). In this I now agree with him, though my reasons are different from his, and require a different theory from his as to the nature of assumptions and beliefs. The question, however, how what I call "understanding a proposition" differs from what Meinong means by an assumption is difficult, owing to our different analysis of the facts. There is certainly an affinity, and Meinong's work certainly suggests the importance of the distinction between understanding a proposition and believing it.

The distinction between understanding and believing is, however, less important for our present purposes than the distinction between understanding and acquaintance. Understanding, if I am not mistaken, is presupposed in belief, and can itself be discussed without introducing belief. Understanding and belief, however, are closely akin as regards logical form, and raise the same logical problems; whereas understanding and acquaintance, as I shall try to show, are very widely different in logical form, and give rise to quite different logical problems.

The theory which Meinong adopts in regard to the logical nature of assumptions and beliefs is a natural one to adopt, and deserves credit for its recognition of the necessity of objects for assumptions and beliefs. His view is, that there is an entity, namely the "proposition" (*Objektiv*), to which we may have the dual relation of assumption or the dual relation of belief. Such a view is not, I think, strictly refutable, and until I had discovered the theory of "incomplete symbols" I was myself willing to accept it, since it seemed unavoidable. Now, however, it appears to me to result from a certain logical naïveté, which compels us, from poverty of available hypotheses, to do violence to instincts which deserve respect. What these instincts are, and how it is possible to respect them, I shall now try to show.

The fundamental characteristic which distinguishes propositions (whatever they may be) from objects of acquaintance is their truth or falsehood. An object of acquaintance is not true or false, but is simply what it is: there is no dualism of true and false objects of acquaintance. And although there are entities with which we are not acquainted, yet it seems evident that nothing of the same logical nature as objects of acquaintance can possibly be either true or false. Of course a judgment or a statement may be true or false in one sense, although it is an event which may be an object of acquaintance. But it is fairly obvious that the truth or falsehood which is attributed to a judgment or statement is derivative from the truth or falsehood of the associated proposition. We say that two men make the "same" statement, meaning that they assert the same proposition; and it is the proposition that makes both men's statements true or both false. The proposition is what they both "mean"—or rather, it is part of what they both "mean". The statement of either of them, considered in itself, is a series of noises; it is only through its "meaning" that it becomes true or false. Thus the opposition of truth and falsehood, in its primary and fundamental sense, is applicable only to propositions, not to particular thoughts or statements.

Now a proposition is, in my opinion, an "incomplete symbol", i.e. some context is necessary before the phrase expressing a proposition acquires a complete meaning. When we take the proposition in the form "beggars being riders", in which the suggestion of assertion has been eliminated, this view is seen not to be paradoxical. The reasons for this view are connected with the instinctive feelings spoken of at the end of the last paragraph but one. We might be induced to admit that *true* propositions are entities, but it is very difficult, except under the lash of a tyrannous theory, to admit that *false* propositions are entities. "Charles I dying in his bed" or "that Charles I died in his bed" does not seem to stand for any entity. It is traditional to say that what is true "corresponds" with reality, and what is false does not. The word "correspond" requires investigation, but in any case it seems plain that a false proposition is not itself an actual entity. A false belief or a false statement is an entity; but it seems obvious that they owe their falsehood to the unreality of something which would be real if they were true. Hence *if* the reality of the proposition were affirmed by the belief, we should have to say that there is such an entity as the proposition when the belief is true, but not when it is false.

The word "proposition" *can*, no doubt, be so used as to make this the case. But if it is so used, then the proposition is not involved in what happens when we believe, or when we "understand a proposition" in the sense explained at the beginning of this chapter. It is obvious that what we call believing or understanding a proposition is a fact of the same logical form whether the proposition is true or whether it is false; for if this were not so, there would be an *intrinsic* difference between true and false beliefs, and mere attention to the mental fact would be capable of showing whether the belief was true or whether it was false. This, however, is unfortunately not the case. We must therefore say that, in the sense in which propositions are involved in believing and in propositional understanding, there is no difference, as regards reality, between true and false propositions. And this in turn, since it is repugnant to admit the reality of false propositions, forces us to seek a theory which shall regard true and false propositions as alike unreal, i.e. as incomplete symbols.

The question of the meaning of "truth" and "falsehood" is one which we shall consider later. At present, we are not concerned with truth and falsehood on their own account, but only with the way in which their opposition throws doubt on the reality of propositions. Our disbelief in their

reality may be reinforced by asking ourselves what kind of entity a false proposition could be. Let us take some very simple false proposition, say "*A* precedes *B*", when in fact *A* comes after *B*. It seems as though nothing were involved here beyond *A* and *B* and "preceding" and the general form of dual complexes. But since *A* does not precede *B*, these objects are not put together in the way indicated by the proposition. It seems, therefore, that nothing which actually is composed of these objects is the proposition; and it is not credible that anything further enters into the proposition. This argument cannot be regarded as very conclusive; still, if anybody thinks he
10 can see an entity which is a false proposition, "I desire it to be produced". Meanwhile, I shall assume that true and false propositions alike are non-entities.

This conclusion, if it is valid, proves that when we understand or assume or believe a proposition, what is involved is not a dual relation of the subject to a single entity, such as Meinong's "Objektiv". This is what makes propositional thought fundamentally different from acquaintance: the logical form of the occurrences involved, whatever it may be, must be unlike that of the dual relations hitherto considered, namely acquaintance, attention, sensation, memory and imagination. It is owing to the novelty of the
20 logical form that we get such essential novelties as truth and falsehood at this stage. It seems probable also on this account that judgment belongs to such a much higher level of mental development than mere sensation, for the logical structure of a judgment, or of any propositional thought, is immensely more complex than that of a sensation.

A *propositional* thought is one which involves a "proposition" in its meaning. An *atomic* propositional thought is one which involves only an *atomic* proposition in its meaning. And an atomic proposition may, for the present, be defined as one whose verbal expression is of the same form as that of an atomic complex.
30   There are various kinds of propositional thoughts, just as there are various kinds of dual relations to objects. Besides understanding a proposition, there are, for example, believing, disbelieving, doubting, analyzing, and synthesizing, to mention only purely cognitive relations—if we went outside what is cognitive, we should have to mention also such relations as desiring and willing. But just as acquaintance is the most comprehensive and fundamental of dual cognitive relations, so *understanding* is the most comprehensive and fundamental of propositional cognitive relations. It is obvious that we cannot believe or disbelieve or doubt a proposition without understanding it. Thus the first step in the analysis of propositional thought
40 must be to understand understanding.

Let us take as an illustration some very simple proposition, say "*A* precedes *B*", where *A* and *B* are particulars. In order to understand this proposition, it is not necessary that we should believe it, or that it should be true. It is obviously necessary that we should know what is meant by the words which occur in it, that is to say, we must have acquaintance with *A* and *B* and with the relation "preceding". It is also necessary to know how these three terms are meant to be combined; and this, as we say in the last chapter, requires acquaintance with the general form of a dual complex. But this is by no means enough to enable us to understand the proposition; in fact, it does not enable us to distinguish "*A* precedes *B*" from "*B* precedes *A*". When we were discussing relations, we said that, with a given relation and given terms, two complexes are "logically possible". But the notion of what is "logically possible" is not an ultimate one, and must be reduced to something that is *actual* before our analysis can be complete. Now although we do not yet know what a proposition is, it is obvious that what we had in mind, when we said that a complex was "logically possible", may be expressed by saying that there is a proposition having the same verbal form. This is still not ultimate, because of our doubt as to how propositions are to be explained; but for present purposes we will treat it as ultimate. Of the two "logically possible" *complexes* "*A* precedes *B*" and "*B* precedes *A*", at most one can be actual; whereas there always are the two *propositions* expressed by these words, in whatever sense there ever are propositions at all. We have now to consider how we distinguish between these two propositions.

Remembering what was said in dealing with relations, we shall say that, in any complex in which the relating relation is time-sequence, we can distinguish two "positions" occupied by the terms of the relation, one of the positions being called the earlier, the other the later. If we wish to mention the earlier term first, we use the word "precedes" for the relation of time-sequence, while if we wish to mention the later term first we use the word "succeeds" for precisely the same relation. It is to be noted that the difference between "precedes" and "succeeds" cannot be explained by reference to dual complexes in general, but only by reference to sequence-complexes. We can see with regard to dual complexes in general that, while the relating relation remains the same, the terms of this relation have two different relations to the complexes in which they occur. But this general knowledge is not presupposed in our understanding of the particular case of earlier and later, which merely requires that we should see the two positions in sequence-complexes. (It is to be observed that "position" is a relation to a complex, not to the relating relation; a term is "earlier" in one sequence-complex, but may be "later" in another, so that "earlier" and "later" are essentially relative to the particular complex concerned.) The propositions required are "*A* precedes in the complex α" and "*B* succeeds in the complex α", where α is a sequence-complex, which must in fact be "*A* precedes *B*". It may be objected that our explanation of the "sense" of a relation will have to be applied afresh to "*A* precedes in the complex α", and that thus we shall be involved in an endless regress. This however is not to be feared, because

A and α differ *logically*, and the statement "α precedes in the complex A" is meaningless; thus there are not in this case two logically possible complexes, and the whole difficulty of "sense" does not arise.

We thus arrive at the result that, since the actual complex α is irrelevant, "A precedes B" means "there is a complex in which A precedes and B succeeds". This proposition is more complicated than the proposition in which the actual complex α is given, i.e. the proposition "A precedes in α and B succeeds in α"; and this in turn is more complicated than either of the two separate propositions "A precedes in α" and "B succeeds in α". Thus if our analysis has been correct, the proposition "A precedes B", which seemed fairly simple, is really complicated owing to difficulties concerned with "sense". These difficulties are not an essential part of the difficulty of discovering what is meant by "understanding a proposition". We shall do well, therefore, to take examples which do not introduce "sense". Among dual relations, there are two sorts of such examples, (1) those where the two related terms are logically different, so that no proposition results from interchanging them, as in the above instance of "A precedes in α"; (2) those where the relation is symmetrical, and the complex is unchanged by interchanging the terms, as in "A resembles B". The first class of examples introduce special difficulties of their own; we will therefore consider the second class.

For the sake of definiteness, let us suppose that A and B are two patches of colour, of distinguishable but very similar shades. In this case, we can say "A and B are similar", which will express absolutely the same proposition as is expressed by "B and A are similar". Thus the relation of similarity, unlike that of time-sequence, gives rise to only one complex with given terms: the verbal difference according as A or B is mentioned first is merely the inevitable result of the temporal or spatial order of our words, and does not correspond to any difference in what the words mean. We therefore escape from all the difficulties associated with sense, and can hope to isolate more successfully the problems involved in understanding a proposition.

In order to understand "A and B are similar", we must be acquainted with A and B and similarity, and with the general form of symmetrical dual complexes. (Whether this form is the same as that of non-symmetrical dual complexes, we need not now inquire.) But these separate acquaintances, even if they all coexist in one momentary experience, do not constitute understanding of the one proposition "A and B are similar", which obviously brings the three constituents and the form into relation with each other, so that all become parts of one complex. It is this comprehensive relation which is the essential thing about the understanding of a proposition. Our problem is, therefore, to discover the nature of this comprehensive relation.

Let us consider successively the following questions:

(1) What can we mean by the "form" of a complex?
(2) Can we, by bringing in the "form" or in any other way, make the "proposition" an entity, i.e. not a mere incomplete symbol, but something which can subsist on its own account, and not only as a fictitious constituent of certain mental complexes?
(3) How can we be sure that acquaintance with the "form" is involved in understanding a proposition? And finally,
(4) What is the logical structure of the fact which consists in a given subject understanding a given proposition?

(1). The natural symbolic expression for the form of a given complex is the expression obtained by replacing the names of the constituents of the complex by letters representing variables, using different kinds of letters for constituents of different logical kinds, or indicating the difference of kind by brackets or some such method. Thus we may indicate the general form of a dual complex by "xRy" or by $R(x, y)$; and we may indicate the general form of a subject–predicate complex by $\alpha(x)$, where α is the predicate and x the subject, or by $x\epsilon\alpha$, where "ϵ" merely serves, like a bracket, to indicate relative position. Such symbols as xRy and $x\epsilon\alpha$ serve admirably for technical purposes, but they do not tell us what the form actually is, or whether it is anything more than a symbol. It is easy to see when two complexes "have the same form"; this will happen whenever there is some one symbol composed wholly of variables, such as "xRy" for instance, from which both can be derived by giving values to the variables. Another way of expressing the same thing is to say that two complexes have the same form if the one becomes the other when the constituents of the other are successively substituted for the constituents of the one. This might be thought to constitute a definition of "having the same form", but in fact it does not; for it is necessary that the substituted term should be in the same position in the new complex as the old term occupied in the old complex, and the sameness of position thus involved cannot be explained without the notion of form.

Although "having the same form" does not seem to be definable without supposing the form to be known, yet it is easier to recognize when two complexes have the same form than to decide what the form is. Since "having the same form" is transitive and symmetrical, we might of course define the form of a complex as the class of all complexes having the same form. Or, if we wish to avoid classes in so fundamental a question, we can say that if, for example, we assert "A and B are similar", we must have in mind some actual complex, say "C and D are similar", with which we are acquainted, and which we will call γ, and we must be really asserting "A and B and similarity form a complex of the same form as γ", where "being of the same form" is taken as a primitive idea. It is, however, obvious that such an explanation will land us in an endless regress; for we shall have to apply a similar treatment to the statement "*A* and *B* and similarity form a complex of the same form as γ", and then to the expanded statement of what this means, and so on. And this instance makes it clear that, if the form enters into the understanding of the corresponding proposition, the form must be something exceedingly simple.

We require of the form that there shall be one form, and only one, for every group of complexes which "have the same form"; also, if possible, it would be convenient to take as the form something which is not a mere incomplete symbol. We may secure these *desiderata* by taking as the form the fact that there are entities that make up complexes having the form in question. This sounds circular, but what is intended is not circular. For example, the form of all subject–predicate complexes will be the fact "something has some predicate"; the form of all dual complexes will be "something has some relation to something". The logical nature of this fact is very peculiar. If we take some particular dual complex xRy, this has three constituents, x, R, and y. If we now consider "something has the relation R to y", we get a fact which no longer contains x, and has not substituted any other entity for x, since "something" is nothing. Thus our new fact contains only R and y. For similar reasons, "something has the relation R to something" contains no constituent except R; and "something has some relation to something" contains no constituent at all. It is, therefore, suitable to serve as the "form" of dual complexes. In a sense, it is simple, since it cannot be analyzed. At first sight, it seems to have a structure, and therefore to be not simple; but it is more correct to say that it *is* a structure. Language is not well adapted for speaking of such objects. But in spite of the difficulties of language, it seems not paradoxical to say that, in order to understand a proposition which states that x has the relation R to y, we must understand what is meant by "something having some relation to something". I shall therefore assume that this may be defined as the "form" of dual complexes, and that similar definitions may be adopted for other forms.

(2). Can we give a definition of a "proposition" which neither brings in anything mental nor makes the proposition an incomplete symbol? At an earlier stage, we provisionally decided this question in the negative, but it is now time to reconsider it. It is to be borne in mind throughout the discussion that false propositions must be allowed for as well as true ones.

We arrived at the proposition, in the first place, as something which a number of mental events have in common. If two men judge that *A* and *B* are similar, or if one man makes this judgment on two occasions, it is obvious that the difference between the two events is only on the subjective side, and that on the objective side there is a similarity consisting not only in the fact that the same objects are concerned, but also in the fact that the different judgments bring the objects into the same relation to each other.

The objective side, it would seem, remains unchanged if a person doubts or desires or wills that A and B are similar. In the former case of two judgments, we changed only the subject, not the relation of the subject to the objects, while in this case we change also the relation of the subject to the objects; but when we abstract both from the subject and from its relation to the objects, what remains seems to be exactly the same in the case of doubt or desire or will as in the case of judgment. It is this common element that we call the "proposition", and wish, if possible, to isolate from its subjective context.

There is one obvious method of eliminating all reference to a particular subject, or to a particular relation of the subject to the objects. Assuming, what we shall shortly try to demonstrate, that understanding, judging, doubting, etc., are multiple relations combining a subject and various objects in one complex, the mental events that we should regard as concerned with the same proposition are all of them complexes of the same form, which result merely from variations of the subject and the relating relation. Thus, if we call the subject S, and the relating relation (of which "understanding" is the one presupposed by all the others) U, and the objects x, R, y (taking the case of a proposition asserting a dual relation for the sake of illustration), and γ the form of dual complexes, the total complex which occurs when the subject has the relation U to the objects in question may be symbolized by

$$U(S, x, R, y, \gamma) \ .$$

If we now proceed to the "form" which results from varying U and S, i.e. to

"there is a U and an S such that $U(S, x, R, y, \gamma)$"

we arrive at something which is the same for all subjects and for all propositional relations which we should regard as concerned with the same proposition. Thus there is no formal obstacle to defining this as the proposition.

The above definition has some merits and some demerits. Its chief merit is that it provides propositions, both true and false, as fast as we can think of them, and that it gives something in common between all the mental events which seem to be concerned with the same proposition. Its chief demerit is that we cannot be sure that there are propositions in all cases in which logic would seem to need them. It is not necessary to our definition that there should actually be a subject which has one of the familiar mental relations to the objects, but it is necessary that there should be some term and some relation by which a complex results having the requisite form and containing the objects in question. It may be possible to prove that there always are such complexes, but I do not at present see how such a proof could be found. In its absence, we cannot know of the existence of propositions other than those that have been actually thought of. It may be said that this does not matter, since any proposition we choose to think of will certainly exist, and therefore no obstacle is set to our thinking. But this seems a somewhat frivolous answer, and we must admit, I think, that the objection in question is serious. I cannot, however, think of anything better calculated to fulfil the purposes for which we want propositions, and I therefore propose to continue to use the word in the above sense.

10   (3). What is the proof that we must understand the "form" before we can understand the proposition? I held formerly that the objects alone sufficed, and that the "sense" of the relation of understanding would put them in the right order; this, however, no longer seems to me to be the case. Suppose we wish to understand "A and B are similar". It is essential that our thought should, as is said, "unite" or "synthesize" the two terms and the relation; but we cannot *actually* "unite" them, since either A and B are similar, in which case they are already united, or they are dissimilar, in which case no amount of thinking can force them to become united. The process of "uniting" which we *can* effect in thought is the process of bringing them

20 into relation with the general form of dual complexes. The form being "something and something have a certain relation", our understanding of the proposition might be expressed in the words "something, namely A, and something, namely B, have a certain relation, namely similarity". I do not mean this as a full analysis, but only as suggesting the way in which the form is relevant. In an actual complex, the general form is not presupposed; but when we are concerned with a proposition which may be false, and where, therefore, the actual complex is not given, we have only, as it were, the "idea" or "suggestion" of the terms being united in such a complex; and this, evidently, requires that the general form of the merely supposed

30 complex should be given. More simply, in order to understand "A and B are similar", we must know what is supposed to be done with A and B and similarity, i.e. what it is for two terms to have a relation; that is, we must understand the form of the complex which must exist if the proposition is true. I do not know how to make this point more evident, and I must therefore leave it to the reader's inspection, in hopes that he will arrive at the same conclusion.

(4). We come now to the last problem which has to be treated in this chapter, namely: What is the logical structure of the fact which consists in a given subject understanding a given proposition? The structure of an

40 understanding varies according to the proposition understood. At present, we are only concerned with the understanding of atomic propositions; the understanding of molecular propositions will be dealt with in Part III. Let us again take the proposition "A and B are similar". It is plain, to begin with,

that the *complex* "*A* and *B* being similar", even if it exists, does not enter in, for if it did, we could not understand false propositions, because in their case there is no such complex. It is plain, also, from what has been said, that we cannot understand the proposition unless we are acquainted with *A* and *B* and similarity and the form "something and something have some relation". Apart from these four objects, there does not appear, so far as we can see, to be any object with which we need be acquainted in order to understand the proposition. It seems to follow that these four objects, and these only, must be united with the subject in one complex when the subject understands the proposition. It cannot be any complex composed of them that enters in, since they need not form any complex, and if they do, we need not be acquainted with it. But they themselves must all enter in, since if they did not, it would be at least theoretically possible to understand the proposition without being acquainted with them. In this argument, I appeal to the principle that, when we understand, those objects with which we must be acquainted when we understand, and those only, are object-constituents (i.e. constituents other than understanding itself and the subject) of the understanding-complex.

It follows that, when a subject *S* understands "*A* and *B* are similar", "understanding" is the relating relation, and the terms are *S* and *A* and *B* and similarity and $R(x, y)$, where $R(x, y)$ stands for the form "something and something have some relation". Thus a first symbol for the complex will be

$$U\{S, A, B, \text{similarity}, R(x, y)\} \ .$$

This symbol, however, by no means exhausts the analysis of the form of the understanding-complex. There are many kinds of five-term complexes, and we have to decide what the kind is.

It is obvious, in the first place, that *S* is related to the four other terms in a way different from that in which any of the four other terms are related to each other. (It is to be observed that we can derive from our five-term complex a complex having any smaller number of terms by replacing any one or more of the terms by "something". If *S* is replaced by "something", the resulting complex is of a different form from that which results from replacing any other term by "something". This explains what is meant by saying that *S* enters in a different way from the other constituents.) It is obvious, in the second place, that $R(x, y)$ enters in a different way from the other three objects, and that "similarity" has a different relation to $R(x, y)$ from that which *A* and *B* have, while *A* and *B* have the same relation to $R(x, y)$. Also, because we are dealing with a proposition asserting a symmetrical relation between *A* and *B*, *A* and *B* have each the same relation to "similarity", whereas, if we had been dealing with an asymmetrical relation, they would have had different relations to it. Thus we are led to the following map of our five-term complex.

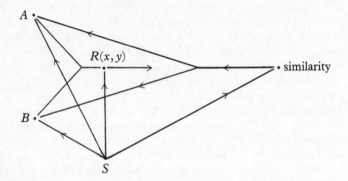

In this figure, one relation goes from S to the four objects; one relation goes from $R(x, y)$ to similarity, and another to A and B, while one relation goes from similarity to A and B. This figure, I hope, will help to make clearer the map of our five-term complex. But to explain in detail the exact abstract meaning of the various items in the figure would demand a lengthy formal logical discussion. Meanwhile the above attempt must suffice, for the present, as an analysis of what is meant by "understanding a proposition".

Chapter II
Analysis and Synthesis

IN THE PRECEDING chapter, we endeavoured, in a somewhat hasty and preliminary manner, to show how it might be possible to find some not definitely refutable theory of what is meant by "understanding a proposition". In this chapter and the next, we shall pursue the same topic, assuming that "understanding" must have the general character assigned to it in the last chapter, and seeking, within this assumption, to secure greater definiteness and to deal with various illustrative special cases.

Analysis and synthesis, which form the topic of the present chapter, are words with a long history and powerful emotional associations. Most of us have been told in youth that analysis is easy and base, whereas synthesis is glorious and difficult. Some of us may have felt inclined to reverse that judgment; but however that may be, it is only by analysis that we can hope to discover what analysis and synthesis are, and therefore only the humble analyst can know in what the glories of synthesis consist. Leaving, therefore, the question of their relative merits, let us proceed at once to a definition of the two processes.

Analysis may be defined as the discovery of the constituents and the manner of combination of a given complex. The complex is to be one with which we are acquainted; the analysis is *complete* when we become acquainted with all the constituents and with their manner of combination, and know that there are no more constituents and that that is their manner of combination. We may distinguish *formal* analysis as the discovery of the manner of combination, and *material* analysis as the discovery of the constituents. Material analysis may be called *descriptive* when the constituents are only known by description, not by acquaintance.

Synthesis may be defined as the discovery of a complex consisting of given constituents combined in a given manner. This, of course, is only possible when there is such a complex. We may speak of an *acquaintance-synthesis* when we become acquainted with the resulting complex; but when we merely come to know that there is such a complex, we shall speak of a *descriptive* synthesis, or of a *propositional* synthesis, because our knowledge will naturally be expressed by a proposition.

We have to consider, in this chapter, what kinds of data are required in order that analysis and synthesis respectively may be possible.

In regard to analysis, one further definition is necessary. It may happen that a complex has complex constituents; we may take as an example the fact that the difference between blue and yellow is greater than the difference between blue and green. This fact consists of a relation between two complexes, namely the difference between blue and yellow and the difference between blue and green. In this case, there is a relating relation which produces the unity of the whole complex, namely "greater", and there is another relating relation, namely "difference", which produces the unity of the subordinate complexes. We will give the name "primary constituents"
10 to the relating relation which produces the unity of the whole and to its terms; we will give the name "secondary constituents" to the primary constituents of primary constituents, and so on. We will give the name "ultimate constituents" to such as have no constituents. We shall define a term as *simple* when it has no constituents; thus the ultimate constituents are simple. The word "constituent", simply, will apply to all constituents of whatever order. The definition of a *complete* analysis given above will thus require a knowledge of all the constituents of whatever order. But we may speak of a *complete primary analysis* when we have discovered all the primary consitutents; and similarly we may define a *complete secondary analysis* and
20 so on. It should be observed that any number of stages of analysis may be possible even with an *atomic* complex, which is constituted by the fact that the unity of the whole depends on one relating relation.

In what follows, it will almost always be the *primary* constituents that will concern us. It is obvious that what can be said generally as regards the discovery of primary constituents only requires repetition in order to apply to the discovery of constituents of any order. Where no confusion can result, I shall sometimes speak of the primary constituents simply as the constituents.

It will be seen that analysis only raises problems because we may be
30 acquainted with a complex without knowing what its constituents are. This fact may, I think, be taken as obvious. Illustrations of it are afforded by the great difficulties in the analysis of sense-data, and by the labour of thought required to discover the more abstract constituents of quite easily apprehended facts—such, for example, as the understanding of simple propositions, which occupied us in the last chapter. We can all understand such a proposition as "*A* precedes *B*", and we can all experience our understanding of it; but to analyze our understanding of it is a very difficult matter. The proposition, therefore, that we can be acquainted with a complex without knowing what its constituents are, I take to be obvious, and to be
40 sufficiently proved by the well-known difficulties of analysis.

There is, however, another proposition, less obvious, and not immediately deducible from the difficulties of analysis: this is the proposition that *we may be acquainted with a complex without being acquainted with its constituents.* This proposition also, I believe, or rather one which is very like it, is true, and it is in any case very important, for many reasons, to discover whether it is true. It is not implied by our previous proposition, for we might be acquainted with the constituents of a complex without being aware that they were its constituents. The arguments in its favour cannot, therefore, be the simple and easy arguments which persuaded us of the truth of our former proposition. Let us now consider what is to be said for and against our new proposition.

There is, to begin with, a reason for doubting whether certainty is attainable on this question. We may have acquaintance with an object, without being acquainted with our own acquaintance. All objects of sense that we do not attend to seem to be instances. And it is logically evident that there must be instances, since otherwise every acquaintance would entail an infinite introspective series, which is absurd. Hence it may happen that we are acquainted with the constituents of a complex without knowing that we are acquainted with them. This fact makes it difficult to produce evidence proving that we are not acquainted with them. It would seem, however, that, when we are acquainted with an object, our acquaintance with it can usually be discovered by an effort of attention—though it must be confessed that, if it could not be so discovered, it is hard to see how we could ever know that it existed undiscovered. In order to circumvent this psychological problem, and to put our main proposition into a form which can be tested, let us restate it as follows: *We may be acquainted with a complex without being able to discover, by an introspective effort, that we are acquainted with the objects which are in fact its constituents.* In this form, our principle is more capable of empirical verification than it was before.

The case of an experience may serve to illustrate the kind of argument which may be brought in support of this proposition. We decided that experiencing a given object is a complex, not because direct inspection reveals any complexity, but because experiencing has properties which we did not see how to account for on any other hypothesis. But although we found no difficulty in being acquainted with an experience, the most attentive introspection failed to reveal any constituent of an experience except the object. Thus if we were right in our analysis of experience, this instance affords a complete proof of our present thesis.

There is a class of arguments in favour of our thesis, derived from spatio-temporal divisibility, which can only be used, if at all, with great caution. It may be argued that, owing to the infinite divisibility of space and time, any sense-datum which has spatial or temporal extension must consist of an infinite number of parts. If so, these parts are necessarily impercepti- ble, since they must be too small for our senses. It will follow, therefore, that every sense-datum which has spatial or temporal extension must be a complex of an infinite number of constituents with which we are not acquainted. Such an argument, however, involves an unduly naïve transference of infinite divisibility from physical space and time to the spaces and time of the senses. In regard to time, we have already seen how physical time can be logically constructed without assuming that a continuous duration actually consists of temporal parts. And in regard to space, it would seem that a similar construction is possible. There seems no reason to assume that, say, a uniform patch of colour occupying a small visual area must be complex; it is quite possible that the infinite divisibility of physical space results from a logical construction out of data which are not infinitely divisible. We shall consider this question at a later stage; for the present it is only introduced to show that any argument, as regards our thesis, which is based upon the infinite divisibility of space and time, requires close scrutiny and is very likely to be invalid.

Cases of apparently continuous change, however, although it is *possible* to account for them on the assumption that they are composed of a large finite number of parts, each internally constant, are much more naturally and easily accounted for on the hypothesis that they are complexes whose constituents we are not aware of. The usual arguments of philosophers who dislike analysis are largely drawn from such examples as the experience of a visible motion. There seems here to be change without any succession of separate states composing the change. Such experiences are only what is to be expected, if we can be acquainted with a complex, such as a motion, without being able to have more than inferential knowledge of its constituents. And the way in which many sensible objects which at first appear simple are found to be complex as soon as they are attended to is much easier to account for on the hypothesis that at first they had constituents with which we were not acquainted than on any other hypothesis known to me.

The analysis of a complex raises different problems according to the nature of the complex. In particular, it makes a difference whether the complex is one which is determinate as soon as its form and its constituents are given, or whether it is one which even then may be one of several. We call a complex "logically possible" when there is a corresponding proposition. Thus for example "A precedes B" and "B precedes A" are both logically possible, though at most one of them can be actual. What is relevant to the problem of analysis is whether, with the same constituents and the same form, several complexes are logically possible, not whether several are actual. In general, in a complex of n terms, there are various "positions" in the complex, corresponding to different relations (generally each of them functions of the relating relation) which the constituents have to the complex. A complex may be called "symmetrical" with respect to two of its constituents if they occupy the same position in the complex. Thus in "A and B are similar", A and B occupy the same position. A complex is "unsymmetrical" with respect to two of its constituents if the two occupy different positions in the complex. An unsymmetrical complex is called "homogeneous" with respect to the unsymmetrical constituents if a logically possible complex results from interchanging them; otherwise it is called "heterogeneous". Thus "A is before B" is unsymmetrical and homogeneous with respect to A and B. But "A is a constituent of α" is unsymmetrical and heterogeneous with respect to A and α. It is only in cases of unsymmetrical homogeneity that a complex is not determined by its form and its constituents.

The relating relation in a complex is always heterogeneous to all the other constituents. Let us denote the other constituents by $x_1, x_2, x_3, \ldots y_1, y_2, y_3,$ 10 $\ldots z_1, z_2, z_3, \ldots,$ where all the x's are homogeneous, and all the y's, and all the z's, but no x is homogeneous with a y or a z, and no y with a z, and so on. If we denote the relating relation by R, the complex may be denoted by

$$R(x_1, x_2, x_3, \ldots y_1, y_2, y_3, \ldots z_1, z_2, z_3, \ldots, \ldots) \ .$$

There will be certain permutation-groups among the x's which leave the complex unchanged. E.g., taking only three constituents, we might have the complex the same for all permutations, or the same when x_1 and x_2 are interchanged, but altered if x_3 is moved, or the same so long as the cyclic order is the same but changed if it is reversed, or changed by any permutation. Only the first of these cases gives *complete* symmetry as regards the x's.   20 The complex is not wholly determinate when its form and its constituents are given, unless it is completely symmetrical with respect to each set of homogeneous constituents. The further formal study of this topic belongs to the theory of permutation-groups, and need not concern us here.

We can now consider the main question which concerns us in regard to analysis, namely: what sorts of facts must we perceive in order to be able to analyze? In order to make sure that we are concerned with a genuine case of analysis, it is necessary to make sure that, in the case considered, the complex is really *given*. Perhaps the best cases are sensational: the discovery of constituents of the visual field, for example; or—to take a case where   30 analysis is harder—the discovery of overtones in a note.

In regard to such cases as the selection of one object out of the visual field, the word "analysis" is often misused. Mere selective attention, which makes us aware of what is in fact part of a previously given complex, without making us aware of its being a part, is not analysis. Chairs and tables, we are told, originally form part of one visual continuum; but even if this be so, we can become aware of them as separate objects without performing any act that can properly be called analysis. All that is necessary is that the area of attention should be narrowed, not that we should realize, as analysis requires, the relation of the new partial objects to the old total one.   40

A whole which is to be analyzed must presumably be first itself an object of attention. The "sensible continuum" of psychologists endeavouring to undo the work of thought is itself a late discovery of thought. All primitive consciousness is selective; the "sensible continuum", which rejects nothing, is the product of the psychologist's scientific impartiality, to which, for the moment, all selection is abhorrent. The visual field as a whole, for example, is not given. No doubt the part of it that we attend to is surrounded by other visual objects, but they grow gradually dimmer, and cannot be regarded as forming altogether a single given object. Before we have anything that can be properly called analysis, we must have a complex given to begin with as an object of attention, whose parts, if they are discovered, do not *merely* become fresh objects of attention, but are recognized as being its parts. Hence if we are to consider analysis of a visual object, we must take an object small enough for the whole of it to be near the centre of our visual field. It will serve to fix our ideas if we take some object as simple as is compatible with the possession of easily distinguishable parts, say a capital T printed in black on a white ground, and ask ourselves what happens when we analyze this object into separate but related constituents.

A capital T will ordinarily be seen as one object whose parts are not separately attended to; indeed, if it forms part of a word, the word will usually be the smallest unit of attention, except to some one who is only just learning to read. We can, however, attend to the T alone, and we can easily perceive that it consists of a vertical and a horizontal stroke, the former being below the latter and beginning approximately at its middle point. All this is so easy to see that it is difficult to realize what a complicated process is involved. The fact that each of the two strokes can be further analyzed, of course introduces further complications; but for the present we will ignore this fact, since it seems possible to regard the two strokes as the primary constituents of the T. Let us call the vertical stroke a and the horizontal stroke b, and let the particular T be called γ. Then the two facts that a is part

of γ and that b is part of γ must obviously be known if γ is to be analyzed. But here we come upon a difficulty. Do we first reach the judgment "a is part of γ", or do we first become acquainted with the complex "a-part-of-γ", and thence arrive at the judgment "a is part of γ"? This raises problems which will be explicitly discussed in connection with self-evident judgments; but our present difficulty can be made plain without much anticipation of what is to be said later. If we first perceive the complex "a-part-of-γ", it would seem as though the very process of analysis which we are endeavouring to explain must be performed in order to pass from this to the explicit judgment "a is part of γ"; thus this judgment, which was to be merely one step in the process of analysis, will itself involve as much analysis as it was to have helped to explain. This method of explaining analysis is therefore impossible. But the view that we begin with the judgment, without first perceiving the complex "a-part-of-γ", leaves it inexplicable how we come to know the judgment, which is certainly not obtained by inference from any other judgment. It would seem, therefore, that the complex "a-part-of-γ" must be perceived in a different way from that in which γ was originally perceived, i.e. it must be perceived *as* a complex, where the interrelated parts are present to consciousness, and not merely discoverable by subsequent attention.   10

There would seem, therefore, to be two kinds of perception of a complex, namely "simple perception", which does not involve acquaintance with the parts, and "complex perception", where the complex is seen *as* a complex of interrelated parts. But if this is the case, then we need not begin our complex perception with the complex "a-part-of-γ", but may begin it at once with γ: there will be a way of perceiving γ as "a-R-b", where R is the relation between a and b in virtue of which they form the complex γ. Let us see whether this suggestion will give a tenable theory of analysis.

Taken in an extreme form, the above theory will involve a very great difficulty, namely: How shall we know that γ, the object of simple percep-   20
tion, is identical with a-R-b, the object of complex perception? This difficulty is so great that I think the theory cannot be entertained unless in a form which makes it appear at least possibly soluble.

I think the solution must be sought by a further use of the relation of *attention*. The difference between simple and complex perception seems to depend upon the number of objects of attention simultaneously present. We spoke earlier as though attention always had *one* object, but this appears to be not the case. When we perceive our T as an unanalyzed whole, it is one object of attention; but if another T is placed alongside of it, we shall naturally say that we see "two T's". In this case, there seem to be two   30
simultaneous objects of attention. And similarly when we have analyzed our T into a vertical and a horizontal stroke, we shall have two objects of attention, namely the two strokes, where before we had only one, namely the T. We may therefore suggest that *complex perception consists in acquaintance with a whole combined with attention to its parts*. It will be natural to say, conversely, that simple perception of a complex consists in attention to the whole combined with acquaintance with its parts. If this is the case, the problem of analysis is merely the problem of transferring attention from the whole to the parts. Let us examine this theory.

In order to be able to know that the object of complex perception is   40
identical with the object of simple perception, we only now require to be able to know that an object to which we attend at one moment is identical with an object with which, at another moment, we have inattentive ac-quaintance. It is certainly the case that we can know this. We have the

experience constantly of becoming attentive to an object which we know was already given in sense before we became attentive to it. This is possible because we can attend to an experience which is in the immediate past, even if we did not attend to it or its object when it was present; and thus we can come to know that the object of this past experience was identical with the object of our present attention. But for this possibility, we could not know that attention selects some but not all of the objects of acquaintance. There is, therefore, no difficulty, on our present theory, in accounting for our knowledge that the object of complex perception is the same as the object of
10 simple perception.

Our present theory seems to accord well with what introspection reveals concerning such an operation as the analyzing of our T. At first, when we attend to it as a whole, our attention has *one* object before it, namely the T; but it would seem that even then we are acquainted with the two strokes of which it is composed, although we are not attending to them. Afterwards, however, it is the two strokes to which we are attending: we are still acquainted with the T, but not attending to it. Finally, in order to know that the T consists of the two strokes, we require a complex perception in which we attend to the T and to the two strokes simultaneously, or in which we
20 perceive the identity of the T with which we have acquaintance in the complex perception and the T to which we attend in the simple perception. All this seems quite in accord with introspection.

It is obvious, however, that if complex perception is to account for analysis, it must not consist merely in simultaneous attention to two objects. Nor can we be content with this together with acquaintance with the complex. Complex perception must involve some consciousness of the relatedness of the two objects. In the complex perception of our T, in which we attend to the two strokes, we are acquainted with their spatial relatedness, though we may not be attending to it. But here the very problem we set
30 out to solve meets us again, not one step advanced towards solution. What is consciousness of the relatedness of two terms? It must not be identified with the simple perception of the complex, for it involves attention to the two terms, which simple perception of the complex does not. The question is: Is there any difference between the complex and "the relatedness of the two terms"? Can we distinguish between the T and the two strokes in a certain spatial relation to each other? We can see why we should use different phrases, because one is appropriate when we are attending to the complex, the other when we are attending to the terms. But apart from this subjective difference, is there any difference between the objects denoted by these two
40 phrases?

I think we must say that there is no difference whatever between the two objects. When there are two strokes in a certain spatial relation, there is a T; the T consists of these two strokes so related; the T *is* these two strokes so

related. I do not think it is possible to discover a vestige of difference between the two objects. Hence in being aware of the relatedness of the two strokes, we are aware of the T. (When I speak of the "relatedness" I do not mean the abstract relation.) It would seem, therefore, that, throughout the process of analysis, we are acquainted with the complex and with its constituents, and that what changes during the process is only the direction of our attention. (I am not denying that we are sometimes acquainted with a complex without having any acquaintance with its constituents; but obviously so long as this state of things lasts, analysis cannot begin.) At first, our attention is directed to the complex; then it passes to the *terms* which are   10
constituents; before the analysis is complete it must pass also to the *relation* which is a constituent. A complete analytic acquaintance with a complex involves acquaintance with the complex together with attention to the terms and the relation which constitute it.

But however *necessary* the above process may be to analysis, it is still not *sufficient*. We might attend to terms and a relation, and be acquainted with a complex, without the terms and the relation being the constituents of the complex. We want to reach a proposition of the form: "This complex consists of these terms so related." This requires a simultaneous attention to the complex and its constituents. In order to judge: "This T consists of two   20
strokes at right angles", we must attend to the T and the strokes and their relation—at least, so it would seem. Thus so far nothing effective has been done in the way of analyzing analysis.

Before proceeding, let us pause to take stock of what has already been said in this argument. Selective attention alone, we decided, is not analysis; what is to be analyzed must be given as one object of attention. To analyze a given complex γ, it would seem that we must know such facts as "a is part of γ". But since this cannot be an inferred judgment, it must be derived from perception of a complex "a-part-of-γ". This requires us to admit a "complex perception" of a complex, as opposed to a "simple perception". These   30
two differ, it would seem, in respect of attention. In both, we are acquainted with the complex, but we only *attend* to it in simple perception, whereas in complex perception of the complex it is the parts that we attend to.

According to the above, our *acquaintance* with the complex is of the same nature in simple perception and in complex perception. Now complex perception was forced upon us by the instance "a-part-of-γ", where the terms and the relation are certainly given. It would seem to follow that, since we can know that a term is part of a complex, all acquaintance with complexes must involve acquaintance with their parts to the extent involved in naming them by means of their parts. That is to say, we do not have to   40
deal with a problem of which the proper statement is "how do we analyze γ (where γ is a given complex)?", but "how do we analyze aRb (where a and R and b are known by acquaintance)?" It would seem that, when a complex

is given, mere attention will enable us to give it a complex name, such as "aRb", though this attention to the constituents is sometimes a very difficult mental feat, and in certain cases is one which seems never to have been performed by human beings.

The question "how do we analyze aRb?" may seem almost childish. It may be said that all the real work of analysis is done when a complex name of this kind has been given. As a matter of psychological experience, this is no doubt true: the effort of attention involved in passing from simple to complex perception of a complex may be very great. But this raises no new
10 epistemological problem. There are, however, certain problems remaining. There are purely logical problems, such as: How is the meaning of a complex name such as "aRb" determined when the meanings of the simple constituent names are known? What is meant by "a is part of aRb"? What is meant by "aRb consists of a and R and b united in the general form of a dual complex"? And if these questions were answered, there would remain the question as to how we come to know the truth of such propositions.

These questions, important as they are, I shall not now discuss. Partly they do not belong to theory of knowledge, partly they belong to a later portion of the subject, partly, wherever they belong, I do not know the
20 answer to them.

On the subject of synthesis, there is very little to be said. The psychological process of synthesis, when it is possible, consists of attending simultaneously to certain terms and a certain relation until we perceive a complex formed of those terms so related. The epistemological problems raised by this process are the same as those raised by analysis, and do not require separate discussion.

Chapter III
Various Examples of Understanding

IN CHAPTER I, we considered only one particularly easy case of under-standing a proposition. In this chapter, we have to consider various examples and difficulties.

The first example I wish to discuss is the understanding of propositions which have no constituents, i.e. where all the constituents have been replaced by apparent variables, and the pure form alone remains. We may take as the type of such propositions the proposition "something is some-how related to something", i.e. "there are an x and a y and an R such that x has the relation R to y" or "xRy is sometimes true". This is much the same proposition as "there are dual complexes". It will be remembered that, according to our theory of the understanding of propositions, the pure form is always a constituent of the understanding-complex, and is one of the objects with which we must be acquainted in order to understand the proposition. If this be true, then the understanding of the pure form ought to be simpler than that of any proposition which is an example of the form. Since we desired to give the name "form" to genuine objects rather than symbolic fictions, we gave the name to the "fact" "something is somehow related to something". If there is such a thing as acquaintance with forms, as there is good reason to believe that there is, then a form must be a genuine object; on the other hand, such absolutely general "facts" as "something is somehow related to something" have no constituents, are unanalyzable, and must accordingly be called simple. They have therefore all the essential characteristics required of pure forms.

Again, the view that a pure form is something which must be understood in order to understand a proposition which has this form, is satisfied by this view of what a form is. To say that we must have acquaintance with "something has some relation to something" if we can understand "this has this relation to that" is by no means a paradox, and seems in fact a truism. What tends to obscure this truism, is the absence of *attention* to the form in ordinary thinking. We may say broadly that it is easier to attend to particulars than to universals, and to universals than to logical forms. But many mental facts involve *acquaintance* with objects to which no *attention* is given except in more abstract kinds of thought. For example, the kind of thought which consists in understanding an atomic proposition containing particulars in some relation involves *attention* to its substantial constituents and *acquaintance* with its form, while the kind of thought which we are at present endeavouring to perform involves *attention* to the form, and *acquaintance* with the characteristic concepts of molecular propositions, such as are involved in the words "and", "or", "not". But *attention* to these concepts will not be required until we come to analyze molecular thought.

It is for this reason that, although the understanding of "something has some relation to something" is logically simpler than the understanding of (say) "*A* is before *B*", it is nevertheless later in the order of psychological development, which appears to be mainly determined by the nature of the objects to which *attention* is given. But since we are concerned mainly with the work of logical analysis of cognitive complexes, we need not be alarmed by an inversion of the psychological order, and we must, therefore, regard the understanding of "something has some relation to something" as logically preceding the understanding of any particular proposition asserting a particular case of a dual relation.

The case of a pure form is instructive for several reasons. To begin with, although "something has some relation to something" is a proposition, and is true, it is nevertheless simple; hence understanding and believing, in this case, must both be dual relations. The question therefore arises: How do they differ from acquaintance? And what becomes of the opposition of truth and falsehood in such cases? Again, there are more purely logical questions (which, however, we must leave on one side), such as: How can an object be at once simple and a "fact", in the sense in which a "fact" is opposed to a simple particular and is the sort of object whose reality makes a proposition true? Why, if pure forms are simple, is it so obviously inappropriate to give them simple proper names, such as John and Peter? These logical questions can no doubt be answered, but for our purposes the epistemological questions are more pressing. Those that concern belief, however, must be postponed until we have discussed belief. We are left, therefore, with the question: Is there any difference between understanding a pure form, such as "something has some relation to something", and being acquainted with this object? And if not, is this kind of understanding radically different from the understanding of propositions concerning particulars?

I do not think there is any difference between understanding and acquaintance in the case of "something has some relation to something". I base this view simply on the fact that I am unable introspectively to discover any difference. In regard to most propositions—i.e. to all such as contain any constants—it is easy to *prove* that understanding is different from acquaintance with the corresponding fact (if any): Understanding is neutral as regards truth and falsehood, whereas acquaintance with the fact is only possible when there is such a fact, i.e. in the case of truth; and understanding of any proposition other than a pure form cannot be, like acquaintance, a two-term relation. But both these proofs fail in the case of a pure form, and we are therefore compelled to rely on direct inspection, which, so far as I can discover, reveals no distinction, in this case, between understanding and acquaintance. Whether, in regard to such propositions, there is any distinction between *belief* and acquaintance, is a question which must be postponed until we reach the discussion of belief.

It is, perhaps, better to give the name "understanding" than the name "acquaintance" to the awareness of such propositions. In the classification of mental facts, various different considerations may be brought to bear. There is, first, the logical form of the mental fact concerned—whether it is a dual or treble or quadruple ... relation. Then there is the logical character of the objects concerned. Then, when both the form of the mental fact and the logical character of the objects are given, there is the actual relating relation which is a constituent of the fact. In considering these grounds of classification, one would naturally have expected that the form of the mental fact would be the source of the most fundamental divisions. In obedience to this supposition, we began with dual relations, acquaintance, attention, etc.; and when we came to propositional thought, it seemed at first as if the change was due to the fact that here the cognitive relations concerned were multiple. This whole point of view, however, is erroneous. The classification of mental facts by the logical character of the objects involved turns out to be far more important than their classification by their own logical form. In connection with analysis, we had occasion to consider a multiple relation called "complex perception"; but although multiple, this relation had more affinities with ordinary acquaintance and attention than with propositional thought, just because its objects were the same as those of ordinary acquaintance and attention. So with regard to understanding: if our analysis in Chapter I of this Part bore even a distant resemblance to the right analysis, different understandings have very different logical forms. Understanding of "something has some relation to something" is a dual complex; understanding of "something has the relation R to something" is a treble complex; understanding of "a has the relation R to b" is a quintuple complex. The distinctive thing that groups these understandings together is the fact that they all involve the pure form of dual complexes among their objects. For this reason, the simplest possible cognitive relation to a pure form belongs to propositional thought, rather than to the kind of consciousness which we considered in Part I.

We thus arrive at a hierarchy of cognitive relations, according to the "abstractness" of the most abstract of the objects involved. If this most abstract object is a particular, we have sensation, imagination, or memory; if a universal, we have conception and complex perception; if a logical form, i.e. a fact containing no constants, we have understanding, belief, disbelief, doubt, and probably many other relations; if the logical form is molecular, we have also inference and the knowledge of the propositions of logic and their instances. The one cognitive relation which seems to preserve a fairly constant character throughout is *attention*, though as the object grows more abstract, attention grows progressively more difficult; perhaps attention to an abstract object is only psychologically possible in combination with attention to other more concrete objects, the number of which tends to increase as the abstract object grows more abstract.

It is an interesting question whether the degree of abstractness of an object can be precisely defined. As a first step towards such a definition, we may distinguish stages of specification in passing from a given abstract object towards a particular which is, in some sense, an "instance" of it. (A complex containing one or more particulars and no general terms, such as "all" or "some", is to be reckoned as a particular.) Thus a universal is removed only one stage from a particular: there are atomic complexes which are particulars of which it is a constituent. But a logical form, even an atomic form, is not a constituent of the particulars which have that form. Thus it is, in some sense, further removed from the particular than the universal is. Finally, a molecular form is not even the form of any actual particular: no particular, however complex, has the form "this or that", or the form "not-this". The question of the definition of "degrees of abstractness" belongs to logic, and we shall not here pursue it further. We shall not assume that this notion has any precisely known meaning, but shall merely employ it as affording suggestions concerning the order of our inquiry.

The importance of the understanding of pure form lies in its relation to the self-evidence of logical truth. For since understanding is here a direct relation of the subject to a single object, the possibility of untruth does not arise, as it does when understanding is a multiple relation. This topic, however, belongs to a later stage: it will be considered again in connection with self-evidence.

The understanding of a pure form is, according to our theory, a logically simpler fact than the understanding of a proposition which is an instance of the form; it is, moreover, part of what actually occurs when we understand an instance. Nevertheless, it is obvious that, in psychological fact, the isolated understanding of a pure form is more difficult than the understanding of an instance. The reason of this seems to be that pure forms are fugitive to attention, and that attention to them is not readily *caused* except by means of instances. This question belongs to psychology, and is only relevant because it might seem, if neglected, to afford an objection to our view that the understanding of a pure form is simpler than the understanding of an instance. It is necessary to realize, once for all, that what is simpler is not necessarily, or even usually, easier than what is more complex. Attention, as a psychical occurrence, is governed by biological considerations: particulars may be good to eat or likely to kill us, and therefore it is useful to pay attention to them; but logical forms are not edible or hostile, and attention to them is not a cause of longevity. This sufficiently explains why it is only a few eccentric persons, unusually relieved from the struggle for existence, whose attention wanders to such unimportant objects.

The next kind of understanding which calls for consideration is the kind which is only one degree less abstract than the understanding of pure form—I mean, the understanding of propositions which assert that there are instances of a given universal. To avoid any difficulties other than those that we wish to discuss at the moment, let us take the case of a symmetrical dual relation, and consider the proposition "something is similar to some- 10 thing". Only two objects are involved in this, namely similarity and the pure form. The understanding of the proposition must, therefore, be logically simpler than the understanding of "A is similar to B". We might express the proposition in the form: "Something has to something a certain relation, namely similarity." Here the pure form occurs explicitly, and all that is added is the words "namely similarity". It would seem, if our general view is correct, that it must be an error to regard our proposition as asserting that there are complexes such as "A is similar to B", since the propositions that deal with complexes are less simple than the proposition which we are examining. What our proposition involves must be a relation of similarity to 20 the form. Thus understanding of such a proposition is a three-term relation of the subject, the form, and the relation. The necessity for the form is, perhaps, rather easier to see in this case than in the case of a proposition such as "A is similar to B". If we try to say simply "there are similarities", it is at once obvious that what is meant is more fully expressed by "something has to something the relation of similarity"; and in these words the form occurs explicitly.

It is to be observed that, if it is *true* that something is similar to something, then there is a single *fact* expressed by these words, and that towards this fact we may have a dual relation of the nature of an acquaintance. This may 30 be called *perceiving* the fact. It cannot be identified, in this case, with understanding the proposition, as it could in the case of the pure form, because here the understanding of the proposition is a three-term relation, and the proposition is of a form which does not logically guarantee truth. And for the same reasons, perceiving the fact cannot be identified with *believing* the proposition.

It might, no doubt, be questioned whether such a proposition as "something has the relation R to something" would have any meaning if it were false, i.e. if, in fact, there were no instances of R whatever. This question is not altogether an easy one. The instances that are discoverable of relations 40 which never hold are none of them atomic relations, that is to say, they are not single relations at all, but results of logical combinations of several relations. It would seem that we never become aware of a single relation

except by the help of instances; hence even if there are any relations of which there are no instances, we can hardly expect to know that there are. But in saying that there are relations of which there are no instances, what we should naturally suppose that we mean would be "there are propositions of the form xRy for values of R for which such propositions are false whatever x and y may be". But with our definition of "proposition", we cannot have any reason to believe that there is a proposition which has never been understood, and we cannot know that a proposition of the form xRy has ever been understood, if the R is one of which there is no instance, and with
10 which consequently no human being is acquainted.

This instance suggests, what is also suggested by many other considerations, that our definition of a proposition is inadequate. It seems plain that "aRb" has "meaning" provided R is the right sort of entity, and that the question whether R is the right sort of entity depends upon its logical character, and not upon the more or less accidental question whether instances of it actually occur. Also, when we say that "aRb" has "meaning", it seems impossible to maintain that we *mean* that somebody understands it. If it has meaning, it *can* be understood; but it still has meaning if it happens that no one understands it. Thus it would seem that we must find
20 some non-psychological meaning for the word "proposition". If such a meaning can be found, a given R may enter into *propositions* of the form "aRb", even if there are no complexes of this form, and no one ever thinks about R. In such a case, the proposition "something has the relation R to something" will have meaning but be false. Thus this kind of proposition does not have the necessary truth that belongs to propositions such as "something has some relation to something."

It follows from our general theory that the understanding of either of the two propositions "a has the relation R to something" and "something has the relation R to b" is simpler than the understanding of the proposition "a
30 has the relation R to b". In the case of a symmetrical relation, the above two propositions are identical, but in the case of an unsymmetrical relation they are different. The fact that the understanding of the above two propositions is simpler than that of "aRb" may be brought into relation with the question of "sense". Let us now consider the understanding of propositions involving non-symmetrical relations; and for the sake of illustration let us take the case of time-sequence. The proposition "something is before something" is, I think, identical with the proposition "something is after something". But "a is before something" is different from "a is after something". Thus we may begin by the understanding of these two
40 propositions.

We decided that, in "a-before-b", a has to the complex a relation which is one function of the relation "sequence", and b has a relation which is another function of the same relation. If we call the complex γ, we will say

"a is earlier in γ" and "b is later in γ", to express these relations. Then "a is before something" means "a is earlier in some complex"; and "a is after something" or "something is before a" means "a is later in some complex". In order to understand this proposition, we need acquaintance with a and "earlier" and the general form of such complexes as "a is earlier in γ". This is the same as the form of "a is part of γ"; it is the form of dual complexes consisting of a simple and a complex (i.e. a relatively simple and a relatively complex). Such complexes, in the language of the preceding chapter, are heterogeneous and unsymmetrical; being heterogeneous, they do not give rise to the difficulties connected with sense. Thus these difficulties have 10 been eliminated from the understanding of "a is before something", but only by introducing the notion of a *complex* in which a is earlier.

The proposition "a is before b" must be interpreted as meaning "there is a complex in which a is earlier and b is later". This involves the word "and", which is one of the words that indicate *molecular* complexes. We cannot therefore deal, at present, with the understanding of this proposition, which must be postponed until we come to deal with molecular propositional thinking. This result is curious, for the *complex* "a-before-b" is atomic, and yet the corresponding *proposition* is not atomic. It is not very easy to believe that such a difference can exist, and perhaps some other theory of "sense" 20 can be found which would avoid such a difference.

But for the difficulty of naming, i.e. of knowing when to speak of *before* and when of *after*, we could explain the understanding of "a is before b" more simply than was done in the above account. We may say: There are two understanding-complexes consisting of the subject, the form "x and y in a relation", sequence, A and B, and of these two complexes, one is called the understanding of "A is before B", while the other is called the understanding of "B is before A". But the difficulty here is that we cannot tell which is to be called which. In order to know this, we must be able to explain the separate word *before*, and this can only be done by the help of a 30 sequence-complex.

A better theory of how to understand relations with sense could probably be found; meanwhile, the above theory seems at least not logically refutable.

Much remains to be said on the subject of the understanding of propositions, but I shall pass on to belief, disbelief, and doubt.

Chapter IV
Belief, Disbelief, and Doubt

S O FAR, WE have been concerned with non-dualistic attitudes towards objects, and with non-dualistic properties of objects. We now at last reach dualistic attitudes and properties: the dualistic attitude of belief and disbelief in this chapter, and the dualistic property of truth and falsehood in the next.

When I speak of "belief", I mean the same kind of fact as is usually called "judgment". I prefer the word "belief", because it has much more definitely the suggestion of a particular dated event which may be studied empirically by psychology. The word "judgment", on the other hand, is generally employed by idealists, and serves to blur the distinction between psychology and logic. Judgment, according to the idealists, is fundamental in logic, and yet is something which could not subsist if there were no minds, though it is independent of this or that mind. We cannot, in our philosophy, give a statement of this view which shall be *primâ facie* tenable. But we may illustrate it by defining a judgment as the fact "that such-and-such a proposition is believed". I.e. the judgment "*A* succeeds *B*" will be the fact (if it is a fact) "There is a subject which believes that *A* succeeds *B*". I do not suggest that this is what idealists mean by judgment, but that it is the nearest approach to their view which is formally possible to us. In this form, it presupposes a discussion of belief, and therefore it is to belief that we must now turn our attention.

The word "belief" is, in one respect, less suggestive of correct views than the word "judgment". It is obvious that judgment involves the sort of thing that is true or false, and not merely single existents, such as tables and chairs. "Belief", on the contrary, is very often supposed to be possible towards the very same kind of objects as can be given in sensation. "Seeing is believing" embodies a confusion from which many philosophers have suffered. This confusion, for example, underlies Hume's account of Belief,[1] which begins with the words:

> The idea of an object is an essential part of the belief of it, but not the whole. We conceive many things, which we do not believe;

[1] *Treatise*, Bk. I, Part III, Section VII.

from which it passes naturally to the well-known conclusion:

> As belief does nothing but vary the manner, in which we conceive any object, it can only bestow on our ideas an additional force and vivacity. An opinion, therefore, or belief may be most accurately defined, A LIVELY IDEA RELATED TO OR ASSOCIATED WITH A PRESENT IMPRESSION.

This account assumes that the object of a belief is the same as the object of an idea. The confusions which have led to this assumption are many, but as it has had disastrous consequences in philosophy, it is important that a sufficient number of them should be set forth.

In the first place, our theory admits that there is a kind of mental fact, called "understanding a proposition", which does not involve the opposition of belief or disbelief, but shares the neutrality of mere acquaintance, and yet consists in a complex of exactly the same form as a belief. When a certain subject understands a proposition and when he believes it, the two complexes differ, according to us, solely in the fact that understanding and believing are different relations: belief in the proposition results from substituting believing for understanding in the complex which is the understanding of that proposition. But understanding a proposition, if our previous theory on this point bore any resemblance to the truth, is a complex of a wholly different form from acquaintance, except in the one case of understanding a pure logical form. Both belief and understanding, except in this one case, have not a single object, the "proposition", but have a plurality of objects, united with the subject in a *multiple* relation. Thus although there is a neutral attitude, namely understanding, which gives complexes having the same logical form as beliefs, yet this attitude is fundamentally different from that of "having an idea of an object", which, in any sense in which we can admit it as fundamental, must be identified with acquaintance, whether of sensation, memory, or imagination, or (in the case of a universal) of conception.

Hume defends himself against the accusation of confusing judgment with conception in a footnote to the above-quoted definition of belief. He says:

> We may here take occasion to observe a very remarkable error, which being frequently inculcated in the schools, has become a kind of established maxim, and is universally received by all logicians. This error consists in the vulgar division of the acts of the understanding, into *conception, judgment* and *reasoning*, and in the definitions we give of them. Conception is defined to be the simple survey of one or more ideas: Judgment to be the separating or uniting of different ideas: Reasoning to be the separating or uniting of different

ideas by the interposition of others, which show the relation they
bear to each other. But these distinctions and definitions are faulty in
very considerable articles. For *first*, 'tis far from being true, that in
every judgment, which we form, we unite two different ideas; since
in that proposition, *God is*, or indeed any other, which regards
existence, the idea of existence is no distinct idea, which we unite
with that of the object, and which is capable of forming a compound
idea by the union.... Whether we consider a single object, or several;
whether we dwell on these objects, or run from them to others; and
in whatever form or order we survey them, the act of the mind
exceeds not a simple conception.

The example of existential propositions, which Hume adduces in the
above passage, has no doubt been a potent ally of the theory which identifies
judgment and conception. William James, whose neutral monism, we
found, involves this same identification, has also, I think, been led to it by
the consideration of existential judgments. We seem to judge that objects of
sense exist, and to add nothing, in so judging, to what is already given in
sense. But the fact is that the whole conception of existence is the result of a
confusion between descriptions and true proper names. Of an actually given
this, an object of acquaintance, it is meaningless to say that it "exists". But
the very same word which, at one moment, is used as a true proper name for
a given object, may be used the next moment as a description. We may say
"this exists", meaning "the object of my present attention exists", or "the
object I am pointing to exists". Here the word "this" has ceased to function
as a proper name, and has become a descriptive word, in which an object is
described by its properties, and the question may be raised whether there is
such an object, since descriptions to which nothing corresponds can be
made up. When we say "the King of England exists" we are not uttering a
tautology, or adding nothing to "the King of England"; we are saying that
there is a person who may be so described. "The King of France does not
exist" is true, but would be a contradiction if "exists" added nothing to "the
King of France". In a word, "*A* exists" adds something to "*A*" if "*A*" is a
description, and is meaningless if "*A*" is a true proper name.

The importance of this result, as regards our present question, is very
great. A great many propositions can be thrown into an existential form:
"some men are wise" may be put into the form "wise men exist"; "the son
of Philip conquered Persia" may be put into the form "the son of Philip who
conquered Persia existed", and so on. Those propositions that cannot be put
into this form can be regarded as denying existence: "all men are mortal"
can be stated as "immortal men do not exist", and so on. So long as it was
thought that the "existence" spoken of in such propositions was something
which could be significantly predicated of an actual given particular, it was

impossible to answer Hume's contention that existence adds nothing to the subject, and therefore it was impossible to show how propositions differ from concepts, and how belief differs from acquaintance.

Closely connected with this question of existence is the question of the relation of the grammatical subject to the real analysis of a proposition. In "immortal men do not exist", there is not an entity, "immortal men", of which non-existence is predicated. "Immortal men" is merely a grammatical constituent of the phrase, which does not correspond to any actual constituent of the proposition, of which a more correct expression is "whatever is human is not immortal". And this applies to many grammatical subjects which pass muster as complex concepts. In such cases the complexity is usually *propositional*, i.e. the propositions which grammatically have these subjects are really molecular, and involve a separation of what appeared to be the parts of one complex subject. Thus it is wholly misleading to suppose that, wherever a grammatical subject is formed by the combination of names of concepts, there must be a complex concept formed by combining the concepts whose names occur in the grammatical subject. This misleading supposition has quite unduly extended the general belief in complex concepts among philosophers, and has obscured the part played by relating relations in forming complexes, as well as the fundamental difference between a concept and a proposition.

In the course of the discussion on belief, Hume mentions the understanding of propositions which are not believed. He says:

> Suppose a person present with me, who advances propositions, to which I do not assent, *that* Caesar *dy'd in his bed, that silver is more fusible than lead, or mercury heavier than gold*; 'tis evident, that notwithstanding my incredulity, I clearly understand his meaning, and form all the same ideas, which he forms. My imagination is endow'd with the same powers as his; nor is it possible for him to conceive any idea, which I cannot conceive; nor conjoin any, which I cannot conjoin.

It might be thought, from this passage alone, that Hume would distinguish between conjoining ideas and conceiving a new complex idea, but this would be a misinterpretation, as appears from the context. But what does appear from the above passage is, that Hume conceives thought as conjoining the *ideas* of objects, while what makes a thought *true* is a conjunction of the *objects*. This gives, of course, a short and easy way of defining falsehood, and of distinguishing between propositions and the facts that make them true. For us, owing to our rejection of "ideas" as a *tertium quid* between subject and object, no such explanation is possible. When we judge that mercury is heavier than gold, *mercury* and *heavier* and *gold* must themselves

be constituents of the event which is our judging: we cannot say that we bring our idea of mercury into some relation with our idea of gold, but that mercury and gold do not themselves stand in the "corresponding" relation. It is curious that authors who believed in ideas were not troubled as to this correspondence of relations. The relation between my idea of mercury and my idea of gold cannot be "heavier", since my ideas are not supposed to have weight. Nor can it be the *idea* of "heavier", since that is not a relation. It must, therefore, be some new relation, in some way related to "heavier", subsisting between my ideas, but not necessarily present to my conscious-
10 ness when I judge. This, however, is obviously absurd. My judging obvi-ously consists in my believing that there is a relation between the actual objects, *mercury* and *gold*, not in there being in fact a relation between my ideas of these two objects. Thus the whole nature of belief must necessarily be misunderstood by those who suppose that it consists in a relation between "ideas", rather than in the belief of a relation between objects. *Something* subjective must be so inseparably bound up with belief as to make it impossible to regard it as a dual relation to a single object, since, if we did so regard it, falsehood would become inexplicable. But the champions of "ideas" introduce the subjective element at the wrong place. It comes in
20 with the subject itself, and is more important than in the case of acquaint-ance because, since belief is a multiple relation, it does not involve any *one* object corresponding to the belief and not involving the subject. But the several objects which are *constituents* of the belief are just as free from reference to the subject as the one object in the case of acquaintance— except, of course, when the belief happens to be about the subject.

What William James says about belief in his *Psychology* is, from our point of view, much the same as what is said by Hume. At the beginning of his discussion[2] he says:

Everyone knows the difference between imagining a thing and
30   believing in its existence, between supposing a proposition and acquiescing in its truth. In the case of acquiescence or belief, the object is not only apprehended by the mind, but is held to have reality. Belief is thus the mental state or function of cognizing reality.... *In its inner nature, belief, or the sense of reality, is a sort of feeling more allied to the emotions than to anything else.*

What has been said already as regards existential propositions applies unchanged to the first part of the above quotation. "Cognizing reality", according to our theory, would more aptly describe acquaintance than belief. Is mistaken belief cognizing of unreality? Are there not beliefs which

40 2 Chap. XXI, "The Perception of Reality", Vol. II, p. 283.

are in no way existential? Is not the whole conception of "existence" inapplicable to just the objects of which we are most certain, namely those given in present acquaintance? And are not imagined objects also "something", with a "reality" of the kind appropriate to such objects? I shall not again enlarge on these questions, but shall pass at once to the *emotion* of belief.

As regards the "emotion" of belief, the only thing that needs to be understood here is that, however real and important it may be as a psychical fact, it does not concern epistemology, and must be noticed only to avoid the confusions which might result from its unobserved intrusion, like an unde-   10
sirable alien whose photograph is furnished to the authorities at the frontier. There is an emotion of conviction, capable of many degrees, arising with judgments that hold our unwavering assent, or with perceptions that put an end to a doubt. But this emotion, though it often accompanies judgments, does not by any means constitute them; in fact, it may be exactly the same in the case of two different judgments. A person of a patriotic disposition will feel exactly the same emotion of conviction in entertaining the belief that his country is the best in the world, as in entertaining the belief that his school or club is the best in the country. The emotion is not a relation to the objects of the belief, but a fresh mental fact, caused, perhaps, by the belief, but   20
quite distinct from it. And it would seem that its intensity is not really proportional to our certainty, but to the energy with which we repel doubt. No one feels much of this emotion in contemplating the facts in the multiplication-table, because doubt of them is not conceived to be possible. But religious and political beliefs, just because they are denied or doubted by so many, rouse the utmost fervour of conviction. Such beliefs, however, are not those which a philosopher should take as his model.

The failure to make a sufficiently radical distinction between belief and presentation has caused difficulties in the theory of erroneous belief, and has led to attempts to introduce the dualism of true and false among objects.   30
There are supposed, by some, to be real and unreal objects, or true and fictitious objects. Such distinctions are always due to the intrusion of belief under various disguises, or at least of the understanding of propositions. One of the most deceptive disguises is the grammatical subject: the golden mountain, or the round square, are thought to be objects, because they can be grammatical subjects; they are therefore declared to be "unreal" objects. All this rests, as already explained, upon a wrong analysis of propositions. The dualism of true and false, with all its attendant distinctions, presupposes propositions, and does not arise so long as we confine ourselves to acquaintance, except, possibly, in the case of abstract logical forms; and   40
even here there is no proper dualism, since falsehood is logically impossible in these cases. But conversely, when we are dealing with belief, we must always bear in mind the dualism of true and false, and avoid theories based

on the unduly cheerful view that all beliefs are true. This very simple test condemns many theories of belief.

The analysis of belief, as was said earlier, must be precisely analogous to the analysis of understanding a proposition. The same constituents enter into a complex of the same form when a proposition is believed and when it is understood. The only difference is that believing is one relation and understanding is another. It is obvious at once that precisely similar arguments apply to both cases, and that any modification which might prove necessary in the theory of the one would be equally necessary in the theory of the other. That the difference lies only in the relations is obvious from the criterion which we applied in distinguishing e.g. sensation from memory: understanding a given proposition is different from believing it, and yet there is no difference as regards the objects involved in the two cases.

We have now to consider a new relation, namely *disbelief*. The main question here is whether disbelief is an unanalyzable relation, or is really belief in the contradictory. When I disbelieve that A and B are similar, am I believing that A and B are not similar, or am I in a new relation, of the same form as belief, to the same objects as when I believe that A and B are similar? It is difficult to find arguments on this point, and it would seem that we must rely on inspection. On the ground of inspection, I hold, though with no great certainty, that disbelief is a new unanalyzable relation, involving merely rejection of the proposition disbelieved, and not consisting in acceptance of its contradictory.

This conclusion may be somewhat reinforced by considering *doubt*. It is fairly obvious, I think, that we may have many degrees of uncertainty concerning a proposition. We may feel nearly sure that it is true, evenly balanced between its truth and its falsehood, nearly sure that it is false; and between these attitudes any number of others seem possible. If all these are, as I believe, indefinable relations to one proposition, it would seem natural to place complete disbelief at the bottom of the scale, to balance complete belief at the top. It would be absurd to pretend that such an argument is conclusive, but when it agrees with inspection it may be allowed to count for something.

The word *doubt* is perhaps not the best word to describe the attitudes intermediate between complete belief and complete disbelief. "Doubt" suggests a vacillation, an alternate belief and disbelief, which is not the attitude I mean to characterize. I mean an attitude, which may be perfectly stable, in which there is an element of uncertainty—what we should describe by saying "I think so, but I don't feel sure". There are, of course, degrees of disbelief as well as degrees of belief; we can combine them in a scale of "certainties", where full belief and full disbelief come together at the top, while complete suspense of judgment comes at the bottom. But even complete suspense of judgment belongs with belief and disbelief rather than with the mere understanding of a proposition. It is a determinate attitude in regard to belief and disbelief, and represents the result of an attempt to decide between the two. Complete uncertainty is obviously a different state of mind from that of a person to whom the yes-or-no attitude has not suggested itself, just as inability to answer a question which has been put is different from not thinking of the question as one to be answered if possible.

Belief, therefore, may have degrees of certainty, from zero up to absolute conviction; and if disbelief differs, as it seems to do, from belief in the contradictory, then disbelief also has degrees of certainty exactly corresponding to those of belief. It must be held that relations which differ in degree are different relations; therefore each degree of belief is a fresh relation, differing from every other degree; and if disbelief is independent, then there are also many relations of disbelief, corresponding to the different degrees. All these relations give rise to complexes having the same form, and therefore no new problems of logical analysis arise out of their multiplicity.

Chapter V
Truth and Falsehood

IN THIS CHAPTER, I shall first state the positive theory which appears to me to have the best chance of being correct, and shall then defend it, partly by answering objections to it, partly by raising objections to other theories.

Truth and falsehood are properties of beliefs and disbeliefs; also of "propositions" in the sense defined in Chapter I; also, derivatively, of sentences and symbols which express beliefs, disbeliefs, or propositions. In order to avoid verbiage, we will confine ourselves to the *truth* of a *belief*. All the essential problems are raised by this case, and a few words on the other cases at the end of our discussion will suffice.

It is obvious that the question whether a belief is true depends only upon its *objects*. If I believe that A is the father of B, the truth of my belief depends upon the physical relations of A and B, and in no way upon me. The belief is true when the objects are related as the belief asserts that they are. Thus the belief is *true* when there is a certain complex which must be a definable function of the belief, and which we shall call the *corresponding* complex, or the *corresponding fact*. Our problem, therefore, is to define the correspondence.

If our complex is one which is completely determined by its constituents, the problem is simple. That is to say, let our belief be

$$\mathcal{J}(S, F, x_1, x_2, \ldots x_n)$$

where $\mathcal{J}$ is the relation "belief" or "judgment", S is the subject, F the form, and $x_1, x_2, \ldots x_n$ the objects of the belief; and suppose that F is a form such that there cannot be more than one complex having this form and composed of given constituents; suppose, that is to say, that no complex having this form is homogeneous and unsymmetrical with respect to any of its constituents. Then, if there is any complex whose constituents are $x_1, x_2, \ldots x_n$, there can be only one; this one may therefore be defined as the *corresponding* complex. If there is such a complex, the belief is true; if not, it is false. A belief of this sort may be called *non-permutative*, because no different belief results from permuting the objects. Thus we may say:

A non-permutative belief is said to be *true* when there is a complex

144

consisting of its objects; otherwise it is said to be *false*.

We have now to show how to extend this definition to permutative beliefs. We are confronted here by a problem which may be stated as a linguistic problem, but is really of great importance in logic. In linguistic terms, our problem is:

> *When several complexes can be formed of the same constituents, to find a method of distinguishing between them by means of words or other symbols.*

In logical terms, our problem is:

> *When several complexes can be formed of the same constituents, to find* 10
> *associated complexes unambiguously determined by their constituents.*

By "associated complexes", here, I mean complexes which exist whenever the original complexes exist, and not otherwise.

In connection with difference of sense in unsymmetrical dual relations, we have already dealt with a particular case of this problem. Before attacking the problem in its general form, let us repeat, briefly, what has been said about the particular case.

The two complexes *A*-before-*B* and *A*-after-*B* are composed of the same constituents, namely *A* and *B* and sequence, combined in the same form. The words *before* and *after* differ, and are not names for the relation of 20 sequence, which is unique, not twofold. What then is meant by *before* and *after*? In the complex *A*-before-*B*, which we will call γ, *A* has one "position" and *B* another; that is to say, *A* has one relation to γ and *B* has another. We may say *A* is *earlier in* γ, and *B* is *later in* γ, where *earlier in* and *later in* are heterogeneous relations, and therefore complexes in which they are the relating relations are completely determined by their constituents. Then "*A*-before-*B*" is the name of that complex (if any) in which *A* is earlier and *B* is later; while "*A*-after-*B*" is the name of that complex (if any) in which *A* is later and *B* is earlier. The distinction between *earlier* and *later* is indefinable, and must be simply perceived. It may be said, of course, that "*A* is 30 earlier in γ and *B* is later in γ" is composed of the same constituents as "*A* is later in γ and *B* is earlier in γ". But these are both *molecular* complexes, and the atomic complexes which enter into them are different; the identity of constituents only appears when we carry our analysis further, to the constituents of the atomic complexes. And this remoter identity of constituents does not raise the problems with which we are at present concerned.

The proposition "There is a complex in which *A* is earlier and *B* later" is one which contains four constituents, namely *A* and *B* and earlier and later. This is a molecular proposition, whose atomic constituents are different from those of the proposition which results from interchanging A and B. Moreover, each of the atomic constituents is non-permutative. It is thus that the two words *before* and *after* become distinguishable, and that language is able to discriminate between the two complexes that may be formed of A and B and sequence.

We may now generalize this solution, without any essential change. Let γ be a complex whose constituents are $x_1, x_2, \ldots x_n$ and a relating relation R. Then each of these constituents has a certain relation to the complex. We may omit the consideration of R, which obviously has a peculiar position.
10 The relations of $x_1, x_2, \ldots x_n$ to γ are their "positions" in the complex; let us call them $C_1, C_2, \ldots C_n$. As soon as R is given, but not before, the n relations $C_1, C_2, \ldots C_n$ are determinate, though unless R is non-permutative, it will not be determinate which of the constituents has which of the relations. If R is symmetrical with respect to two constituents, two of the C's will be identical. If R is heterogeneous with respect to two constituents, two of the C's will be incompatible. But in any case there are these relations $C_1, C_2, \ldots C_n$, and each constituent has one of these relations to γ.

Unless the relation happens to be non-permutative, γ is not determined when we are given R and $x_1, x_2, \ldots x_n$. But it is determined when we are
20 given also the positions of $x_1, x_2, \ldots x_n$, i.e. when we are given

$$x_1 C_1 \gamma \cdot x_2 C_2 \gamma \cdot \ldots \cdot x_n C_n \gamma \, .$$

Thus there is one complex at most which has the given constituents in the given positions. We may describe this as "*the* complex γ in which R is the relating relation, and $x_1 C_1 \gamma, x_2 C_2 \gamma, \ldots x_n C_n \gamma$". In ordinary language, the positions of the constituents in the complex are indicated by inflexions, by the order of words, and by the use of pairs of terms such as *before* and *after*. But such methods of expression, except in the case of pairs like *before* and *after*, are not sufficiently explicit for a symbolism which is to be a help in philosophical analysis. If such symbolism is to be obtained, it must be by
30 means of our relations $C_1, C_2, \ldots C_n$ or something analogous.

It is to be observed that the relations $C_1, C_2, \ldots C_n$ are not determined by the general *form*, but only by the relation R. So far as the general form "xRy" is concerned, the position of A is the same in "A-before-B" as in "A-after-B". It is only after the relation R has been assigned that positions can be distinguished.[1] Although, therefore, the various possible positions are determinate when R is given, they are not functions of R. That is to say, there are not n relations $T_1, T_2, \ldots T_n$, such that, whatever R may be, C_1 has the relation T_1 to R, C_2 has the relation T_2 to R, and so on. $C_1, C_2, \ldots C_n$ are a

---

[1] The position of R, unlike that of the other constituents, *can* be assigned relatively to the
40   form; this is what enables us to speak of it as the relating relation.

system of relations, determinate when R is given, but requiring to be simply recognized in each case, and not describable in general terms.

When $C_1, C_2, \dots C_n$ are given, conversely, R is determinate. Thus our complex γ can be described unambiguously without mentioning R, as simply "the complex γ in which $x_1 C_1 \gamma, x_2 C_2 \gamma, \dots$ and $x_n C_n \gamma$". If we have decided, once for all, that when R is the relating relation, the term which has the C_1-position is to be mentioned first, then the one with the C_2-position, and so on, we can denote the complex γ by the symbol

$$R(x_1, x_2, \dots x_n) \ .$$

But this symbol, though it has a certain notational convenience, is not sufficiently explicit for philosophical purposes. For philosophical purposes, the symbol

$$(\imath \gamma) \cdot x_1 C_1 \gamma \cdot x_2 C_2 \gamma \cdot \dots x_n C_n \gamma$$

is preferable, because it does not make a more or less concealed use of the spatial order of $x_1, x_2, \dots x_n$.

By means of the above account of "positions" in a complex we can give a non-permutative complex associated with the complex γ, namely: "There is a complex α in which $x_1 C_1 \alpha, x_2 C_2 \alpha, \dots x_n C_n \alpha$". Here "$\alpha$" is an apparent variable. Instead of the one relation R, we now have the n relations $C_1, C_2, \dots C_n$. The new complex is molecular, and is non-permutative as regards its atomic constituents $x_1 C_1 \alpha, x_2 C_2 \alpha, \dots x_n C_n \alpha$; also each of these atomic constituents is non-permutative because it is heterogeneous. Whether any difficulties arise from the fact that the molecular complex is still permutative with respect to the constituents of its atomic constituents, is a question which must be left until we come to deal with molecular thought. But it seems fairly evident that no difficulties can arise from this fact.

The necessity for the above process is concealed by the fact that it is presupposed in ordinary language. When different complexes can be composed of the same constituents, it is essential that language should distinguish between them. Hence language cannot well express what is prior to these distinctions. If we are to name one out of several complexes composed of the same constituents, we can only do it by means of some such process as the above; hence such a complex always has rather a description than a complex proper name. But since names for unsymmetrical relations always take account of difference of sense, it is very hard to express what can be known before this distinction is taken into account.

Having now obtained a non-permutative complex associated with any given complex, we can see how to avoid the difficulties, as regards the theory of truth, which arise from permutativeness. In stating a proposition, there is

always an indication, whether by the order of words, or by inflexions, or in some other way, as to the positions which the objects are to occupy in the "corresponding" complex whose existence is asserted. It follows that what is directly asserted is the non-permutative associated complex. When we assert "A is before B", we are asserting "there is a complex γ in which A is earlier and B is later." It is impossible to find a complex name which shall name this complex γ directly, because no direct name will distinguish it from "B-before-A". Complex names, in fact, are only *directly* applicable to non-permutative complexes, where the mere enumeration of simple names
10 determines the complex meant. Thus the only propositions that *can* be *directly* asserted or believed are non-permutative, and are covered by our original simple definition. Owing to the above construction of associated non-permutative complexes, it is possible to have a belief which is true if there is a certain permutative complex, and is false otherwise; but the permutative complex is not itself the one directly "corresponding" to the belief, but is one whose existence is asserted, by description, in the belief, and is the condition for the existence of the complex which corresponds directly to the belief. In the case we took, if I have a belief whose objects appear verbally to be R, x_1, x_2, ... x_n, there are really other objects,
20 expressed by inflexions, order of words, etc., and what I am really believing is: "There is a complex γ in which $x_1C_1\gamma$, $x_2C_2\gamma$, ... $x_nC_n\gamma$". In the sense already explained, this proposition is non-permutative, and, except in so far as belief in molecular propositions introduces new complications, our first simple account of the correspondence which constitutes truth applies to it. The actual complex γ itself, whose existence is affirmed by description in our associated molecular complex, cannot be directly named, and does not directly correspond with our belief, or with any possible belief. We may have acquaintance with it, and we may have descriptive knowledge of it; but a complex name for it must be descriptive, not simply composed of the
30 names of the constituents. Belief only reaches it at the second remove, by corresponding with its associated non-permutative complex. It is this that makes permutative complexes so difficult to deal with and such fertile sources of error.

Our positive theory of truth has now been enunciated. It remains to consider the arguments for and against it.

It must be confessed, to begin with, that its range is as yet very limited. We have seen that, when a complex is permutative, there is no atomic belief corresponding to the complex; and although we have seen how a belief is possible which is not atomic and is true when there is such a complex and
40 false otherwise, yet this belief, because it is not atomic, raises problems which we do not wish to consider until the next Part. Thus the only beliefs with which we can deal at present are those whose truth demands the existence of an atomic non-permutative complex. This includes beliefs in

subject–predicate propositions, and in propositions asserting symmetrical relations or relations which, where they are not symmetrical, are also not homogeneous. We may revert to our former instance, "*A* and *B* are similar". The belief in this proposition is *true* when there is a complex whose constituents are *A* and *B* and similar, while otherwise it is *false*. This is the theory which we have to examine.

The chief ground in favour of such a theory must always be that it satisfies our feelings as to what is obvious concerning truth, and that it adds nothing except analysis. Now if we ask: "When is the belief that *A* and *B* are similar *true*?" the only possible answer is: "When *A* and *B* are similar"—that is to say, when there is a complex composed of *A* and *B* and similarity. It would seem, therefore, that we have merely expressed what is obvious. This is the whole of the positive argument in favour of our theory. What remains to be done is to show that other proposed theories are inadequate, and that any objections we can discover to our theory can be answered.

Theories of truth other than the above may be divided into two classes, according as they do or do not define truth by a *correspondence*. Of theories which do not define truth by a correspondence, we may distinguish two, as being specially wide-spread, namely (1) the coherence-theory, and (2) pragmatism. Of theories which use a correspondence, there are two sorts, namely those which (as ours does) define falsehood by the absence of a correspondence, and those which define falsehood by correspondence with an object of a different kind from the object which corresponds in the case of truth. Of the first sort, we shall not consider other forms than ours; of the second sort, there are two, namely those which admit real and unreal objects for the correspondence, and those which admit true and false objective "propositions" for the correspondence. We have thus four theories to consider successively.

(1). *The coherence-theory* is generally advocated—for example in Mr. Joachim's *Nature of Truth*—in connection with a logic wholly different from ours. The chief arguments against it are arguments against the logic with which it is commonly associated; but we shall here assume these arguments, and confine ourselves to a statement and a refutation which assume our logic.

A certain relation of "coherence" is supposed given or defined—no matter how—between beliefs, this relation being symmetrical and transitive. It is then supposed that the relation of coherence holds between any two beliefs which belong to the field of the relation—in other words, that any two beliefs which are coherent with themselves are coherent with each other. Hence the field of coherence forms one group, of which any two members are mutually coherent. This group of beliefs is called *true*, while other beliefs are called *false*.

The coherence-theory is not stated in the above form by any of its advocates. I have, however, stated nothing beyond what is required to insure that all beliefs shall be divided into two mutually exclusive groups, the true and the false, together with the doctrine, accepted by all advocates of coherence, that any two true propositions are mutually coherent. We may therefore take the theory, in the form above stated, as a sufficient text for criticism.

The difficulty of the coherence-theory lies in pointing out any relation, not defined in terms of truth, which holds between every pair of true beliefs and between no pair of false beliefs. The beliefs in dreams may be mutually
10 coherent, in any sense of the word which seems admissible. It is true that they are not coherent with the beliefs of waking life; but that gives no reason why dreams should be rejected rather than waking life. If we knew of one belief which could be known to be true independently of coherence, we could regard the system of true beliefs as the system of beliefs cohering with that one; but if truth is to be *defined* by coherence, such a course is not open to us. If there is more than one group of coherent propositions, and if all true propositions form *one* group, then plainly coherence alone does not insure truth. Hence a false proposition must not be coherent even with itself. The coherence-theory in fact involves something very like the doctrine of pre-
20 Kantian rationalism, that all false propositions are self-contradictory. The only logic, however, which has so far proved adequate to producing this result, has, like the Djyun that fetched water, continued its work too long, and proved in the end that *all* propositions are self-contradictory. With the application of this result to the special case of the coherence-theory, we may leave this subject and pass on to our next theory of truth.

(2). *Pragmatism*, or at least the pragmatic theory of truth, may be defined as the theory that the truth of a belief is constituted by some characteristic of its consequences. This way of stating the theory is hardly fair to William James, in whom it was bound up with neutral monism, and with the view
30 that belief does not differ from "entertaining an idea" except emotionally. We have already discussed both these views; but one remark seems appropriate at this point. William James recognized "acquaintance" in the case of sense-perception, but not in the case of memory or imagination. He would not have said, as we should, that these always are acquaintance with *something*, though perhaps not with anything precisely similar to some sense-datum. Memory, imagination, and conception were, to him, indirect ways of cognizing sense-data: they were *true* when they were calculated to lead to expected sense-data, and *false* otherwise. The rest of his pragmatism, I think, grew from this root. But to us, this doctrine is impossible,
40 in virtue of our earlier discussions. We must, therefore, if we are to discuss any form of pragmatism at this stage, discuss a form which recognizes that a belief is a unique kind of mental fact, involving a different sort of relation to objects from any involved in presentation or in "entertaining an idea".

Let us endeavour to state the pragmatic theory of truth in a form at once as general and as precise as possible. It is not necessary to say that the consequences of the belief must be "good"—we will merely suppose that there is *some* property α which they have if the belief is true but not if it is false. There is very considerable difficulty as to what is meant by "consequences". It seems fairly plain that *logical* consequences are not what is meant. The theory boasts of being psychological, and therefore cannot take account of logical consequences which perhaps no one perceives; moreover logic itself must submit to the pragmatic test. Thus the consequences intended must be *causal*. Now all statements as to the effects of particular events must have a sort of rough-and-ready on-the-whole in-the-long-run kind of character, because in any given case the normal effect may be prevented by something else. We cannot say that a belief is false in a particular instance, because its normal effect has been prevented by some exceptional extraneous circumstance. We shall have to say, therefore, that belief in a certain proposition is true when, as a rule, in the long run, its consequences, on the whole, have the property α which we regard as distinctive of truth.

Concerning this theory, it is, in the first place, utterly incapable of precision. How many exceptions are allowed by "as a rule"? How great a lapse of time is involved in "the long run"? How great a majority of consequences having the property α is required by "on the whole"? Yet without these qualifying phrases the theory becomes immersed in paradox. Again, how are we to discover the effects of a belief? A few immediate effects may be fairly obvious, as for example when a man faints on hearing himself sentenced to death. But remoter consequences must always be very conjectural, and yet without taking account of them the theory will not work. A third objection is that the theory, contrary to the expressed intention of its advocates, becomes, after all, a very complicated and very arbitrary form of correspondence-theory. A belief is *true* when there is a certain corresponding *fact*, namely that its consequences (with the necessary qualifications) have the property α. But why a belief should be called "true" in this case, it is impossible to see. If there were any objection to correspondence-theories in general, it would apply to this theory as to others; but the objections of vagueness, difficulty of discovery, and arbitrariness are peculiar to this theory. Almost the only argument alleged in its favour is, that it is supposed to afford an easy criterion of truth; how false this supposition is, the above brief remarks have, I hope, sufficed to show.

(3). I come now to theories of twofold correspondence, i.e. of correspondence of true propositions with one sort of object, and false propositions with another sort of object. And first we will consider the view that true and false propositions correspond respectively with real and unreal objects. This view seems bound up with the existential view of judgment. If every proposition is of the form "*A* exists", then a proposition is true when its subject is real, and false when its subject is unreal. There must, on this view, be unreal objects, because propositions of the form "*A* exists" certainly are sometimes believed when they are false, yet, on this view, there must be an object *A*, or else the proposition "*A* exists" would be meaningless, which it plainly often is not. Hence we can divide objects into real ones, which exist, and false ones, which do not. True propositions are those asserting the existence of real objects, and false propositions are those asserting the existence of unreal ones.

10   There is, to begin with, a trivial objection, which is that the theory, as above stated, forgets negative propositions. In their case, truth implies the unreality of the subject, while untruth implies its reality. This addition is easily made to the theory, but the serious objections remain unaffected by it.

The objections are (a) that many propositions are not existential, (b) that when a proposition is existential, its grammatical subject does not represent an actual constituent of the proposition, which, when rightly analyzed, contains no constituent corresponding to the grammatical subject, (c) that there cannot possibly be such things as unreal objects, and that any theory which assumes or implies that there are must be false. All these objections

20   have been explained at length already, and need not detain us now. It is only necessary to observe that what has been said about unreality applies unchanged when it is called by some title of politeness, such as "being for me" or "being for thought", which represent merely the vacillating regret in pronouncing sentence of non-existence on life-long friends. And the same applies to any philosophy which believes, in any ultimate way, in a realm of "possibles" which are not actual. The view that the possible is something, but not quite so much something as the actual, and that error consists in mistaking the possible for the actual,[2] is only rendered possible by the wrong analysis of sentences which results from confusing descriptions with

30   proper names.

(4). A second form of twofold correspondence theory regards beliefs as having objects of a different kind from the objects of presentations, and divides the objects of belief into two classes, the true and the false. In order to differentiate this theory from its predecessor, we must suppose that propositions (as we will call the objects of belief) are not fictitious when they are false, any more than when they are true: there are such objects in either case. Meinong, whose theory approximates to this type, in the end falls under our previous heading, for he seems to hold that, although "there are" false propositions, yet false propositions do not subsist, whereas true prop-

40   ositions do subsist. The theory in question has, however, been held; for

---

2 A view which seems to be that of Professor Stout, "The Object of Thought and Real Being", *Proceedings of the Aristotelian Society*, 1910–11.

example, there is an author who states it in the following terms: "There are, apart from and independently of judgment, true and false propositions, and either kind may be assumed, believed, or disbelieved."[3] This theory has an engaging simplicity, and it is hard to find conclusive arguments against it. Nevertheless, I believe it is false.

The arguments in favour of the view which are employed in the above article all depend upon the assumption that, when a molecular proposition which is true appears to contain atomic constituents which are false, the apparent atomic constituents must really be constituents. We cannot enter into this question until we come to Part III; for the present, I shall assume by anticipation that a different analysis of such molecular propositions is possible.

The arguments against the view we are considering are not of a very definite kind. There is a strong natural conviction that when a judgment is false there is not, in the world of objects, *something*, pointed to by the judgment, which there is when the judgment is true. Most of the ways of giving effect to this natural conviction are demonstrably false, but the way advocated in the first part of this chapter is, so far as I know, not demonstrably false. Again, it is very difficult to believe that there are objective falsehoods, which would subsist and form part of the universe even if there were no such thing as thought or mind. But the chief objection is that the difference between truth and falsehood, on the theory in question, has to be accepted as ultimate and unanalyzable, whereas it seems obvious that the difference between truth and falsehood must be explicable by reference to *fact*, i.e. to what is actually in the universe whatever we may see fit to believe. I do not pretend that these arguments are logically compelling; they seem, however, sufficient to make us prefer, if possible, a theory which dispenses with objective falsehoods. And to me, now, it seems obvious, as a matter of inspection, that belief is a multiple relation, not a dual relation, so that belief does not involve a single object called a "proposition". But I should not insist upon this argument if it stood alone.

There are a variety of objections which may be urged against our account of truth and falsehood. Most of these involve questions which concern molecular propositions, and which therefore must be postponed. There are, however, three kinds of objections which may be briefly considered at this stage. (1) It may be said that the correspondence between belief and fact is arbitrary in our account. (2) It may be asked how truth and error can ever be distinguished if our account is correct. (3) It may be said that, after all, there must be non-mental "propositions" as opposed to complexes, and that therefore beliefs had better be interpreted as dealing with propositions.

(1). Is the correspondence of belief and fact arbitrary in our definition?

---

3 "Meinong's Theory of Complexes and Assumptions (III)", *Mind*, n.s. No. 52, p. 522.

The word "arbitrary" is not a very easily definable word. But the feeling underlying the question may be made definite as follows: The word "truth" has a known meaning, in the sense that, if we understand a belief, we understand also the proposition that the belief is "true". Hence it is not open to us to give any definition we choose of the word "true", and defend ourselves on the ground that definitions are merely verbal conventions. What we call a definition of truth is really an *analysis* of it, and the analysis must commend itself to us as an analysis of what we were already meaning by "truth". Now it may be said that our definition fails in this. It may be said that we might equally have taken any other complex as the one which must exist if our belief is to be true. In fact, the association of belief and complex may be said to be too external in our definition. I do not think this is the case. Where non-permutative complexes are concerned, *the* complex formed of the objects of our belief seems as intimately associated with our belief as anything purely objective can be; and it seems quite evident that the truth or falsehood of a belief depends on something purely objective. Where permutative complexes are concerned, our process of obtaining associated non-permutative complexes was rather elaborate, and no doubt open to objection. One special objection is that, in order to regard the associated complex as non-permutative, we have to regard its atomic constituents, $x_1C_1\gamma$, $x_2C_2\gamma$, etc., as really its constituents, and what is more, we have to regard the corresponding propositions as constituents of the proposition "there is a complex γ in which $x_1C_1\gamma$, $x_2C_2\gamma$, etc." This seems to demand a mode of analyzing molecular propositions which requires the admission that they may contain false atomic propositions as constituents, and therefore to demand the admission of false propositions in an objective sense. This is a real difficulty, but as it belongs to the theory of molecular propositions we will not consider it further at present.

(2). It may be asked how truth and error can be distinguished if our account is correct. We might retort by asking how they can be distinguished if any other account hitherto given is correct. Pragmatism, which prides itself on its supposed capacity for dealing with this question, is really, as we have seen in this chapter, in a much worse position than we are. Monistic idealism maintains a view from which it follows that we cannot know the truth of anything until we know the truth of everything. The inductive philosophy has never been able to explain how it ascertained the validity of inductive inference. And so on. But a *tu quoque* is not a very desirable form of argument, and I think a better reply is possible.

To begin with, we have contended that it is possible to have acquaintance with a complex. Seeing A and B together, we may have acquaintance with the complex "the similarity of A and B". This will, on our theory, assure us of the truth of the belief that A and B are similar. Thus our form of correspondence-theory, together with our doctrine of the direct perception of complexes, seems unusually fitted to account for the possibility of belief which is *knowledge*, and for the way in which perception gives rise to such belief.

It must be admitted, however, that no belief can amount to *knowledge* unless some beliefs are *self-evident*, in the sense that they are certainly true and are not inferred from other beliefs. The belief that *A* and *B* are similar, when we are directly acquainted with the similarity of *A* and *B*, will be a case in point. The conception of self-evidence is fundamental in distinguishing *knowledge* from *belief* and from *true belief* (which is not necessarily knowledge). Although we have dealt with belief and with truth and falsehood, we have not yet dealt with knowledge, in the sense of knowledge of truths, as opposed to knowledge of objects, which is acquaintance. In a "theory of knowledge", it may seem strange to have postponed the consideration of knowledge so long. But in fact "knowledge" is a difficult and complicated concept, and many preliminaries are required before it can be successfully studied. In the next chapter, we shall begin this study by the consideration of self-evidence.

(3). The last of the above objections to our theory, namely that non-mental "propositions" are, after all, indispensable, belongs to logic, not to theory of knowledge. It is, to my mind, much the most serious of the three objections, and much the hardest to meet. I do not profess to be able to answer all the arguments in favour of "propositions" in this sense. I can only say that, to me personally, no such entities are visible, and the admission of such entities—which must be capable of falsehood as well as truth—runs counter to the rejection of unrealities, fictions, and mere possibilities which seems to me, on general grounds, necessary and vital to all sound philosophy. Until, then, the arguments in favour of non-mental "propositions" are presented in some more unanswerable form than any now known to me, I shall continue to reject them, and to believe that the apparent reasons in their favour are fallacious, even if I cannot always detect the fallacy.

Chapter VI
Self-Evidence

THE SUBJECT OF self-evidence is one of the most perplexing in the whole of Epistemology. Logic, psychology, and metaphysics all have something to contribute to it, but their various contributions are *primâ facie* conflicting. It is easier to see that there must be such a thing as self-evidence than it is to see what it is. The endeavour to define self-evidence brings to a head the conflict between the objectivity of truth and the subjectivity of belief by which the scepticism of every age has been
10 nourished. I do not pretend to be able to decide this secular conflict. But we shall find it not without interest and profit to explore the strength and weakness of the opposing forces.

The broad definition of self-evidence is that it is *knowledge which we possess independently of inference*. So defined, it might include knowledge of single objects by acquaintance; but although such knowledge is important in connection with self-evidence, it does not raise the problems which we have to discuss, and is therefore better excluded from the definition. We shall add, therefore, that self-evident knowledge is to be knowledge of *propositions*, not of single objects. In fact, since "acquaintance" serves for
20 cognition of single objects, it will be convenient to define "knowledge" as cognition of *propositions* only, and is therefore only occurring in *propositional* thinking.

The above definition would be admirable if we knew what is meant by "knowledge". But unfortunately the definition of "knowledge" is very difficult, and it seems highly probable that it must involve self-evidence: we may find that what we "know" is what is self-evident to us and what we infer from what is self-evident to us. "True belief" is not the definition of knowledge. We may have some wholly unwarrantable belief, such as that a particular horse will win the Derby, and our belief may turn out to have
30 been true; but it is not on that account to be called knowledge. Some people believe that Home Rule will do good, some believe that it will not do good; one party in this opposition must be believing truly, but it would be absurd to say that either party had knowledge. We require, in knowledge, some power of logical resistance, some more than subjective stability against doubt, which may easily be absent in beliefs that merely happen to be true. Now this resistance and stability would seem always to rest, in the last

resort, upon self-evidence. Hence we must define self-evidence without mentioning "knowledge" in our definition.

Self-evidence cannot be defined except by reference to a particular subject, or to some psychological conditions. If anything is self-evident, it must be the knowledge immediately derived from sense; yet this is not self-evident until the moment of sensation. Hence it is not the nature of the proposition concerned that determines whether it is to be self-evident, for the proposition is just the same before sensation as it is after. It may be that there are discoverable kinds of propositions which are *capable* of self-evidence, i.e. that all self-evident propositions belong to certain kinds and not to others; but actual self-evidence is a property which is relative to a given subject at a given moment, and does not belong to the proposition *per se*. It is better, therefore, to speak of self-evident *beliefs* than to speak of self-evident propositions.

A self-evident belief must be independent of inference. I do not mean that it may not be ascertained by means of inference in the first instance, but that, when ascertained, it must be able to stand by itself without the help of the inference. Many abstract beliefs are obtained by inference from particular cases, and then become luminously obvious in their own right. This luminous obviousness is a *sine quâ non* of self-evidence.

But besides this psychological characteristic, self-evident beliefs must also be *true*. We want self-evident beliefs to be the foundations of *knowledge*, and although some true belief is not knowledge, all knowledge is true belief. If we demanded merely the psychological characteristic of obviousness, we should escape all our difficulties, but we should not have found anything important to the theory of knowledge. We want, if possible, to find a class of beliefs which can be known to be true. For this purpose, we must so frame our definition of self-evidence as to insure that beliefs which have this characteristic are true.

We do not want, however, to include truth explicitly in our definition of self-evidence. If we do this, we are still left with the problem of discovering which of our beliefs possess truth and which do not, which is the very problem we hoped to solve by means of self-evidence. What we are seeking, therefore, is some characteristic, other than truth, which shall insure the truth of our beliefs without requiring that we should already know them to be true. Now luminous obviousness, by itself, seems, as a matter of empirical fact, to be insufficient to insure truth; at least, if it is to be sufficient, it must be very carefully defined and limited.

Let us now turn to the logical side of our problem. If there is to be knowledge, there must be knowledge which is independent of inference. This is the logical ground for saying that there can be no knowledge unless there is self-evidence. Let us see whether there is any escape from this necessity.

The vulgar imagine that, in a science, every term ought to be defined and every proposition ought to be proved. But since human capacity is finite, what is known of a science cannot contain more than a finite number of definitions and propositions. It follows that every series of definitions and propositions must have a beginning, and therefore there must be undefined terms and unproved propositions. The undefined terms are understood by means of acquaintance. The unproved propositions must be known by means of self-evidence.

It is sometimes sought to evade this conclusion by denying the linear character of inference. Some—notably the monistic idealists—argue that all perfected inference is circular. Others, who advocate an inductive empiricism, contend that the apparent order of inference is never the real order, but that the truth of the premisses is only rendered probable by the conclusions to which they lead. It is not necessary, for our present purposes, to deny either of these views, for neither, we shall find, enables us to dispense with self-evidence.

Let us take first the view that all inference is circular. In that case, to take a simplified scheme, we have (say) four propositions p, q, r, s, of which p implies q, q implies r, r implies s, and s implies p. We may also suppose, if we like, that every other possible implication holds between these propositions. But all this affords no ground for believing any of them: however many mutual implications there may be, they may all be false. What *is* proved is that all are true *if* any one of them is true. Thus if we have some reason, though not a conclusive one, for believing each separately, their mutual implications make the probability that they are all true greater than the antecedent probability that any separate one was true. This is important in many problems, but it is not relevant in our present problem. We must not, in our present problem, assume that we have an indubitable knowledge of propositions concerning probability, and thence prove that some propositions have a good chance of being true. The question as to how we acquired our indubitable knowledge of probability will have to be asked, and then we shall be forced ultimately to admit self-evidence as our only defence. The theory that all inference is circular, therefore, though it may alter the region in which self-evidence is to be sought, will not enable us to dispense with self-evidence as the ultimate source of our knowledge.

We have now to consider the inductive argument, that the premisses are rendered probable by the conclusions to which they lead, and are not really the grounds on which we believe the conclusions. This contention rests on a confusion between logical and epistemological premisses. Given a body of propositions which are all known to be true, or all known to be probable, and of which some are deducible from others, the best order, from a purely logical point of view, will be that in which there are the fewest and simplest premisses. But in theory of knowledge, where we wish to consider how these propositions are known, the order is likely to be quite different. Our premises will have to be self-evident, and it is not generally the case that the simplest logical premises are so evident as some of their consequences. It may happen that, as the inductive empiricist contends, the simplest logical premises are only rendered *probable*, not *certain*, by the self-evidence of the propositions which would be their consequences in a pure logical order. But this can afford no argument against self-evidence as the source of knowledge, since, if the whole body of propositions in question is to be accepted, self-evidence must belong to the propositions which are epistemological premises and which give inductive probability to the purely logical premis- 10 ses. Thus here again self-evidence remains epistemologically fundamental.

It may be said that the whole attempt to get behind belief to something more solid, and worthy to be called knowledge, is futile; that we believe and disbelieve at random, because we live a life of undisciplined impulse; but that, if we are seeking a philosophic detachment, we ought to realize that it is only to be found in a complete abstinence from belief, as from other forms of slavery to illusion. A less moralizing and more satirical scepticism may content itself with questions. How, it will ask, since you admit that you are sometimes wrong, can you know that you are not always wrong? How can you test beliefs except by other beliefs? And even if all your beliefs were 20 coherent in one logical whole, which they probably are not, what illumination assures you that the truth must be coherent and the coherent may be true? Why should not the world be incoherent? Why not regard belief as merely an ineradicable propensity of the human animal, like eating and sleeping?

To these questions there would seem to be no answer. The position of the sceptic who questions without denying is impregnable. All our arguments must appeal to some supposed common ground, something which the other side will admit; if nothing is admitted, argument ceases and refutation is impossible. The extreme sceptical position remains, therefore, one which is 30 philosophically tenable.

But the sceptical philosophy is brief; it begins and ends in questioning. By its nature, it cannot argue, or seek to establish any result, even its own tenability. Therefore its philosophical interest is soon exhausted, and we turn to the other hypothesis, according to which we do know some propositions. In short, we abandon the fundamentally questioning attitude, which is sometimes represented as alone truly philosophical, for the analytic attitude, which, in the main, accepts facts at their face value, and does not seek for a justification of the whole in something outside the whole. This attitude may not have any theoretical superiority over the other, but it at 40 least leads to a more complicated philosophy, and therefore claims a longer attention.

As soon as we adopt the analytic attitude, we are met by the fact that some

beliefs are recognized as erroneous, and that, therefore, some means of discriminating among beliefs is supposed to exist. It would seem that there must be logical grades among beliefs, and that those which survive the discrimination by which some are rejected must achieve a higher status than they had before. In short, within the system of beliefs, there must be means of giving more weight to some than to others, since without such means it would have been impossible to reject certain beliefs rather than others. If it could be shown that self-evidence, in some sense which insures truth, belongs to certain beliefs but not to all, the discrimination involved in
10 rejecting some as erroneous might be justified.

The necessity of self-evident beliefs if there is to be any knowledge is well stated by Meinong:[1]

In the circumstance that a conviction by no means guarantees the actuality of the proposition [Objektiv] which it apprehends, there lies a sort of danger for the whole of our knowledge. How then do we know about the actuality of the propositions in question? Obviously never otherwise than by judgments. But how do these judgments help us, if they in turn may be false just as easily as, perhaps more easily than, true? This does not, it is true, exclude the possibility of
20 judging truly. But if it depended only on chance, that once in a way, so to speak, the right judgment and the right proposition should come together, then in the end it could also be only a chance when a man holds a judgment which is true to be true. For the impulse, given with every judgment, to hold it to be true, belongs to false judgments no less than to true ones. Such consequences, which would be equivalent to abandoning all confidence in our judging, and so to the sacrifice of all knowledge, can only be avoided, as far as I see, by two presuppositions, first, that there are judgments in whose nature it lies to be true, secondly that we are capable of
30 recognizing the truth-nature in such judgments by means of judgments of the same nature.

Such judgments Meinong calls "evident", and he points out that it is evident that an evident judgment cannot be false. His view seems to be that "evidence" is an intrinsic property of certain judgments, and that judgments which have this property can be seen to have it by inspection, in fact that it is evident that they have it. By assuming that evident judgments are always true, we thus acquire a basis for distinguishing knowledge from mere belief. He spends little time on the analysis of evidence, but passes on to the enumeration of certain kinds of evident judgment.

40 1 *Über die Erfahrungsgrundlagen unseres Wissens* (Berlin, 1906), p. 32.

It should be observed that we cannot *prove* that evident judgments are true by appealing to the fact that it is evident that they are true. Such a proof would, of course, be a vicious circle. Evidence must be in itself a guarantee of truth, and cannot be used to prove that it is a guarantee. It must somehow lie in the nature of self-evidence that judgments which have this characteristic are free from the liability to error. Whether this is so, and how we can know it, are difficult questions. But before attacking these questions, it will be well to consider whether self-evidence can be analyzed, or whether there is some discoverable characteristic which is always associated with self-evidence.

Self-evidence may be regarded as consisting in some relation to acquaintance, or as a cognitive relation other than belief but implying it, or as a predicate of beliefs. Let us consider these views successively.

(1). It may be said that a judgment is self-evident when it is contemporaneous with acquaintance with the corresponding complex. For example, if we see a patch of red surrounding a patch of white, the judgment that the red surrounds the white will be self-evident. This view has the merit that it secures the truth of self-evident judgments while yet making their self-evidence discoverable by inspection. According to this view, all self-evidence consists in analysis of what is given: when (say) a complex aRb is given, the judgment that a has the relation R to b is self-evident.

That judgments made under the above circumstances are self-evident is, I think, true, and it seems possible to maintain that their self-evidence *consists* in their being so made. As Meinong points out, it must sometimes, if not always, be evident that a judgment is evident, and this condition, so far as I can see, is fulfilled if the above is taken as a definition. If b is a belief, it is suggested that "b is evident" means "b is simultaneous with perception of the corresponding complex". Hence the belief that b is evident will be evident if it is simultaneous with the perception of b's simultaneity with the perception of the complex corresponding to b. This may very well be the case fairly often, and therefore it may fairly often be evident that a judgment is evident.

There are, however, difficulties in the way of taking the above as a definition. Take the question of correspondence. We say that a judgment is evident if we perceive the corresponding complex. We do not say that it is evident if we perceive its correspondence with a certain complex, but only if we perceive the complex which does in fact correspond, though we may not know that it does. But this seems to leave self-evidence altogether too extraneous a property of judgments. It might quite well happen that we did in fact perceive the corresponding complex, without the judgment feeling different from other judgments, unless perception of the corresponding complex causes the judgment to have some intrinsic property. But if any such intrinsic property is so caused, it may be capable of other causes. And I think it is undeniable, on grounds of inspection, that evident judgments do feel different from other judgments.

Take, again, the analytic judgments which we considered in Chapter II of this Part, such as "a is part of the complex aRb". If we derive the evidence of such judgments from perception of the corresponding complex, we have to suppose that, if they are to be evident, we must perceive the complex "a-part-of-aRb". This view, though perhaps not definitely refutable, makes analysis very complicated, and introduces great difficulties into the theory of the correspondence which defines truth.

10 Such evident judgments as knowledge of the laws of contradiction and excluded middle would, I think, be very hard to fit into our formula for self-evidence. But as they, even in particular cases, introduce molecular propositions, we will not consider them at present. Let us leave the question whether our suggested definition of self-evidence is adequate undecided until we have considered other possible definitions.

(2). We may hold that self-evidence is constituted by a special propositional relation, different from belief but implying it. Just as attention is a kind of intensified acquaintance, so, it may be suggested, self-evidence is a kind of intensified belief. It may be said that, beyond ordinary belief, there 20 is a kind of absolute certainty, leaving no possible room for doubt. Of course the obvious objection to this view would be that whatever we happen to be believing at the moment appears to us to be certain at the moment, if we have a real belief and not merely a degree of doubt which is all but certainty. But it would be said in reply that most belief is a mere unreflective assent, and that there is another kind of belief, which is capable of surviving critical scrutiny and adverse argument, because it makes what is believed strictly indubitable.

Let us examine this view, first in the interests of the sceptic, then in the interests of the believer in knowledge.

30 The view is one which the sceptic will welcome warmly. "Assuming", he will say, "that there is some hyper-dogmatic kind of judgment, which resists all our efforts to bring it under the domain of rational doubt, all the phenomena are fully accounted for. It is intelligible, to begin with, why the delusion that we possess knowledge is so widely diffused. Let a man once become the victim of an indubitability, and he will become utterly and absolutely convinced that he possesses a piece of truth from which no mere argument shall divorce him. If he drinks too much and thinks he sees rats, if he eats too little and thinks he sees angels, if he eats and drinks normally and thinks he sees tables and chairs, he is equally obsessed by indubitabilities."

40 But it is also intelligible why the sceptic, though still victimized by the indubitable in his unprofessional moments, is able, on a calm survey, to perceive the groundlessness of even the most indubitable beliefs. For, though he may be unable to doubt what is to him indubitable, when it is

present to his mind, he may nevertheless succeed in doubting the general proposition "that the indubitable must be true". "Indubitability", he will say, "is a merely subjective property, belonging, at different times, to the most opposite beliefs. At one time, it is indubitable that the world is bad, that ingratitude and selfishness are all but universal, and that we alone maintain a heroic endurance and a stoical oblivion of our own outraged rights. At another time, under the influence of more sleep or better digestion, the contradictory of these propositions becomes equally indubitable." But the sceptic regards his moments of undoubtingness as the moments when instinct seizes him: it is only when he returns to the doubt whether what is indubitable is always true that he feels again the companionship of reason. "Action", he will say, "is what man shares with the brutes, and indubitable beliefs belong in essence with action. But thought is man's distinctive prerogative; and the more inconclusive it becomes, the more it is permeated by difficult doubt, the more completely is it purified from the taint of action, and the nearer it approaches to the ideal of contemplation. Let us recognize undoubtingness, therefore, as, like rage and hate and lust, one of the unfortunate passions to which our animal ancestry exposes us, but from which it is the business of the philosopher to free himself to the utmost possible extent."

So far the rhetorical sceptic, whose desire for literary effect has led him into a somewhat naïve attitude towards Darwin and *delirium tremens*. Let us now speak again in our own proper person, as advocates of knowledge. The truth in what the sceptic urges is that no merely subjective characteristic, such as indubitability, whether resulting from a special kind of belief-relation or in any other way, can possibly give a guarantee of *truth*. It will account abundantly for men's belief that they have truth; but the better it accounts for this, the more it strengthens the sceptic's case, unless at the same time it gives a *reason* for certainty, and not merely a psychological account of certainty. Now a *reason* for certainty *must* involve reference to the *facts*. But an *ascertainable* reason for certainty must involve reference to ascertainable facts. Now the only way of ascertaining facts (except by judgment, which is liable to error) is by acquaintance. Hence if self-evidence is to be defined in such a way as to give a reason justifying certainty as regards our beliefs, it must be defined by means of acquaintance with facts connected with the beliefs. From this argument, so far as I can see, there is no escape. Hence, though indubitability should belong to self-evident judgments, their *definition* must not be by indubitability, but rather by some such method as we considered under our first heading.

(3). We must, however, still examine our third suggestion, that self-evidence is a predicate of some beliefs. There is a good deal to be said in favour of this view. It seems as if we could recognize a self-evident belief by the way it feels, without reference to anything outside itself. Meinong, though he does not enlarge on the analysis of self-evidence, seems to take this view. But the argument by which we refuted our second suggestion remains equally conclusive against our third. *Truth* is not an intrinsic predicate of judgments, for obviously their truth depends upon facts, not upon the character of the judgment as a mental occurrence. Thus if there is any intrinsic predicate of judgments which implies that they are true, it remains to be inquired how we can know this. It would be a *petitio principii* to argue that we know it because it is itself a judgment having the predicate in question. Hence the fact that the predicate in question is a guarantee of truth must be somehow inferred from something which we know otherwise than through its possession of this predicate. There must, therefore, be some other definition of self-evidence, by means of which it can be known (if it is true) that this predicate insures truth. Thus once more we are brought back to some form of correspondence with perceived fact as the only possible source of self-evidence.

It may be thought, however, that a similar argument could be employed against a definition of self-evidence by correspondence. How do we know, it may be said, that a judgment must be true if it corresponds with fact? Is this self-evident? And if so, do you mean merely that it is perceived to correspond with fact? But such an answer exposes you to the very *petitio principii* that you have urged against other definitions of self-evidence.

The reply to this is that correspondence with fact is the *definition* of "truth", not merely a criterion. Hence when a judgment corresponds with fact, it is true by definition, not as the result of an inference. When a judgment is *perceived* to correspond with fact, it is indubitable; thus indubitability accompanies self-evidence, but does not constitute it, and may exist where self-evidence is absent. But owing to the fact that a self-evident judgment is indubitable, we do in fact firmly believe what is self-evident. It is in this way, through the fact that perceived correspondence causes belief, that beliefs which deserve to be called "knowledge" arise. This explains at once why there are self-evident beliefs, and why self-evidence, where applicable, is a criterion of truth.

Our argument so far has shown us (1) that self-evident judgments must be defined by some characteristic which is discoverable by inspection of what is given when such judgments are made, (2) that they must be so defined as to insure their truth, (3) that it is impossible to insure their truth except by reference to acquaintance with fact. Although, therefore, subjective certainty will, at least usually, belong to them, yet neither certainty nor any other subjective characteristic suffices to *define* them, and their definition must be by reference to perception of some complex which insures their truth. We are thus brought back to our first theory, or something like it, as giving the right definition of self-evidence. It remains to examine several forms of this theory, and to consider which of them is the best.

The general requisites of our arguments as to self-evidence are satisfied by any definition which makes self-evidence depend upon perception of some complex which only exists when the judgment is true. Besides what we call *the* corresponding complex, there are many other complexes which only exist when the judgment is true. One such complex suggests itself in this connection, namely the complex which consists of the correspondence of the judgment with the fact. Since this correspondence is what constitutes truth, we may be said, in this case, to *perceive* the truth of the judgment. Shall we say that this is what makes a judgment self-evident?

There is some danger of confusing the *fact* that a judgment is self-evident with the *knowledge* that it is; and when we are said to know its self-evidence, it may be meant that we perceive it, or that we judge (truly) that it is self-evident, or that its self-evidence is self-evident to us. We have thus four things to distinguish: (1) the fact of self-evidence, (2) the perception of it, (3) the judgment of it, (4) the self-evidence of the judgment of it. It is only the *fact* of self-evidence that directly concerns us, since, when that is defined, the others follow. The only importance of mentioning the others is in order to remind us that they are different from the fact.

Shall we say that a judgment is self-evident when we perceive the corresponding complex, or only when we perceive its correspondence with this complex? And in the latter event, need we perceive its correspondence with an actual complex, or only with some complex? It will be observed that "truth" is defined as correspondence with *some* complex; thus perception of the correspondence of a judgment with *some* complex is what constitutes perception of the truth of the judgment. If, therefore, it is this perception that defines self-evidence, then a judgment is self-evident when we *perceive* its truth. This view is one which seems worthy to be adopted if possible.

The view that a judgment is self-evident whenever we simultaneously perceive the corresponding complex, which is the view we considered first, suffers from the defect that it makes self-evidence consist in such a very external characteristic. If we judge and simultaneously perceive the corresponding complex, without being conscious of the correspondence, it is difficult to see how this can give to our judgment the characteristic of self-evidence. It may be said that this constitutes the self-evidence of the judgment as a fact, but not the knowledge (in any of our three relevant senses) of its self-evidence. But I do not think this can be maintained. Mere simultaneity is in any case too external: it must be simultaneity in *one* experience. But even simultaneity in one experience cannot suffice: the relevance of the complex to the judgment must also be given in experience, otherwise the two fall apart, and we cannot account for the fact that a self-evident judgment *feels* different from one which is not self-evident. Suppose we are in a theatre before the beginning of the play: we shall believe that the curtain will rise, but this belief is not self-evident. At a certain moment, we see it rising, i.e. we perceive the corresponding complex; at this moment our belief *may* become self-evident, but I think it only *does* do so if we perceive the correspondence of the curtain rising with our belief. Thus it seems that perception of the correspondence itself is essential to self-evidence.

As to our second question, namely whether we must perceive correspondence with an actual complex, or only the fact of there being a corresponding complex, it is difficult to find any way of deciding it; for when we perceive the first we perceive the second, and it is doubtful whether we ever perceive the second without perceiving the first. There seem therefore to be no grounds of choice. I choose, arbitrarily, in favour of the second. Thus a judgment is self-evident when, at the time of making it, the person who makes it perceives its correspondence with some complex. Since this is defined as its truth, we arrive at the following definition:

> *Self-evidence* is a property of judgments, consisting in the fact that, in the same experience with themselves, they are accompanied by acquaintance with their truth.

This definition, so far as I can see, satisfies all the conditions that we have found ought to be satisfied by a definition. And since there are self-evident judgments according to this definition, we have thus a means of making a beginning of knowledge as opposed to mere belief; for the definition shows that self-evident judgments are by nature incapable of falsehood, and therefore deserve the name of knowledge.

Chapter VII
Degrees of Certainty

IT IS A commonplace that all our knowledge is in some degree liable to error, and that we are fallible even in our most dogmatic moments. Nevertheless, we feel far more certainty with regard to some beliefs than with regard to others; and this difference does not disappear with reflection, though the beliefs of which we are most certain in the end may be different from those of which we were most certain at the beginning. The question I wish to discuss in this chapter is whether there is any logical justification for different degrees of certainty, i.e. whether there is any *ground* for believing some things more firmly than others. The question is important, because conflicts sometimes occur among our beliefs, and it is then a question which of them we shall abandon. If none of them are quite certain, it would be useful to know whether we have any reason to prefer the more certain; and this question requires an investigation of the question whether degrees of certainty have, or can have, any logical basis.

We may introduce the discussion by considering what sort of certainty is actually derived from self-evidence. Of course, when our definition of self-evidence is strictly applicable, our belief has the highest possible degree of certainty, for we cannot perceive the truth of a belief unless the belief is true. But before we can obtain a relatively fixed and isolated belief, expressed in words and registered mentally for future use, many mental operations have to be performed, and in all these there is some risk of error. Let us take the case of a judgment of sense, i.e. of a judgment such as "A is to the right of B", where A and B are patches of colour in one field of vision. Here sensation gives (by the help of selective attention) the complex A-to-the-right-of-B, and reflection enables us to perceive the correspondence of this complex with our judgment. Hence, if we perceive this correspondence and make our judgment, then our judgment is self-evident, and is entitled to the highest certainty. But in order to state and register our judgment, A and B must be remembered; we must be sure that it was precisely those patches, not others near them, that were concerned; very soon, A and B themselves will fade from memory, and we shall have to substitute descriptions of them, which involve possibly erroneous beliefs. In this way, any judgment of sense, however self-evident at first, is liable to change its character in unnoticed ways, and thus loses its complete certainty very quickly.

In regard to logical judgments and judgments concerning universals, there is, it is true, much less ground for uncertainty when they have once been self-evident. That something has some relation to something, or that red and blue have that in common which makes us call them both colours, are propositions not referring to particular parts of time, and therefore as capable of self-evidence at one moment as at another. It is therefore theoretically possible to preserve their self-evidence by continued attention. But even in such judgments as these, there are remote possibilities of error if we look merely to the words which express the judgments, for it is possible that we may forget the meanings of the words and, trusting to our memory that they once expressed a truth, interpret them now in a way which is false. Such possibilities have little logical importance, but they have some practical importance, and they increase the urgency of our present problem, which is: To find a definition of degrees of certainty, which will give a reason, in cases of conflict, for preferring a more certain judgment to a less certain one.

Our problem must not be confused with that of probability. That a proposition has a certain degree of probability, is a new proposition, which we may believe with any degree of certainty from the highest to the lowest. Our problem is concerned in seeking something analogous to self-evidence as being nearly certain is analogous to being quite certain. We are not considering certainty about the probability of a proposition, but uncertainty about the proposition itself.

Meinong[1] considers in this connection the case of memory. He points out that the trustworthiness of memory in general cannot be deduced from any other knowledge, although, of course, if memory in general is admitted, a particular case of memory may be tested by means of other cases. It follows that memory must be, in part at least, immediate knowledge, in the sense of being uninferred, and yet is found, by lack of mutual consistency of recollections, to be liable to not infrequent errors. If, then, we are to have anything resembling knowledge concerning the past, it would seem that there must be something analogous to self-evidence in the power of yielding beliefs otherwise than by inference, but differing by the fact that the beliefs are not quite certain. We find, in fact, that our memories, quite independently of argument, are more or less certain: we feel convinced of what happened a moment ago, but very doubtful indeed concerning what we can barely remember. And we feel that this is reasonable; but why it is reasonable, is a very difficult question.

Meinong, after explaining the impossibility of proving the general trustworthiness of memory without assuming it, proceeds as follows (p. 70):

1 *Loc. cit.*, p. 68ff.

It occurs to no one to await a demonstration before trusting his memory; every one knows that he is justified in such trust even without a proof, i.e. on the ground, not of mediate, but of immediate evidence.

Only this evidence stands, to begin with, in quite astonishing opposition to the fact that memory, not so very seldom, is deceptive, and that therefore a prudent person does not rely with full confidence on his recollections, but never quite loses sight of the possibility that he may be mistaken. But just here we have to take account of what gives judgments of memory such a characteristic place in our knowledge, and also primarily interests us in the present connection. These judgments are not made with certainty, or, more exactly: a man who does not wish to overstep his right in this matter must not make them with absolute certainty, though this happens often enough in practice. These judgments are, rather, in their nature only presumptions [Vermutungen], although, under favourable circumstances, such strong ones as to be hardly, or even not at all, perceptibly removed from certainty. The evidence, therefore, which belongs to them according to the above, is not evidence for certainty, but *evidence for presumption*. For there is, as can be seen e.g. in the region of calculable probability, the opposition of justifiable and unjustifiable judging, not only when we judge certainly, but also when we judge uncertainly. And something may be rightly presumed, which nevertheless does not happen, and so is false, which can of course never happen with justifiable certainty. This presumptive evidence, which involves the probability of the Objective of the judgment just as conclusive evidence involves its truth, I hold to be a fundamental fact of epistemology.

The above passage brings out very clearly the epistemological importance of the problem which Meinong is discussing, and I do not see how to escape his conclusion, though I think his allusion to probability is a mistake, and I think we ought to exempt from uncertainty that part of the near past to which "immediate" memory reaches. It will be remembered that in Part I, Chapter VI, when we were discussing the perception of time, we derived our knowledge of the past entirely from *immediate* memory, not because this is the only source of our beliefs about the past, but because all other memory is fallible, and must, therefore, be supposed, since dual cognitive relations do not admit error, to begin with judgments, or at any rate with some kind of propositional thought. We will define the "immediate" past as the past which can be reached by immediate memory, and the "remote" past as the past which is not immediate. It may be doubted whether there is any sharp line of demarcation between them, but in any case there are portions of time well within the one, and portions well within the other. We have now to consider our beliefs concerning the remote past—i.e. all the past before the last thirty seconds or so. All that is to be said about "evident presumptions" may be said by reference to this special case, i.e. to our memory of the remote past.

The theory of "evident presumptions" might seem to be forced upon us by Meinong's arguments. There are, however, some very grave objections of a general kind to the theory. When we were discussing self-evidence, we found that no theory was satisfactory which defined it by a purely psychological characteristic, without reference to fact; for, if there was no reference to fact, there could be no reason why self-evident judgments should be true. The same applies, it seems to me, to "presumptions". Memory, we are to suppose, consists of a number of "evident presumptions", which cannot all be true because they conflict *inter se*. But what reason have we for supposing that *any* of them are true? They *seem* true, but we know that this seeming is deceptive. To say that we are to accept, in cases of conflict, those we feel most sure of rather than the others, is wholly arbitrary. What has our feeling sure to do with the facts? We do, however, decide somehow, by means which it is hard to think wholly irrational, that some of our memories are mistaken, some true, and others still doubtful. If these means of deciding are not wholly irrational, evidence for presumption, like evidence for certainty, must be defined by some relation to facts with which we are acquainted. It cannot therefore be an ultimate analysis, however excellent it may be as a first account of what happens.

The case of memory is, I think, much more complicated than Meinong supposes. In cases of erroneous memory, what seems to happen is that something imagined is mistaken for something remembered. Now we decided that imagination differs from memory and sensation by the fact that it does not imply (though it also does not exclude) a time-relation of subject and object. If, then, something which has actually been experienced becomes again an object of acquaintance, but without any given time-relation to the subject, it is now an object of imagination, not of memory. Since imagination seems limited, as regards simples, to objects which have been given in sense, all imagination is compounded of acquaintances with objects which have been experienced and therefore might be remembered, but in fact are not remembered. The question thus arises: what exactly is the mental occurrence which distinguishes remote memory from imagination?

Time-relations to the subject seem to be twofold: there is pastness in general, and there are definite temporal distances. Within the immediate past, different distances can, I think, be immediately perceived: an event which happened a second ago seems less remote than one which happened five seconds ago. Temporal order within the immediate past could, in fact, be inferred from these relations of distance, if it were not otherwise known.

But our power of thus immediately perceiving temporal distances is very limited; beyond the immediate past, events remembered are simply past, and their greater or less distance from the present is a matter of inference. Now when we are considering a remote memory, we have to distinguish those cases (if any) in which the pastness is given in acquaintance, so that there is a given complex leading to the self-evident judgment "this is past", from those other cases where an object is given in an acquaintance which involves no time-relation to the subject, and is then judged, without the help of any time-acquaintance, to be an object which occurred in the past. In this latter case, the object, so far as it is given in acquaintance, is an object of imagination; it is only through the addition of a judgment that it becomes an object of remote memory. Besides this distinction as regards the manner of our knowledge of the time-relation, there is another as regards the manner of our knowledge of the object. The object believed to be in the remote past may be not given in acquaintance, but only known by description. When we pass from imagination to memory by judgment, this seems usually the case: we do not believe that what existed was identical with what we imagine, but only that it may be described in terms of our image, by means of the kind of resemblance which commonly exists between sense-data and the images that we regard as images "of" those sense-data. This resemblance raises difficult questions which do not concern our present problem; I shall therefore say no more about it now.

We have thus, apart from perceptions of time-distance, four kinds of memory to distinguish, according as the pastness is given or judged, and according as the object is given or described. We will distinguish the first pair as "perceptive" memory and "judgment" memory; the second pair as "acquaintance" memory and "descriptive" memory. Thus:

"Perceptive acquaintance-memory" consists in perceiving a complex of the form "A in the past", where A is known by acquaintance.

"Perceptive descriptive memory" consists in perceiving a complex of the form "the existence of the object of such-and-such a kind in the past", where the kind is usually determined by resemblance to an image which we have now.

"Judgment-acquaintance-memory" consists in judgments of the form "A is in the past", where A is known by acquaintance, and the judgment is not derived from perceptive acquaintance-memory with A.

"Judgment-descriptive memory" consists in judgments of the form "the object of such-and-such a kind is in the past", where the judgment is not derived from a perceptive memory.

I do not know whether all these four kinds of remote memory actually occur; but if memory and its fallibility are to be investigated, it is necessary to bear in mind that all these four kinds are possibilities to be considered.

In considering whether these four kinds all occur, let us proceed backwards.

Judgment-descriptive memory occurs, very obviously, in such a case as the following: I find my imagination haunted by a scene which has the dimness and vagueness commonly characteristic of imagination, and which there- fore, as it stands, will not be thought to be *identical* with any set of sense-data. But suddenly it occurs to me that this scene is not *mere* imagina- tion, but "represents" something that actually happened to me. Thus I judge it to be memory. It is *descriptive* memory because the image only *resembles* what happened; it is *judgment* memory because—at least so we
10 assume—the first reference of our image to a past event is by a judgment. Such memory is quite peculiarly fallacious. Indeed the converse phenome- non to the above is not uncommon, where we mistake an imagined scene for a descriptive memory, and suddenly become aware—or at least begin to believe—that the scene is *merely* imaginary, and does not represent any- thing that really happened. Very remote memories, such as those of child- hood, generally belong to this class. Unless corroborated otherwise, pru- dent people place very little reliance on such memories.

Judgment-acquaintance-memory is more difficult to find an instance of. Perhaps, however, it occurs as part of judgment-descriptive memory when
20 this uses a present image in its description. There probably are respects in which an image is expected to be *identical* with the thing it "represents"— formal relations, spatial order, etc. For instance, an image of two men will contain the same sort of duplication of parts that belongs to the sense-datum called "seeing two men". Thus in respect of these elements which are identical, a judgment-memory which is on the whole descriptive will be an acquaintance-memory. There is another case which probably involves ele- ments of judgment-acquaintance-memory, and that is the case of the illu- sion that what is happening has happened before. But this illusion does not as a rule go the length of belief; and if it did, we should only think that
30 something exactly similar had happened before, and should therefore only have a *description* of the supposed previous occurrence. Similarly as regards the identity between image and sense-datum "represented", this does not extend to particulars, and therefore does not involve acquaintance with any actual particular which previously existed. Although, therefore, I see no reason to deny that judgment-acquaintance-memory occurs, I also see no reason to assert that it does.

Perceptive descriptive memory will occur if, in such a case as we considered in connection with judgment-descriptive memory, it is at some moment *self-evident* that our image "represents" a past event. It may occur without
40 this being self-evident in the sense defined in the previous chapter, if we ever perceive the complex "this representing some past event", where "this" will presumably be an image. That is to say, perceptive descriptive memory will occur in any case where we immediately perceive the sort of

connection of our present image with the past which is involved in calling it an image "of" something past. This is the sort of experience which we might describe by saying that our image gives us a "feeling of pastness". I am inclined to think that this is the usual case of remote memory. But as a rule, the actual perception of the time-complex is very brief, and is quickly succeeded by the more stable and more easily revived *judgment* of memory. Thus this case of memory is, in practice, not easy to distinguish from judgment-descriptive memory. It will be seen that perceptive memory is infallible, while judgment-memory is fallible. Thus the facility with which the two may be confused makes errors of memory hard to avoid. But if, as I 10 believe, perceptive descriptive memory is the usual case, it will follow that memory is usually trustworthy, and that, in a case which is not known for certain to be a case of perceptive memory, there is yet a probability in favour of its correctness.

Perceptive acquaintance-memory occurs in immediate memory, which, however, contains also, if we were right in what we said above, a perception of temporal distance from the subject. The perception of temporal distance does not greatly concern our present inquiry, and may be ignored. We have, then, to ask ourselves whether perceptive acquaintance-memory extends beyond the narrow range of the immediate past. I think not. I think that this 20 kind of memory is coextensive with immediate memory, and is indeed the analysis of immediate memory. Objects further in the past seem to be no longer given in acquaintance, but only indirectly accessible through images known to have a reference to the past. A particular with which we are acquainted is either a sense-datum, or a datum of immediate memory, or an image. It may happen, however, in exceptional cases, that the image has all the characteristics of a sense-datum, and is in fact identical with that "of" which it is the image. It may also happen in exceptional cases that immediate memory extends much further into the past than it usually does. These are purely empirical questions, the answer to which in no way affects our 30 analysis.

There is, however, one point in the psychology of memory which helps to explain what our account might otherwise seem incapable of explaining, namely the apparent gradual transition from immediate to remote memory. Between acquaintance-memory and descriptive memory there is, as a matter of logical form, an absolute gulf, with no possibility of gradual transition. But in the image which an event leaves behind it, there is a gradual transition: its intensity and brilliance and general resemblance to a sense-datum decays as time goes on, very rapidly at first, then more slowly. If it is by a description in terms of this image that we know the past sense-datum, it 40 is intelligible that we think our knowledge of the past decays gradually. What really happens is that the present image which "represents" the past event comes gradually to be less and less like the past event, and thus there is something which *seems* like a quantitative decay of acquaintance with the past, but is really acquaintance with an image growing progressively less like the past but known throughout to be "representative" of the past.

Let us now return, after this long excursion, to the question of degrees of certainty, as illustrated by the case of memory. A memory-judgment may be based upon perceptive memory, and is then certainly true, or it may originate in judgment-memory, in which case it may be false. (When I speak of its "originating", I mean, on this occasion; of course, if it is true, it must have been originally an acquaintance, but that does not enter into our present question.) Let us dismiss the judgment-memory, as not worthy to be called "knowledge" even when it happens to be correct. (It is to be observed that, when I speak of memory, I include no beliefs about the past which are inferred from other beliefs. Inferred beliefs about the past may be knowledge, but in that case, among the premises from which they are inferred, there will always be some memory-judgments based on perceptive memory.) Thus our store of uninferred knowledge concerning the past will consist of memory-judgments based on perceptive memory. Such judgments, we know, are true. But does that give us any right to rely implicitly upon this or that memory-judgment? In other words, can we ever be sure that a given memory-judgment is based on perceptive memory, not on judgment-memory?

The question of degrees of certainty, which has escaped us so long, reappears here. For a moment, perceptive memory gives us assurance. If we can reach the memory-judgment while perceptive memory still lasts, we have certainty as regards the memory-judgment. But if the perceptive memory is very fugitive, as it often is, our memory-judgment will soon come to be based, not upon the original perceptive memory, but upon remembering the perceptive memory. This remembering may itself be of any of our four kinds. If it is perceptive acquaintance-memory, we may still feel quite certain of what we originally remembered; but in any other case, we ought to feel a certain doubt. In the case of judgment-memory, this is obvious. In the case of perceptive descriptive memory, where we remember our memory by means of an image which gradually grows less like the memory which it "represents", the image gives less and less information about the original memory, and therefore must give less and less assurance as to the nature of the fact originally remembered. And apart from the complication introduced by remembering a memory, in all cases of descriptive memory based on images, our knowledge as to what is remembered has a certain vagueness, due to the vagueness of the relation of "representing" which connects the image with the past fact. This seems to account for our indestructible certainty that there was a past, which we know to have existed in virtue of memory, in spite of the fact that particular memories often prove to be wrong. The representative nature of the image, according to our

theory, is immediately known in descriptive perceptive memory; no doubt
the accuracy of the representation must be known within limits, if memory
by images is to give any information. But the limits may sometimes be wide,
and thus any unduly precise statement as to what is remembered will be
uncertain. It would seem, therefore, that the ultimate source of the uncertainty which is still present in perceptive memory by images, is the vagueness of the representative character of images. Degrees of certainty, therefore, in this case at least, are not an ultimate property of judgments, but are
derived from vagueness. We ought not to pass an uncertain judgment that
such-and-such a thing happened, but a certain judgment that something
like such-and-such a thing happened. From this it is theoretically possible
to pass to probability-judgments. Thus it would seem that what we took to
be an uncertain judgment about something is really a certain judgment
about something else.

The subject of vagueness is of some importance, and has not been
sufficiently considered. Let us endeavour to define it, taking the case of
memory-images for purposes of illustration.

Suppose the question comes up how tall a certain absent person is. We
may endeavour to decide the question by calling up an image of him. It may
be easy from the image to decide that he is over 5 ft. 8 in. and under 6 ft. 2 in.
But it may be impossible to decide from the image whether he is over or
under 6 ft., though we may feel "nearly certain" that he is under 6 ft. Let us
assume that there are people present whose heights are respectively 5 ft. 8
in., 5 ft. 9 in., 5 ft. 10 in., 5 ft. 11 in., 6 ft., 6 ft. 1 in. and 6 ft. 2 in. We will
call these people A, B, C, D, E, F, G. Our image enables us to judge that the
absent man is taller than A and shorter than G. We *think* he is taller than B
and shorter than F, but do not feel sure; D seems the most likely height, but
B, C, E and F are possible. How is this state of affairs to be analyzed?

It *might* be said that our image is of a certain definite height, but we are not
sure that the man is of the same height. This, however, does not seem to fit
the facts. The image will be more nearly of some exact height in a good
visualizer than in a bad one, but even in the best visualizer it will not be
distinguishable with any certainty from either of two given heights both of
which can be easily distinguished from a height half way between them. It
has therefore a certain vagueness which does not belong to sense-data. What
we call "height" in an image is perhaps not the same as height in a
sense-datum, but it has some relation to height in a sense-datum, since it
enables us to pass some judgments as to the height of the absent man. This
relation, whatever it is, is part of what makes the image "representative". It
would seem that there are as many heights of images as of sense-data, for it
would be a different image that would assure us that the absent man was
between 5 ft. 9 in. and 6 ft. 3 in. But each image is capable of "representing"
a number of different heights. Perhaps there is one which it represents best,

while those on either side are represented gradually less and less well. However this may be, the relation of "representing", which holds between images and sense-data, is not one-one; a whole stretch of objects may be represented by a given image, and a whole stretch of images may represent a given object. This fact seems to constitute the logical analysis of "vagueness". What has been said about height is obviously applicable to any similar series, such as colours, tones, etc.

What has been said above about the uncertain judgments of memory will be found, I think, to apply equally to all other cases of uncertainty. That is to say, there is no such thing, if we were right, as an uncertain judgment: there is only a judgment of uncertainty. In the case of the man whose height we try to decide from our image of him, it is uncertain whether he is over or under 6 ft. But this is not an uncertain judgment that he is over 6 ft., together with an uncertain judgment that he is under 6 ft. It is a single judgment, capable of just as great certainty as any other. If this conclusion is sound, Meinong's notion of "presumptions", as something falling short of the decidedness of judgments, is not ultimate, but resolves itself into what we may call the "judgment of approximation", or sometimes into the "judgment of probability", which are distinguished by the nature of their objects, not by the manner of judging. I do not feel any great confidence in this conclusion, but on the whole it seems more probable than any other.

It should be observed that the question of error is wholly distinct from our present question. Judgments in which we have the most absolute confidence sometimes turn out to have been erroneous. As we saw in discussing self-evidence, error cannot be excluded by any purely subjective characteristic such as the feeling of certainty, but only by that immediate contact with facts which we obtain in acquaintance. The question of criteria for the exclusion of error is not one with which we can deal at the present stage; but from what has been said already, it is obvious that such criteria must have reference to acquaintance, and must be undiscoverable so long as we remain within the sphere of judgment.

Before passing on to the consideration of molecular thought, let us sum up what has been said in this Part on the subject of atomic thought.

An atomic complex, broadly, is one in which there is a single principal relating relation, i.e. the complex can be analyzed into certain terms (which may be complex) related by a single relation. An atomic propositional thought is a complex formed by a multiple relation of a subject to certain objects, where nothing is involved in the objects which may not occur in an atomic complex, but the "form" of some atomic complex does occur, while no "form" of any molecular complex occurs.

What is called "understanding a proposition" is a relation of a subject to certain objects, which are (1) the form of certain atomic complexes (2) entities of the same logical kinds as the constituents of such complexes, sufficient in number and kind to form one such complex. A given proposition will be the fact (if it is a fact) of there being a complex of the form of an understanding, where the objects are given, but the subject and the relating relation are arbitrary.

The question of analysis, we found, is complicated by the doubt as to whether we can be acquainted with a complex without being acquainted with its constituents. What seemed empirically certain was, that we may be acquainted with a complex without being able to discover that we are acquainted with its constituents; but it is not possible to assert positively that we are ever not acquainted with its constituents. We found that there are two ways of perceiving a complex, which we called respectively *simple* and *complex* perception. In simple perception, we attend to the complex itself, and do not attend to its parts, whether or not we are acquainted with them. In complex perception, we attend to the parts, and are acquainted with the whole without attending to it. It is by means of complex perception that we are able to give a complex name to a complex, composed of the names of its constituents suitably combined. When we have become able to give a complex name, the judgments that this and that and the other are constituents of the complex are self-evident.

In considering the understanding of propositions, a specially interesting case is afforded by the atomic propositions of pure logic, which have no constituents; in this case, understanding is a dual relation, the object-term being a pure form. This fact seems to be connected with the self-evidence of logical propositions. The understanding of such propositions is the logically simplest kind of understanding. Next to this comes the understanding of propositions which merely assert that there are instances of such-and-such a universal. The understanding of unsymmetrical atomic complexes, such as "a-before-b", raises special problems, and appears to be not an atomic understanding.

In connection with belief, which we considered next, we emphasized the necessity of regarding it, and propositional thought generally, as consisting in a *multiple* relation, not a *dual* relation, and as thus radically different from conception or any form of acquaintance. The assimilation of belief to conception, we found, has been the source of many false theories, from Hume onwards. It has been encouraged by a wrong analysis of "existence", and has produced inextricable confusions in the theory of error. Belief, we decided, and disbelief also, is a relation producing precisely the same form of complex as is produced by understanding, and raising no new logical problems.

Truth and falsehood, which we considered next, we defined by the presence, in the case of true belief, of a certain definable correspondence with a complex consisting of the objects of the belief, while in the case of falsehood there is no such complex. The chief difficulty lay in defining the correspondence in the case of unsymmetrical homogeneous complexes, but we overcame this by constructing associated non-homogeneous complexes which exist when the original complexes do but not otherwise. We were thus able to state our theory finally in the simple form: A belief is true when its object-terms form a complex; if not, it is false. This theory we endeavoured to strengthen by a criticism of various other theories which have been proposed.

The subject of self-evidence, which we considered next, is important as introducing us for the first time to something which may be called *knowledge* as opposed to mere belief. We found that there must be some beliefs of whose truth there can be no doubt, though they are not obtained by inference; if this were not the case, there could be no such thing as knowledge. Such beliefs, we found, must be recognizable by inspection, and yet not defined by any purely psychological characteristic. They must therefore involve reference to facts with which we are acquainted. The definition we arrived at is: A belief is self-evident when we are acquainted with its truth, i.e. with the fact that there is a complex composed of its object-terms. We saw that there are beliefs which are self-evident in this sense, and that sometimes it is self-evident that they are self-evident.

Finally we considered degrees of certainty, and decided, though with some hesitation, that this is not an ultimate notion, but that what appears to be an uncertain judgment is really a certain judgment differing as regards its objects. This conclusion we reached largely by an analysis of memory which is not immediate, and of the way in which a memory-image represents a past datum.

Bibliographical Index

THE WORKS REFERRED to by Russell, and by the editors using the author-date system, are cited here in full. The year in italics following the author's name is that of the edition described, or else that of first publication. Full bibliographical data are not provided for pre-1800 titles. After each citation is an index of the pages on which the work is mentioned. Page numbers in roman type refer to Russell's text; page numbers in italics to editorial matter.

The bulk of Russell's working library is housed in the Russell Archives at McMaster University. The phrase "(Russell's library.)" indicates relevant volumes in that library.

The Bibliographical Index does not list unpublished correspondence referred to in the Introduction.

AYER, A.J., W.C. KNEALE, G.A. PAUL, D.F. PEARS, P.F. STRAWSON, G.J. WARNOCK AND R.A. WOLLHEIM, 1956. *The Revolution in Philosophy*. London: Macmillan; New York: St Martin's Press.
Referred to: *xiii*n.

BLACKWELL, KENNETH, *1973*. "Our Knowledge of *Our Knowledge*". *Russell*, no. 12: 11–13.
Referred to: *ix*n.

—— 1974. "Wittgenstein's Impact on Russell's Theory of Belief". Unpublished M.A. thesis, McMaster University.
Referred to: *vii*n.

—— *1981*. "The Early Wittgenstein and the Middle Russell". In Block *1981*.
Referred to: *ix*n.

—— AND ELIZABETH RAMSDEN EAMES, *1975*. "Russell's Unpublished Book on Theory of Knowledge". *Russell*, no. 19: 3–14, 18.
Referred to: *viii*n.

BLOCK, IRVING, ed., *1981*. *Perspectives on the Philosophy of Wittgenstein*. Oxford: Basil Blackwell.
Referred to: *ix*n.

BROAD, C.D., *1924*. "Critical and Speculative Philosophy". In *Contemporary British Philosophy: Personal Statements (First Series)*. Edited by J.H.

179

Muirhead. London: George Allen & Unwin; New York: Macmillan.
Referred to: *vii*.

CHISHOLM, RODERICK M., *1974*. "On the Nature of Acquaintance: A Discussion of Russell's Theory of Knowledge". In Nakhnikian *1974*.
Referred to: *viiin*.

CLARK, RONALD W., *1975*. *The Life of Bertrand Russell*. London: Jonathan Cape and Weidenfeld & Nicolson.
Referred to: *viiin*.

COSTELLO, HARRY T., *1957*. "Logic in 1914 and Now". *The Journal of Philosophy*, 54: 245–64.
Referred to: *xxiv*.

COSTELLOE, KARIN, *1914*. "An Answer to Mr. Bertrand Russell's Article on the Philosophy of Bergson". *The Monist*, 24: 145–55. (Russell's library.)
Referred to: *xxiii*.

DEWEY, JOHN, 1916. *Essays in Experimental Logic*. Chicago: The University of Chicago Press. (Russell's library.)
Referred to: *xxvin*.

EAMES, ELIZABETH RAMSDEN, *1969*. *Bertrand Russell's Theory of Knowledge*. London: George Allen and Unwin.
Referred to: *viiin*.

—— *1975*. "Phillip E.B. Jourdain and the Open Court Papers". *ICarbS*, 2: 101–12.
Referred to: *ixn*.

—— *1979*. "Response to Mr. Perkins". *Russell*, nos. 35–6: 41–2.
Referred to: *ixn*.

—— *See also* BLACKWELL, KENNETH, AND ELIZABETH RAMSDEN EAMES.

ELIOT, T.S., *1914*. Unpublished seminar notebook. Houghton Library, Harvard.
Referred to: *xn*., *xxiiin.–xxivn*.

FLORENCE, P. SARGANT, *1977*. "Cambridge 1909–1919 and Its Aftermath". In *C.K. Ogden: A Collective Memoir*. Edited by P. Sargant Florence and J.R.L. Anderson. London: Elek Pemberton.
Referred to: *xxiiin*.

GRIFFIN, NICHOLAS, *1980*. "Russell on the Nature of Logic (1903–1913)". *Synthese*, 45: 177–88.
Referred to: *ixn*.

—— *1982*. "Russell's Multiple-Relation Theory of Judgment". Unpublished paper read at Foundations of Logic Conference, University of Waterloo.
Referred to: *ixn*.

HOLT, EDWIN B., WALTER T. MARVIN, WILLIAM PEPPERELL MONTAGUE, RALPH BARTON PERRY, WALTER B. PITKIN AND EDWARD GLEASON SPALDING, *1912*. *The New Realism: Coöperative Studies in Philosophy*. New York: Macmillan.
Referred to: 16n., 24.

HUME, DAVID, *1888*. *A Treatise of Human Nature*. 2 vols. Edited by T.H. Green

and T.H. Grose. London: Longmans, Green. (Russell's library.)
Referred to: 136, 137, 138, 139.

JAMES, WILLIAM, *1890*. *The Principles of Psychology*. 2 vols. London: Macmillan.
(Russell's library: 1891 [i.e. 3rd] impression.) Reprinted in his *1975–*.
Referred to: 17, 55, 72n., 140n.

—— *1912*. *Essays in Radical Empiricism*. London, New York and Bombay:
Longmans, Green. (Russell's library.) Reprinted in his *1975–*.
Referred to: 15n., 17, 18, 19, 20, 27.

JOACHIM, HAROLD H., *1906*. *The Nature of Truth*. Oxford: at the Clarendon Press.
Referred to: 149.

KEYNES, JOHN MAYNARD, *1921*. *A Treatise on Probability*. London: Macmillan.
(Russell's library.)
Referred to: xxixn.

LACKEY, DOUGLAS, *1981*. "Russell's 1913 Map of the Mind". *Midwest Studies in
Philosophy*, 6: 125–42.
Referred to: ixn.

LENZEN, VICTOR, *1914*. "Epistemology". Unpublished seminar notebook. RA REC.
ACQ. 133b.
Referred to: xn., xxii, xxiii, xxiv, xxv, xxix, xxx, xxxiii, xxxvi.

—— *1914a*. "A Theory of Judgment". Unpublished term paper for B. Russell's
epistemology seminar, Harvard University. Bancroft Library, University of
California, Berkeley; copy in RA (REC. ACQ. 133a).
Referred to: xn., xxv.

—— *1971*. "Bertrand Russell at Harvard, 1914". *Russell*, no. 3: 4–6.
Referred to: xxivn.

MACH, ERNST. "A Theory of Heat". Unpublished translation, in Open Court
papers, of *Die Principien der Wärmelehre; historisch-kritisch entwickelt*.
Leipzig: Johann Ambrosius Barth, 1896.
Referred to: xxviin.

—— *1897*. *Contributions to the Analysis of the Sensations*. Translated by C.M.
Williams. Chicago and London: Open Court. 1st German ed., 1866.
Referred to: 15n., 16.

MAXWELL, GROVER, *1974*. "The Later Bertrand Russell: Philosophical
Revolutionary". In Nakhnikian *1974*.
Referred to: viiin.

McGUINNESS, BRIAN, *1972*. "Bertrand Russell and Ludwig Wittgenstein's 'Notes
on Logic' ". *Revue internationale de philosophie*, 26: 444–60.
Referred to: viiin., xxin.

—— *1974*. "The *Grundgedanke* of the *Tractatus*". In *Understanding Wittgenstein*.
Edited by Godfrey Vesey. (Royal Institute of Philosophy Lectures, Vol. 7.)
London: Macmillan.
Referred to: ixn.

MEINONG, ALEXIUS, *1899*. "Über Gegenstände höherer Ordnung und deren

Verhältniss zur inneren Wahrnehmung". *Zeitschrift für Psychologie und Physiologie des Sinnesorgane*, 21: 182–272. Reprinted in his *1968–78*, Vol. 2. Referred to: 41, 42.

—— *1906. Über die Erfahrungsgrundlagen unseres Wissens.* (Abhandlungen zur Didaktik und Philosophie der Naturwissenschaft, Band 1, Heft 6; Sonderhefte der *Zeitschrift für den physikalischen und chemischen Unterricht.*) Berlin: Julius Springer. Reprinted in his *1968–78*, Vol. 5. Referred to: 160, 168n., 169.

MONTAGUE, WILLIAM PEPPERELL, *1912.* "A Realistic Theory of Truth and Error". In Holt *et al.*, *1912.* Referred to: 24.

NAKHNIKIAN, GEORGE, ed. *1974. Bertrand Russell's Philosophy.* London: Duckworth. Referred to: *viiin.*

PEARS, D.F., *1975* "Russell's Theories of Memory". In his *1975b.* Referred to: *ixn.*

—— *1975a.* "Wittgenstein's Treatment of Solipsism in the *Tractatus*". In his *1975b.* Referred to: *ixn.*

—— *1975b. Questions in the Philosophy of Mind.* London: Duckworth. Referred to: *ixn.*

—— *1977.* "The Relation between Wittgenstein's Picture Theory of Propositions and Russell's Theories of Judgement". *Philosophical Review*, 86: 177–96. Reprinted in *Wittgenstein: Sources and Perspectives.* Edited by C.G. Luckhardt. Ithaca, N.Y.: Cornell University Press, 1979. Referred to: *ixn.*

—— *1979.* 'Wittgenstein's Picture Theory and Russell's *Theory of Knowledge*". In *Wittgenstein, the Vienna Circle and Critical Rationalism: Proceedings of the Third International Wittgenstein Symposium.* Edited by H. Berghel, A. Hübner and E. Köhler. (Schriftenreihe der Wittgenstein-Gesellschaft.) Vienna: Hölder-Pichler-Tempsky. Referred to: *ixn.*

—— *1981.* "The Logical Independence of Elementary Propositions". In Block *1981.* Referred to: *ixn.*

—— *1981a.* "The Function of Acquaintance in Russell's Philosophy". *Synthese*, 46: 149–66. Referred to: *ixn.*

PERKINS, JR., R.K., *1979.* "Russell's Unpublished Book on Theory of Knowledge". *Russell*, nos. 35–6: 37–40. Referred to: *ixn.*

PERRY, RALPH BARTON, *1912. Present Philosophical Tendencies: A Critical Survey of Naturalism, Idealism, Pragmatism and Realism together with a Synopsis of the*

Philosophy of William James. London, Bombay and Calcutta: Longmans, Green.
Referred to: 16n., 21, 29, 30.

RUSSELL, BERTRAND ARTHUR WILLIAM, 3RD EARL, *1903. The Principles of Mathematics*. Cambridge: at the University Press. 2nd ed., London: George Allen & Unwin, 1937.
Referred to: 84n., 87n.

— *1904*. "Meinong's Theory of Complexes and Assumptions". *Mind*, n.s. 13: 204–19, 336–54, 509–24. Reprinted in his *1973*.
Referred to: 153.

— *1905*. "On Denoting". *Mind*, 14: 479–93. Reprinted in his *1956*.
Referred to: *xii*.

— *1905a*. Review of Meinong *1904*. *Mind*, n.s. 14: 530–8. Reprinted in his *1973*.

— *1906*. "What is Truth?" *Independent Review*, 9: 349–53. Review of Joachim *1906*.

— *1906a*. "The Nature of Truth". *Mind*, n.s. 15: 528–33. Review of Joachim *1906*.

— *1907*. Review of Meinong *1907*. *Mind*, n.s. 16: 436–9. Reprinted in 1973.

— *1907a* "On the Nature of Truth". *Proceedings of the Aristotelian Society*, n.s. 7:28–49. Sections I and II reprinted as "The Monistic Theory of Truth" in his *1910*.

— *1908*. "Transatlantic 'Truth' ". *Albany Review*, n.s. 2: 393–410. Reprinted as "William James's Conception of Truth" in his *1910*.

— *1910*. *Philosophical Essays*. London, New York and Bombay: Longmans, Green. New ed., London: George Allen & Unwin, 1966.

— *1910a*. "On the Nature of Truth and Falsehood". In his *1910*.

— *1910b*. "La Théorie des types logiques". *Revue de métaphysique et de morale*, 18: 263–301. Reprinted in English in the Introduction to Vol. 1 of Whitehead and Russell *1910–13* and in Russell *1973*.

— *1910–13. See* Whitehead and Russell *1910–13*.

— *1911*. "L'Importance philosophique de la logistique". *Revue de métaphysique et de morale*, 19: 281–91. *See* his *1913* for a translation.
Referred to: *xin.*, *xliii*.

— *1911a*. "Knowledge by Acquaintance and Knowledge by Description". *Proceedings of the Aristotelian Society*, n.s. 11: 108–28. Reprinted in his *1918*.
Referred to: *xliii*, 36n.

— *1911b*. "Le Réalisme analytique". *Bulletin de la Société française de philosophie*, 11: 53–82.
Referred to: *xn.*, *xliii*.

— *1911c*. "Sur les Axiomes de l'infini et du transfini". *Société mathématique de France: Comptes rendus des séances*, no. 2: 22–35. Translated into English as "On the Axioms of the Infinite and of the Transfinite" in I. Grattan-

Guinness. *Dear Russell—Dear Jourdain: A Commentary on Russell's Logic, Based on His Correspondence with Philip Jourdain*. London: Duckworth, 1977.
Referred to: *xliii*.

—— *1912. The Problems of Philosophy*. (Home University Library of Modern Knowledge, No. 35.) London: Williams and Norgate, [n.d.].
Referred to: *vii, xi, xii, xiii, xix, xliii*.

—— *1912a*. "On the Relations of Universals and Particulars". *Proceedings of the Aristotelian Society*, n.s. 12: 1–24. Reprinted in his *1956*.
Referred to: *xliii*.

—— *1912b*. "The Philosophy of Bergson". *The Monist*, 22: 321–47. Reprinted as "Bergson", Bk. 3, Chap. 28, in his *A History of Western Philosophy*. New York: Simon and Schuster, 1945.
Referred to: *xliii*.

—— *1912c*. "The Essence of Religion". *Hibbert Journal*, 11: 46–62. Reprinted in *The Basic Writings of Bertrand Russell, 1903–59*. Edited by Robert E. Egner and Lester E. Denonn. London: George Allen & Unwin, 1961.
Referred to: *xi, xliii*.

—— *1912d*. Review of James *1912*. *Mind*, n.s. 21: 571–5.

—— *1912e*. "On Matter". Paper read at Cardiff. Unpublished manuscript. RA 220.011360.
Referred to: *xliii*.

—— *1912f*. "What is Logic?" Unpublished manuscript. RA 220.011430.
Referred to: *xliii*.

—— *1913*. "The Philosophical Importance of Mathematical Logic". Translation of his *1911* by Philip Jourdain. *The Monist*, 23: 481–93. Reprinted in his *1973*.
Referred to: *xin*.

—— *1914. Our Knowledge of the External World as a Field for Scientific Method in Philosophy*. Chicago and London: Open Court. Revised ed., London: George Allen & Unwin, 1926.
Referred to: *vii, x, xiii, xviii, xxi, xxiv, xxvi, xxvii, xxviii, xlvii*.

—— *1914a*. "Mysticism and Logic". *Hibbert Journal*, 12: 780–803. Reprinted in his *1918*.
Referred to: *xiii, xxiii, xlvi*.

—— *1914b*. "On the Nature of Acquaintance":

[Part I.] "Preliminary Description of Experience". *The Monist*, 24 (Jan.): 1–16. Reprinted in his *1956* and as Part I, Chap. I, of this volume.

[Part] "II. Neutral Monism". *The Monist*, 24 (April): 161–87. Reprinted in his 1956 and as Part I, Chap. II, of this volume.

[Part] "III. Analysis of Experience". *The Monist*, 24 (July): 435–53. Reprinted in his *1956* and as Part I, Chap. III, of this volume.
Referred to: *xxi, xxii, xxiii, xxvi, xxvii, xxix, xxxi, xxxiii, xlvi*.

—— *1914c.* "Definitions and Methodological Principles in Theory of Knowledge". *The Monist*, 24 (Oct.): 582–93. Reprinted as Part I, Chap. IV, of this volume.
Referred to: *xviiin.*, *xxiv*, *xxvin.*, *xxix*, *xxxi*, *xxxiii*, *xxxiv*, *xlvii*.

—— *1914d.* "The Relation of Sense-Data to Physics". *Scientia*, 16: 1–27. Reprinted in his *1918*.
Referred to: *xxiii*, *xxv*, *xxviii*, *xxix*, *xlvi*.

—— *1914e.* "Preface". In Henri Poincaré. *Science and Method*. Translated by Francis Maitland. London, Edinburgh and New York: Thomas Nelson and Sons, [n.d.].
Referred to: *xxiii*.

—— *1915.* "Sensation and Imagination". *The Monist*, 25 (Jan.): 28–44. Reprinted as Part I, Chap. V, of this volume.
Referred to: *xxvi*, *xxviii*, *xxix*, *xxxi*, *xlvii*.

—— *1915a.* "On the Experience of Time". *The Monist*, 25 (April): 212–33. Reprinted as Part I, Chap. VI, of this volume.
Referred to: *ix*, *xviiin.*, *xxiv*, *xxvi*, *xxviii*, *xxix*, *xxxiii*, *xlvii*.

—— *1916. Justice in War-Time*. Chicago and London: Open Court, 2nd ed., 1917.
Referred to: *xxvii*.

—— *1916a. Principles of Social Reconstruction*. London: George Allen & Unwin. U.S. ed. as *Why Men Fight: A Method of Abolishing the International Duel*. New York: The Century Co., 1917.
Referred to: *xxviin.*

—— *1918. Mysticism and Logic and Other Essays*. London, New York and Bombay: Longmans, Green.

—— *1918–19.* "The Philosophy of Logical Atomism". 8 lectures. *The Monist*, 28 (Oct. 1918): 495–527; *ibid.*, 29 (Jan.–July 1919): 33–63, 190–222, 345–80. Reprinted in his *1956*.
Referred to: *vii*, *viiin.*, *xxxv*, *xlvii*.

—— *1919. Introduction to Mathematical Philosophy*. London: George Allen & Unwin; New York: Macmillan.
Referred to: *xxxvi*, *xxxvin.*

—— *1919a.* "On Propositions: What They Are and How They Mean". *Aristotelian Society Supplementary Volume*, 2: 1–43. Reprinted in his *1956*.
Referred to: *xxxvi*.

—— *1919b.* "Professor Dewey's 'Essays in Experimental Logic' ". *The Journal of Philosophy, Psychology and Scientific Methods*, 16: 5–26. Review of Dewey *1916*. Reprinted in *Dewey and His Critics: Essays from the Journal of Philosophy*. Edited by Sidney Morganbesser. New York: The Journal of Philosophy, 1977.
Referred to: *xxvin.*

—— *1921. The Analysis of Mind*. London: George Allen & Unwin.
Referred to: *xxxvi*.

—— *1922*. "Introduction" to *Tractatus Logico-Philosophicus*. German translation in Wittgenstein *1921*; in English, with revisions, in Wittgenstein *1922*. Referred to: *xxxvi, xxxvii*n.

—— *1927*. *The Analysis of Matter*. London: Kegan Paul, Trench, Trubner; New York: Harcourt, Brace. Referred to: *viii*n.

—— *1944*. "My Mental Development". In Schilpp *1944*. Referred to: *xiv*n.

—— *1956*. *Logic and Knowledge: Essays, 1901–1950*. Edited by R.C. Marsh. London: George Allen & Unwin. Referred to: *x, xxxv*n.

—— *1959*. *My Philosophical Development*. London: George Allen & Unwin. Referred to: *viii*n., *ix*n.

—— *1967*. *The Autobiography of Bertrand Russell*. Vol. I: *1872–1914*. London: George Allen & Unwin. Referred to: *vii*.

—— *1968*. *The Autobiography of Bertrand Russell*. Vol. 2: *1914–1944*. London: George Allen & Unwin. Referred to: *viii*n., *ix*n., *xviii, xxxv, xxxvi*n.

—— *1973*. *Essays in Analysis*. Edited by Douglas Lackey. London: George Allen & Unwin.

—— *1983–*. *The Collected Papers of Bertrand Russell*. London: George Allen & Unwin.

—— *1983*. *Cambridge Essays, 1888–99*. Edited by Kenneth Blackwell, Andrew Brink, Nicholas Griffin, Richard A. Rempel and John G. Slater. Vol. 1 of his *1983–*.

SCHILPP, PAUL ARTHUR, ed., *1944*. *The Philosophy of Bertrand Russell*. (The Library of Living Philosophers, Vol. 5.) Evanston and Chicago: Northwestern University.

SEARLE, JOHN R., *1957–58*. "Russell's Objections to Frege's Theory of Sense and Reference". *Analysis*, 18: 137–43.

SHAKESPEARE, WILLIAM. *Macbeth*. Referred to: 59.

SOMMERVILLE, S.T., *1979*. "Types, Categories and Significance". Unpublished PH.D. thesis, McMaster University. Referred to: *ix*n.

—— *1980*. "Wittgenstein to Russell (July, 1913). 'I Am Very Sorry to Hear . . . My Objection Paralyses You' ". In *Language, Logic and Philosophy: Proceedings of the Fourth International Wittgenstein Symposium*. Edited by Rudolf Haller and Wolfgang Grassl. (Schriftenreihe der Wittgenstein-Gesellschaft.) Vienna: Hölder-Pichler-Tempsky. Referred to: *ix*n.

STOUT, GEORGE FREDERICK, *1901*. *A Manual of Psychology*. 2nd ed. (The

University Tutorial Series.) London: W.B. Clive, University Tutorial Press. (Russell's library: 3rd ed., 1913.)
Referred to: 21n., 55, 59.

—— 1911. "The Object of Thought and Real Being". *Proceedings of the Aristotelian Society*, n.s. 11: 187–205.
Referred to: 152n.

THOMPSON, MICHAEL *1975*. "Some Letters of Bertrand Russell to Herbert Wildon Carr". *Coranto*, 10: 7–19.
Referred to: *xxxv*.

THORPE, JAMES, *1972*. *Principles of Textual Criticism*. San Marino, Calif.: The Huntington Library.

TWAIN, MARK [pseud.], *1969*. *Mark Twain's Mysterious Stranger Manuscripts*. Edited by William M. Gibson. Berkeley and Los Angeles: University of California Press.

UNWIN, PHILIP, *1972*. *The Publishing Unwins*. London: Heinemann.

URMSON, J.O., *1956*. *Philosophical Analysis: Its Development between the Two World Wars*. Oxford: at the Clarendon Press.
Referred to: *viiin*.

WARNOCK, G.J., *1958*. *English Philosophy Since 1900*. (The Home University Library of Modern Knowledge, No. 234.) London: Oxford University Press.
Referred to: *xiiin*.

WHITEHEAD, ALFRED NORTH, AND BERTRAND RUSSELL, *1910–13*. *Principia Mathematica*. 3 vols. Cambridge: at the University Press. 2nd ed., 1925–27.
Referred to: *vii, viii, ix, x, xi, xii, xiii, xiv, xv, xviin., xxxvii, xliii*, 13n.

WIENER, NORBERT, *1914*. "A Contribution to the Theory of Relative Position". *Proceedings of the Cambridge Philosophical Society*, 17: 441–9. (Russell's library.) Reprinted in Vol. 1 of his *Collected Works: With Commentaries*. Edited by P. Masani. Cambridge, Mass., and London: The MIT Press, 1976.
Referred to: 77n.

WITTGENSTEIN, LUDWIG, *1913*. "Notes on Logic, September 1913". Translated [as version 1] and rearranged [as version 2] by B. Russell. Manuscript and typescript of version 1 in RA; published in Wittgenstein *1979*, App. 1. Version 2 1st published in *The Journal of Philosophy*, 54 (1957): 231–45; reprinted in 1st ed. (1961) of his *1979*, App. 1.
Referred to: *xxi, xxiii, xxxvii*.

—— *1921*. "Logisch-Philosophische Abhandlung". Introduction by B. Russell. *Annalen der Naturphilosophie*, 14: 185–262. Translated into English as his *1922*.
Referred to: *xxxv, xxxvii*.

—— *1922*. *Tractatus Logico-Philosophicus*. Translated by C.K. Ogden. Introduction by B. Russell. (International Library of Psychology, Philosophy and Scientific Method.) London: Kegan Paul, Trench, Trubner.

(Russell's library.)

Referred to: *xxxvi–xxxvii*.

— *1971. Protractatus: An Early Version of* Tractatus Logico-Philosophicus. Edited by B.F. McGuinness, T. Nyberg and G.H. von Wright. Translated by D.F. Pears and B.F. McGuinness. Oxford: Basil Blackwell.

Referred to: *xxxvn*.

— *1974. Letters to Russell, Keynes and Moore.* Edited by G.H. von Wright and B.F. McGuinness. Oxford: Basil Blackwell.

Referred to: *ixn.*, *xixn.*, *xxn.*, *xxin.*

— *1979. Notebooks 1914–1916.* 2nd ed. Edited by G.H. von Wright and G.E.M. Anscombe. Translated by G.E.M. Anscombe. Oxford: Basil Blackwell. 1st ed., 1961.

Referred to: *xxin*.

WOOD, ALAN, *1957. Bertrand Russell: The Passionate Sceptic.* London: George Allen & Unwin.

Referred to: *xxiiin*.

General Index

PAGE NUMBERS IN roman type refer to Russell's text; page numbers in italics to editorial matter. Editorial matter has been indexed only for proper names and philosophical subjects.

For authors, see also the Bibliographical Index.

abstract
    beliefs 157
    fact(s) 25, 33, 38, 42, 44
    ideas: Berkeley and Hume on 91, 95
    objects 57, 84–5, 89, 131–2
    thought 55, 57, 129–30
acquaintance
    with abstract objects 84–5, 89; with
    complexes 82–4, 120–2, 154, 177; with
    facts *xxxiii*; with logical form 99, 100,
    101, 113, 129–31; with subject 36–7;
    with universals 5, 79, 95–6, 100, 101
    analysis of 5, 44, 45, 100
    definition of 35
    and introspection 121
    James on 5, 55, 150
    kinds of 5, 38, 79
    Mach on 5
    and memory 71–2, 172–3
    nature of, summarized 99–101
    and proper names 7–8, 37, 39–40
    reality of its objects 48–9
    rival theories of 5
    and self-evidence 161, 164
    and understanding 108, 130–1
    see also experience; presence
act (of presentation) 42, 43
action vs. contemplation 163
affirmation 108
    Meinong on 107
Allen (George) & Unwin Ltd. *x*
ambiguity 6, 21–2, 46, 69–70
analysis
    and attention 123–4, 125–8
    complete 119, 120
    definition of 119
    when insufficient 27
    material vs. formal 119

method in 33
and philosophy 146, 159
and possibility 27, 111
problems of 120, 128
and self-evidence 161
and symbolism 146
theory of 125
and time 64, 66
    see also construction
Annahme: Meinong on 107–8
apparent variable 71, 129, 147
a priori
    Kant on 22
    odium of 6
Aristotelian Society *xii*
arithmetic 11, 13, 30
    see also number(s)
association of ideas 15
assumptions: Meinong on 107, 108
astronomy 44, 106
atomic thought, summarized 176–8
attention
    and abstract objects 132
    and acquaintance 39–40, 79, 121
    and analysis 123–4, 125–8
    of eccentric persons 133
    and experience 8–9
    and logical form 129–30, 132–3
    object of 69
    as relation 40, 100
awareness 7–8, 35, 72
axiom of time 76n.

"before" and "after" 85–8
being: *see* existence
belief
    abstract 25, 157
    analysis of 23–5, 46, 142, 144

189